BUSINESS ACUMEN FOR STRATEGIC COMMUNICATORS

Business Acumen for Strategic Communicators

This book tackles the top question I hear from communicators all over the world. What is the one x-factor that gives communications leaders the guts to speak up and shape critical C-suite affairs? If you're in business, there are few things more important than understanding how businesses really work. Stepping up your business acumen is always time well invested.

— **Stacey M. Tank**, Chief Transformation & Corporate
Affairs Officer, Heineken N.V.

Business Acumen for Strategic Communicators is an important read for anyone building a career in public relations. The book provides a compelling view into how business I.Q. makes communicators better at their craft, and how it lays the groundwork necessary to bring an informed, powerful voice to corporate decision-making. It is thought-provoking while also providing important, practical advice.

— **Andy Polansky**, Chairman & CEO, IPG DXTRA &
Executive Chairman, Weber Shandwick

Understanding and explaining how business works is one of the most important tools that a strategic communicator can have. This book gives those looking to enter strategic communications, and those already in the field, great tools and skills to advance their careers. If you want to take a leading role in your organization, this is the book for you.

— **Chris Roush**, Quinnipiac University

Matt Ragas and Ron Culp have provided communicators with a trifecta of business knowledge. Their first book provided the what, their second book explained the why, and now *Business Acumen for Strategic Communicators: A Primer* gives us the how of developing business acumen in our field. Once again, Ragas and Culp have made the language of business accessible to educators, students, and professionals alike.

— **Sandra Duhé**, MBA, Ph.D., Southern Methodist University, USA

BUSINESS ACUMEN FOR STRATEGIC COMMUNICATORS

A Primer

BY

Matthew W. Ragas
DePaul University, USA

and

Ron Culp
DePaul University, USA

United Kingdom – North America – Japan
India – Malaysia – China

Emerald Publishing Limited
Howard House, Wagon Lane, Bingley BD16 1WA, UK

First edition 2021

Reprints and permissions service
Contact: permissions@emeraldinsight.com

British Library Cataloguing in Publication Data
A catalogue record for this book is available from the British Library

ISBN: 978-1-83867-662-9 (Print)
ISBN: 978-1-83867-659-9 (Online)
ISBN: 978-1-83867-661-2 (Epub)

ISOQAR certified
Management System,
awarded to Emerald
for adherence to
Environmental
standard
ISO 14001:2004.

Certificate Number 1985
ISO 14001

INVESTOR IN PEOPLE

This book is dedicated to our students and alumni, and to all the educators, professionals and mentors who help develop the future leaders of our field.

CONTENTS

PART V: BUSINESS MODELS

PART VI: PRACTICE MAKES PERFECT

LIST OF FIGURES

LIST OF TABLES

LIST OF SIDEBAR CONTRIBUTORS

Valerie Barker Waller	YMCA of America
Katie Boylan	Target
Joe Cohen	Axis Capital
Carol Cone	Carol Cone ON PURPOSE
Bob Feldman	ICF Next
Catherine Hernandez-Blades	Aflac
Shelly Lazarus	Ogilvy & Mather
Maril MacDonald	Gagen MacDonald
Kelly McGrail	MARS, Inc.
John Onoda	Onoda Consulting
Linda Rutherford	Southwest Airlines
Rodrigo A. Sierra	American Medical Association (AMA)
Grant Toups	ICF Next
Karen van Bergen	Omnicom Group

FOREWORD

Linda Rutherford

As 2007 was drawing to a close, I got my most frightening assignment ever. As a young leader in our communications group at Southwest Airlines, I was asked to take on getting our Annual Report written – there was a desire to change up the writing style, make the language more consistent and help tell a better story of all of the airline's achievements for that year.

Oh, super. I'd managed to skate along for nearly 15 years at Southwest Airlines on my journalism background – someone who could find just the right words to explain a complex story to the masses. Or so I thought. All of a sudden, my vocabulary was being overwhelmed with terms like forward-looking statements, earnings before interest and taxes and one of my favorites: compound annual growth rate (CAGR). When CAGR was thrown around verbally as we were prepping for the annual report sections, I quietly laughed to myself, thinking: what in the world does a "kegger" have to do with finance? That's when I did what all former journalists come communications pros do – I Googled it. Then, I spent the holidays hunkered down for weeks cramming on all things finance. My investor relations partners were incredibly patient with me and I learned a great deal in a short amount of time.

That experience was enlightening. It taught me that our communications profession is dynamic: that I had *not* learned all I needed to know in college, and that if I wanted to contribute at a higher level, I had to be committed to lifelong learning.

And the learning keeps on coming. I believe 2020 will go down in history as the "lost year," and especially for those industries hardest hit by the impact of COVID-19. Our travel demand went from "robust to bust" in the span of just a few weeks. It called for a whole new approach to crisis communication (being informative and conveying what we are calling controlled uncertainty); writing new playbooks for rebuilding the business and getting travelers comfortable about getting on a plane again; and pursuing clever financing options to maintain our liquidity without taking on too much debt.

We've seen some hopeful signs of recovery, but this will be a long road back to our "new normal," and the story is still being written on what that ultimately looks like. It has been a great lesson in humility – we simply must never rest on our laurels.

Matt Ragas and Ron Culp recognized that fact several years ago. They embarked on a journey to better equip communicators with tools, concepts and even handy glossaries so that we could up our game and have a better understanding of how business really works – in its glorious highs and most certainly in its lowest of lows. Today, we're all familiar with the term "trusted advisor." Thanks to their two previous works, *Business Essentials for Strategic Communicators* and *Mastering Business for Strategic Communicators*, we have resources to more fully understand the fundamentals of business models, financial reports and elements of corporate strategy – all with a mission to help us earn the trust of our business peers in HR, strategy, finance, marketing and operations.

In this latest work, *Business Acumen for Strategic Communicators*, Matt and Ron keep challenging us to learn and grow because the sands of business are shifting again. Industry disrupters, economic downturns, the rapid pace of change, the rise of the activist stakeholder, the growing sophistication of communications agencies, the digital/social influence – all these things and more mean we need to keep learning.

Southwest Airlines Founder Herb Kelleher once said, "if you don't change, you die." He knew instinctively that the airline he founded in 1971 could not remain static or it would not be relevant to the changing wants and needs of air travelers. The same goes for all of us as communicators.

Those of us in the business world today are beyond being seen as "just spokespeople" for our organizations. We have the "seat at the table" but the expectations have grown. Increasingly, our roles as communications advisors mean we need to have a pulse on all aspects of business. As "keepers of the corporate soul," we are being tapped to provide a holistic viewpoint on pivots in the business model – not just write the news release to talk about it.

The Page Society – a premier organization dedicated to the growth and development of the world's top communications professionals – has a new model by which we can measure our ability to influence our organizations in a few key areas. Page's research into "The CCO as Pacesetter" explores the expanding roles and expectations for communicators as businesses and organizations wrestle with heady topics like societal value creation, corporate culture and brand stewardship (Arthur W. Page Society, 2019a). Further, communications leaders are expanding capabilities in the digital space beyond content creation and into publishing and listening capabilities, and thinking through the needed talent and structures to support those functions for the enterprise.

This book explores the dynamism of our chosen profession; it looks at the latest ways communicators should effectively work across the enterprise and be ready to step into a new role, that of "chief integration officer." More than ever, communicators are being asked to break down functional silos and work collaboratively to bring their holistic view of an organization's stakeholders into the larger context of decisions made about people, performance and policies.

We need to live up to that challenge, now more than ever, and this book will help you do that. Happy reading!

Linda Rutherford
Senior Vice President & Chief Communications Officer
Southwest Airlines Co.

PREFACE

Be an eternal student and learn the client's business.

These two timeless pieces of professional advice from the late Betsy Plank, often called the "First Lady of Public Relations," have perhaps never been more prescient as the strategic communication profession enters a new decade (*PRWeek*, 2015; Public Relations Society of America, Inc., 2019). A longtime resident of Chicago, Plank was a trailblazing public relations executive with a deep commitment to public relations education, including co-chairing the precursor to the Commission on Public Relations Education and playing a central role in the formation of the Public Relations Student Society of America.

After decades of arguing that communication needs a seat at the leadership table and to advise those "in the room where it happens," this has become more the reality in recent years. Earning and keeping the trust of stakeholders and creating societal value – not just financial value – has become an imperative for many chief executive officers and C-suite leaders. The concomitant rise of the chief communications officer (CCO) in many larger organizations has resulted in strategic communication finally becoming more *strategic* – not just being responsible for crafting messages that announce C-suite decisions, but serving as trusted advisors to the C-suite in the formulation of such decisions. This shift and elevation of the communication function has accelerated the mix of competencies expected of not just CCOs, but of everyone in the profession, as they seek to work more effectively with often MBA-trained businesspeople.

The book you are holding in your hands or reading on your screen represents our latest effort to help boost the confidence and business acumen of strategic communication professionals, particularly younger practitioners and students. The world has changed significantly since the publication of our first book, *Business Essentials for Strategic Communicators: Creating Shared Value for the Organization and its Stakeholders*, some seven years ago.

Since the publication of *Business Essentials*, a growing number of colleges and universities have overhauled their curriculum to include coursework on business acumen. Similarly, more agency and in-house training programs are emphasizing business acumen.

We are grateful for the feedback of the countless educators, students and professionals who helped shape this book. Diversity, equity and inclusion (DE&I) is a defining issue of our time. We have made an intentional effort to feature more diverse voices in this book.

Business Acumen is divided into five sections: an introduction to strategic communication and business acumen; a look at three guiding approaches to business that are increasingly prevalent in the C-suite; the people at the core of the relationships within and among business and society today; a dive into the essentials of the money and the numbers for communicators; a look at the business models of agencies and consultancies, and in-house communication teams and departments; and a final chapter on business acumen and professional development, which is chock full of actionable advice for putting into practice beyond the pages of the book.

Students and professionals alike are starved for time today as they juggle competing demands and more available media options than ever before. In the business world, this has even impacted the pace and length of meetings. Increasingly, *less is more*. With *Business Acumen*, we have tried to adopt a writing style that is conversational and accessible, as well as to make the chapters as concise as possible. The net result is to allow the reader to complete at least one chapter per sitting and to give you a sense of accomplishment and progress after each reading.

Every chapter includes an "Expert Insight" sidebar essay authored by a senior communication leader. At the end of each chapter, there are a set of discussion questions and keywords to review. Back by popular demand, *Business Acumen* features an updated and expanded glossary of business terms. To become fluent in the language of business means learning its vocabulary. The reference section is also updated and expanded. The subtitle of this book is very much intentional. Our goal with this book is for it to serve as *a primer* on developing your business acumen. We hope you will use the extensive reference section to help you dive deeper into the subject matter. We always welcome your feedback and comments.

In conclusion, two more timeless pieces of advice from Betsy Plank come to mind: invest something in the profession you practice and consider work as grown-up play. In this spirit, we hope you find this book to be a worthy investment by us back into a field which has provided us with so much opportunity and satisfaction. Further, we hope this book shows that learning about the world of business doesn't need to be boring – and dare we say it – can even be fun.

Matt Ragas
Ron Culp
DePaul University
Chicago, IL.

ACKNOWLEDGMENTS

Book collaborations are common in academia, but writing three books together in seven years is a feat that can only be achieved when the authors are passionate about the subject, share a mutual respect for each other and have plenty of colleagues and friends who enthusiastically support their efforts. We are blessed on all three counts as our latest book, *Business Acumen for Strategic Communicators: A Primer*, now builds on our first two joint efforts – *Business Essentials for Strategic Communicators: Creating Shared Value for the Organization and its Stakeholders* and *Mastering Business: C-suite Insights from Strategic Communications Leaders*.

We are grateful to the educators at more than 40 colleges in the United States and abroad who are using our books to help communications students understand the vital role of business in society. Increasing the business acumen of communicators is the goal of our books, since applying this knowledge will elevate the role, respect and influence of our profession on society.

Almost before the ink was dry on *Mastering Business*, our editor, Charlotte Maiorana, expressed interest in this book. Without a doubt we could not have done this without Charlotte, editorial assistant Katy Mathers and the talented Emerald Publishing team. We are also forever grateful to the diverse group of some 60 strategic communication professionals who enthusiastically provided their wise counsel and advice that you will read in the following pages. We are especially indebted to Linda Rutherford for her illuminating foreword.

Since beginning this mission, we have been personally humbled by the encouragement from professionals, students and colleagues who have urged us to write, speak and teach about business acumen. Nowhere was that support more gracious and enthusiastic than at the institution we've loved since both of us first walked onto the DePaul University campus roughly a decade ago. From interim provost Salma Ghanem and acting dean Lexa Murphy to our colleagues in the College of Communication, we are inspired by their laser focus and commitment to the success of our students and alumni, especially during difficult and stressful times. Other partners in the effort to elevate the stature and business acumen of strategic communication and public relations pros are the many academic and professional groups, including those to which we belong – Arthur W. Page Society, Association for Education in Journalism and Mass Communication, Institute for Public Relations, the Museum of Public Relations, National Investor Relations Institute, Publicity Club of Chicago, Plank Center for Leadership in Public Relations and the Public Relations Society of America.

We thank our families and friends for their support, help and encouragement of this book. Our partners in life, Traci Ragas and Sandra Culp, have patiently endured hundreds of conversations throughout this and prior projects, and they occasionally chimed in at just the right moments to improve a word choice, delete an unnecessary comma or suggest that we take a break.

These acknowledgments began with a brief mention of the mutual respect the authors have for each other. Our instantly congenial academic kinship and shared values have grown into a mutual admiration society and perfectly balanced collaborative partnership. Ron is impressed by Matt's near encyclopedic business knowledge, organizational skills and his ability to translate often complex subjects into clear, coherent sentences. Matt admires Ron's steadfast commitment to teaching, mentoring and helping lift up others, as well as his eminent career in government, corporations and agencies where he built decades of knowledge and relationships that have helped create an invaluable perspective for our three books.

Finally, our thanks and respect to you, the reader, of this book. The fact you have chosen to devote your valuable time to reading it demonstrates your commitment to increasing your own business acumen, which we hope will both increase your confidence and enhance your career.

PART I

INTRODUCTION

1

STRATEGIC COMMUNICATION AND BUSINESS ACUMEN

Actions (often) speak louder than words.

This timeless phrase has perhaps never been more salient or relevant. With the rise of social and digital media, the world is more transparent, and organizations are being held more accountable. By itself, *talk is cheap*. Stakeholders and society today support organizations that don't just "talk the talk" but "walk the walk." Even better, the *walking* helps drive the *talking*. Such a societal bias for action provides strategic communications professionals with a unique opportunity to not just craft messages on behalf of organizations and clients, but also to advise these organizations and their leaders in the C-suite on values-driven policies and behaviors.

At times, the past can be instructive for the future (Kerrigan, 2020; Miller, 2017; Weindruch, 2016). Arthur Page was a corporate public relations (PR) and communications pioneer. He was one of the first communications executives to serve on the boards of directors and trustees of major corporations and non-profit organizations (Block, 2019). For example, from 1931 to 1948, Page served on the board of AT&T, then one of the world's largest and most powerful companies. He also advised a host of US presidents from Teddy Roosevelt to Dwight Eisenhower (Block, 2019). Page's approach to communications and business is memorialized in The Page Principles, which were developed by the founders of the Arthur W. Page Society (2019b), a professional organization for senior communications leaders. The first Page Principle is "always tell the truth." The second Page Principle is "prove it with action." Page was quoted many times during his life as saying that effective corporate communication is 90% *doing* and just 10% talking about it (Block, 2019).

As memorialized in a song from the hit Broadway musical *Hamilton*, everyone wants to get inside "The Room Where It Happens." Arthur Page was one of the first corporate communicators to get to do so. AT&T was one of the first large corporations to recognize the value and untapped potential of communications beyond simply managing publicity (Miller, 2017; Weindruch, 2016). In the 1980s, PR executive Marilyn Laurie became the first woman in the top policymaking councils of AT&T, then a Fortune 10 company (D. Martin, 2020). Today many corporations and chief executive officers (CEOs) are recognizing how effective strategic communication can help make or break an enterprise (Weindruch, 2016). In some ways, the C-suite has issued the communications profession a license to lead (Ragas & Culp, 2018a).

It is now up to the communication field to take full advantage of this opportunity and demonstrate that it deserves to contribute to *strategic decision making* – advising on organizational actions and not just words (Berger, 2019; Berger & Meng, 2014).

EVOLUTION OF PR AND STRATEGIC COMMUNICATIONS

The late Harold Burson, a father of corporate PR and a founder of what is now BCW Global, succinctly argued that the PR and communications field has progressed through three stages (Burson, 2017; Christian, 1997). Communicators used to be asked by business leaders simply, "how do I say it?" – to announce business decisions *after* they had already been made. Over time, communicators began being asked, "what do I say?" Decisions were still often made in another room, but communications professionals were gaining greater respect and influence within organizations. Today, more C-suites are asking communications professionals, "what do I do?" – thereby giving communicators a voice beyond message crafting and into strategic decision making. While the level of influence varies by organization (APCO Worldwide, 2016), more senior communicators are being asked to advise and counsel those "in the room where it happens" (Arthur W. Page Society, 2016b, 2017, 2019a; Bolton, Stacks, & Mizrachi, 2018; Neill, 2015; Ragas & Culp, 2018a, 2018b). With the rise of the chief communications officer (CCO), the senior communicator in some organizations is now sitting at the leadership table as a member of the executive committee and/or the C-suite (Bolton et al., 2018; Harrison & Mühlberg, 2015).

Given this evolution, to be most effective and best prepared to live up to the *strategic* part of *strategic communications*, communications leaders and their teams, as well as their agency partners, need to have a stronger business IQ (Feldman, 2016; Penning & Bain, 2018; Ragas & Culp, 2014a, 2018b). The Arthur W. Page Society, whose membership is made up of senior communications leaders from around the world, has conducted an extensive research program into the opportunities and challenges facing today's CCO and communications departments. This includes interviews with 20 CEOs of large corporations about the roles and expectations of the CCO and the corporate communication function. Page's (2017) research finds that total business knowledge by the CCO and senior communications leaders is now "table stakes" (p. 4).

More specifically, this C-suite research (Arthur W. Page Society, 2017) concludes that:

> *In years past, CEOs have expressed hope that their CCO would know all about their enterprise's business in order to more strategically apply communications to advance its goals. Now, many CEOs require their CCO to be knowledgeable about the business – from strategy to operations – so they are able to provide strategic input on issues that span business functions. This is especially true at enterprises with communications departments that are well established and have a broad mandate. (p. 4)*

Former CCO Charlene Wheeless, the 2020–2021 chair of the Page Society, says that it is important to understand how the company you work for makes money and to learn the *business* of business (personal communication, July 12, 2020). "This is the holy grail of every company," says Wheeless, a strategic communications consultant to senior executives and previously the vice president of global corporate affairs for Bechtel Corporation, one of the world's largest engineering, procurement, and construction companies. "When you know how a company makes money (and loses it), you are much more likely to make better decisions, and much less likely to appear as the tone deaf communications person."

"The CEOs we work with are looking for communications leaders who can articulate the business case for every recommendation they make," says

Jean Allen, a Page Society member and a partner and head of the global communications practice for Heidrick & Struggles, an executive search firm (personal communication, September 12, 2019). "Gone are the days when a program would fly without a clear connection to the strategic goals of the enterprise."

When strategic communicators become trusted business advisors and counselors to the C-suite, the results for business, stakeholders, and society can be significant. For example, NIKE has been both lauded and criticized for its 2018 decision to feature former NFL quarterback turned civil rights activist Colin Kaepernick in its 30th anniversary campaign for "Just Do It" (Youn, 2019). In 2016, Kaepernick gained international attention after he began "taking a knee" during the national anthem before NFL games to protest racial inequality and police brutality against Black people in the US Kaepernick and the San Francisco 49ers parted ways in March 2017. He has remained unsigned and in retirement since (L. Thomas, 2020).

Despite some initial backlash, the "Dream Crazy" anniversary campaign featuring Kaepernick and other athletes who have overcome the odds to be successful, not only racked up awards, but NIKE credits the campaign with driving positive business results (Youn, 2019). Yet, this campaign reportedly almost *didn't happen.* According to a published report (Creswell, Draper, & Maheshwari, 2018), NIKE had considered just the year before dropping the controversial Kaepernick as a spokesperson. Nigel Powell, the head of communications for NIKE, vocally opposed the possible move and argued this would have been viewed very negatively by younger consumers. NIKE decided to keep Kaepernick. Later, NIKE's ad agency partner, Wieden & Kennedy, persuaded the company to feature Kaepernick as the face of its anniversary campaign.

In 2020, NIKE doubled down on its commitment to social justice. Following the brutal death of George Floyd, which galvanized Black Lives Matter (BLM) protests around the United States, NIKE unveiled several days later a "For Once, Don't Do It" anti-racism video (Ebrahimji, 2020). NIKE then announced a $40 million commitment over four years to supporting organizations focused on racial inequality, social justice, and greater access to education (L. Thomas, 2020). NIKE subsidiary Jordan Brands and basketball Hall of Famer Michael Jordan separately announced plans to donate $100 million over 10 years to these causes. Finally, NIKE CEO John Donahoe reportedly recommitted to the firm getting its "own house in order" by growing a company culture "where diversity, inclusion and belonging is valued and is real" (L. Thomas, 2020, para. 5).

STRATEGIC MANAGEMENT FUNCTION AND BUSINESS ACUMEN

Not so surprisingly, business acumen is increasingly acknowledged as a critical competency for communications professionals, particularly in contributing to strategic decision making and organizational leadership matters (Berger, 2019; Neill & Schauster, 2015; Penning & Bain, 2018; Roush, 2006). However, senior communications leaders indicate that young professionals often do not receive enough training in this area. For example, a survey of senior leaders (all members of the Page Society) found that roughly 8 out of 10 respondents (85%) placed *very high* importance on "business 101" coursework as part of a communication education, but almost as high of a percentage (81%) felt that college and university communications programs were *not* placing sufficient curricular emphasis on this area (Ragas, Uysal, & Culp, 2015).

More educators are getting the message. Many of the top textbooks within PR and strategic communications now highlight the importance of business literacy as part of the development of communications graduates into future leaders (e.g., Bowen, Rawlins, & Martin, 2019; Kelleher, 2020; Page & Parnell, 2019; Swann, 2014; Wilcox, Cameron, & Reber, 2015). For example, Wilcox et al. (2015) highlight in their popular introductory textbook, *Public Relations: Strategies and Tactics*, the following essential career skills: (1) writing skills, (2) research ability, (3) planning expertise, (4) problem solving ability, (5) business/economics competence, and (6) expertise in social media. These educators explain that "the increasing emphasis on public relations as a management function calls for public relations students to learn the 'nuts and bolts' of business and economics" (Wilcox et al., 2015, p. 27). Swann (2014) also highlights the need for graduates to develop business acumen, writing in *Cases in Public Relations Management*, another major textbook, that "one factor preventing some public relations practitioners from entering the ranks of management is a lack of understanding of basic business principles, management strategies, and number-crunching" (p. 5).

In its 2018 report on undergraduate PR education, the Commission on Public Relations Education (2018) recommended business literacy as a new, additional recommended area of study. The Commission, which is a joint effort of academics and professionals from a wide range of communication organizations, recommended five new areas of study in total: business literacy, content creation, data analytics, digital technology, and measurement and evaluation. These areas are in addition to a recommended now six-course minimum sequence for PR majors: introduction/principles of PR, research methods, writing, campaigns and case studies, supervised work experience or internships, and ethics. The Commission on Public Relations Education (2018) defines business literacy as "providing students with a working knowledge of the fundamentals of corporate accounting and finance, economic thinking, capitalism, markets and financial communications" (p. 63).

A large industry-wide survey of PR and communications professionals found that possessing business acumen was rated as one of the 12 most important skills/areas of expertise for the next generation of communicators (Krishna, Wright, & Kotcher, 2020). More specifically, the most important skills/areas of expertise in rank order, out of 32 items, were as follows: (1) writing; (2) listening; (3) research/measurement skills; (4) creative thinking; ability to deal with online reputation crises; ability to communicate effectively in today's environment of disinformation (all tied); (5) creativity; (6) ability to build a modern crisis response plan; (7) digital storytelling; and (8) possessing business acumen; and social listening (tied). Notably, further analysis found that top/senior management (e.g., CCOs) in this survey rated possessing business acumen as significantly more important than middle managers (Krishna et al., 2020). The authors of this study believe that "senior executives' experience and broader worldview of the business world contributed to this difference" and conclude that "business literacy then needs to be built into basic curricula by public relations faculty so future generations are well-versed in the language of business, as recommended by senior managers" (Krishna et al., 2020, p. 50).

In *Mastering Business for Strategic Communicators*, more than 20 current or former CCOs provided career advice on serving as trusted advisors/counselors to business leaders across the enterprise (Ragas & Culp, 2018b). In reviewing the chapter contributions, Ragas and Culp (2018b) note that these senior leaders often defined themselves as *businesspeople with an expertise in communication*. When discussing business acumen, several contributors invoked Stephen Covey's (2004) famous phrase: "seek first to understand to be understood." Stated simply, a communicator must first fully understand the business problem or opportunity; only after doing so is their counsel then more likely to be on target, be understood, and followed.

One such contributor to *Mastering Business* is Peter Marino, the former chief public affairs and communications officer for MillerCoors. Marino was promoted to running an entire operating unit of Molson Coors Beverage Company. He serves as the president of emerging growth for the multinational beverage company that is one of the world's largest brewers by volume. "As PR evolves and continues to make a more strategic impact on the business, all PR professionals need to think of themselves as businesspeople first who specialize in communications," explains Marino (personal communication, June 24, 2019). "As the profession becomes more business literate, the more value we can provide our clients. When we combine business thinking across the enterprise with our artful skills in communications, there's no limit to the impact we can have moving forward as PR professionals."

DEFINING BUSINESS ACUMEN IN STRATEGIC COMMUNICATIONS

Business acumen is a sought-after competency for businesspeople across fields, whether working in startups, corporations, or non-profit organizations (Charan, 2017; Cope, 2012). But what does business acumen specifically mean *in the context of strategic communications*? A group of 40 senior leaders in corporate communications were convened via a Delphi panel method to deliberate on this subject and reach consensus answers (Ragas, 2019a). More than 8 out of 10 (81%) panelists had more than 20 years of communications industry experience and half (50%) had more than 30 years of experience. The most commonly held senior title by the panelists during their careers was CCO (34%), followed by vice president (29%), president (18%), CEO or executive vice president (both 16%), and senior vice president (8%). These corporate and agency senior leaders are responsible for collectively having helped hire, develop, and manage thousands of communications professionals.

A high level of agreement was reached among the Delphi panel about what business acumen means in a communication context and which specific knowledge falls under this domain for strategic communication professionals (Ragas, 2019a). The panel concluded that:

> *Business acumen means becoming knowledgeable about business functions, stakeholders and markets that are critical to the success of one's organization or client; using this understanding to assess business matters through a communications lens; and then providing informed strategic recommendations and actions. As such, professionals should demonstrate a commitment to ongoing learning about a range of business subjects, including interpreting financial statements and information; strategy; operations; supply chain; organizational behavior, culture and structure; marketing and sales; human resources; technology, data and analytics; economics; legal, public policy and regulatory; stakeholder management; and corporate governance and social responsibility.*

Fig. 1.1 provides a visual representation of this statement in model form. As shown on the model, at the base or foundation of the model is becoming knowledgeable in interpreting financial statements and financial information (i.e., learning the core language of business).

Fig. 1.1: Business Acumen Model for Strategic Communication Professionals.

Business Acumen Model

Provide informed strategic recommendations and actions

Assess business matters through a communications lens

Business Functions   Business Stakeholders   Business Markets

Business Subjects

- Strategy
- Operations
- Supply chain
- Organizational behavior, culture, structure

- Marketing and sales
- Human resources
- Technology, data and analytics
- Economics

- Legal, public policy and regulatory
- Stakeholder management
- Corporate governance and social responsibility

Interpret financial statements and financial information *(learn the language of business)*

Source: Ragas (2019a).

The terms business acumen and business literacy are related, but they should not be used interchangeably. Business literacy is a necessary, but not sufficient condition of business acumen. Someone who is business literate has at least an intermediate level of proficiency in understanding, speaking, and translating the language and concepts of business. Someone with business acumen not only has a more advanced level of proficiency but applies this knowledge and understanding through providing strategic counsel and advice that drives business actions.

"Companies are under scrutiny 24/7. CEOs don't have time to think in terms of communications or marketing or advertising solutions," explains Bill Heyman, CEO and founder of Heyman Associates, an executive search firm that specializes in senior-level communications and marketing searches (personal communications, June 20, 2019). "You have to understand the whole enterprise, tap the right subject matter expert to explain whatever you don't know, and then credibly tie your advice and plan to the bottom line. It's smart to start building those skills as early as possible."

PERCEIVED BENEFITS OF BUSINESS ACUMEN

The senior leaders on the Delphi panel also identified valuable professional, organizational, and societal benefits to strategic communications professionals developing business acumen (Ragas, 2019a). According to the panel, professional benefits may include greater career growth, advancement and job mobility, including being more likely to serve in a business advisor/counselor capacity and potentially rising to CCO-level positions during their careers. Turning to organizational benefits, the panel concluded that, when the professional serves as a business advisor/counselor, the organization may have better alignment of business and communications strategy, which can drive superior business results. Finally, in deliberating on societal benefits, the panel concluded that, when the professional serves as a business advisor/ counselor, there may be better integration of business and social goals for the organization, which can result in better stakeholder relationships and organizational reputations.

Fig. 1.2 provides a visual representation of the panel's summary statement regarding the presumed benefits of strategic communication professionals developing business acumen.

The growth outlook for the strategic communications profession and related disciplines is bright, but competition for the best jobs remains intense. There are nearly 500 mass communication and journalism programs in US colleges and universities (Gotlieb, McLaughlin, & Cummins, 2017). The largest number of enrollments within these programs is in strategic communication sequences (i.e., PR, advertising, PR and advertising combined, or a related area). This means there are thousands of new graduates being produced. Shifting to the professional world, within the United States alone, there are approximately 600,000 professionals working in PR, advertising, promotions, and marketing positions (U.S. Bureau of Labor Statistics, 2020). Looking internationally, PR and strategic communication are among the fastest growing professions in Europe and Asia (Commission on Public Relations Education, 2018).

Sharpening one's business knowledge and skills can be an important way for younger strategic communication professionals to differentiate themselves in the competitive job market, advance their careers, and build stronger relationships with senior executives. "Business acumen is the key

---

Fig. 1.2:   Three Presumed Benefits of Business Acumen for Strategic Communicators.

Three Presumed Benefits of Business Acumen

PROFESSIONAL	ORGANIZATIONAL	SOCIETAL
The communications professional may experience greater career growth, advancement and job mobility (including potentially rising to leadership roles within the function and beyond). They may gain more trust and credibility among organizational management and be more likely to serve in a trusted business advisor/counselor capacity.	When the communications professional serves as an advisor/counselor, the organization may gain a competitive advantage, including better alignment of business strategy and communications strategy, which can drive superior business results.	When the communications professional serves as an advisor/counselor, there may be better integration of business and social goals for the organization. Communications can foster a values-based, purpose-driven mindset that can drive better stakeholder relationships and organizational reputations.

Source: Ragas (2019a).
Note: About 97% of the Delphi panel "strongly agreed" or "agreed" with this third-round statement. *Delphi consensus* ranges from 55% to 100% agreement with 70% often considered the standard (Avella, 2016).

to career advancement, especially for women in this industry. Often times, the main difference between being considered for a top tier versus middle management role is your ability to understand how the business works and use that to drive actionable results," says Dionne Gomez, vice president of corporate affairs, Zeno Group and a recipient of a *PR News* Rising PR Stars 30 & Under award (personal communication, June 30, 2019).

"The ability to recognize and understand business needs with clients creates a deeper connection and helps deliver greater results," says Chelsea Michael, a vice president in the headquarters of global PR and marketing agency FleishmanHillard and a *St. Louis Business Journal* "30 under 30" honoree (personal communication, July 29, 2019). "My understanding of business concepts has led to stronger relationships with client CEOs and CMOs, and has put PR at the forefront of key business decisions."

LOOKING AHEAD

The future of the strategic communication field is generally bright. In a world that demands transparency and in which organizations must earn the trust and respect of social media-empowered stakeholders, the need for effective strategic communications counsel has perhaps never been stronger (Berger, 2019; Bolton et al., 2018; Kerrigan, 2020; Ragas, 2019a). This represents a great opportunity for communications to lead. Of course, the field is not without its challenges. Strategic communications areas, such as PR and advertising, will almost certainly converge more with marketing departments and functions in the years ahead (Burton, 2019; USC Annenberg Center for Public Relations, 2019).

Chief marketing officers (CMOs) and MBA-trained marketing professionals typically are fluent in the "business of business" and often are members of the C-suite and/or advisors to it (Haran & Sheffer, 2015). Disciplines adjacent to strategic communication, such as investor relations, also desire to serve as trusted advisors and counselors to the C-suite (National Investor Relations Institute, 2019). Of course, as Aaron Burr laments in *Hamilton*, not everyone gets inside (or stays within) "the room where it happens." This said, with a re-doubling of efforts by the communication profession into training, developing, and mentoring talent (Penning & Bain, 2018), coupled with an action-oriented commitment to diversity, equity, and inclusion (Brown, Waymer, & Zhou, 2019; Wallington, 2020), the profession is poised to develop future leaders who are better prepared for such potential opportunities and challenges in the years ahead.

KEY TERMS

Arthur W. Page Society

Business acumen

Business literacy

Chief communications officer
    (CCO)

Chief marketing officer (CMO)

Chief executive officer (CEO)

Commission on PR Education (CPRE)

C-suite

Delphi panel method

Executive committee

Investor relations

MBA

Page Principles

Strategic communications

DISCUSSION QUESTIONS

(1) The Page Society argues that organizations need to "provide it with action." What are examples of organizations proving it with action? What about organizations falling short?

(2) Harold Burson says PR and communications has evolved through three stages in its history. In your opinion, which stage (or stages) is the field in currently? Explain.

(3) Do you think business acumen will become more or less important as a competency for strategic communication professionals in the future? Why or why not?

(4) Besides business acumen, what competencies do you think will be critical to the success of strategic communication professionals today and in the future? Explain.

(5) What do you think the future holds for the strategic communication profession? Will communication professionals rise in influence or decline in influence in organizations?

By Kelly McGrail, Vice President, Leadership Communications at Mars, Incorporated

Being an excellent communicator provides many opportunities. But, combining those skills with business acumen is the key to unlocking a career as a credible advisor and strategic partner to management.

One could pursue an MBA to develop this acumen. But, you can also create your own path of learning and development on the job. My early career gave me the opportunity to walk factory floors in steel-toed boots, develop marketing plans, see how an innovation pipeline worked, and partner with the finance team to address tough questions on business performance. Look to create these kinds of opportunities for yourself.

Get in the Trenches and Create a Network

Getting into the trenches with your colleagues is a great way to tap into their expertise, learn, and create a network. Be curious about how the business works. For example, if you have the chance to tour a factory or a supply chain, ask about critical challenges. Explain why you are seeking to understand, and build relationships with the people who can be subject matter experts for you when you need them.

Find a Business Mentor

A mentor can share context and explain nuances which may not be obvious without the benefit of experience. My best mentor encouraged me to have a point of view from the perspective of a business leader, not just a communication specialist, and didn't judge if I was off base – he coached. Find someone who can provide perspective, serve as a sounding board, and connect you with others. And, demonstrate your respect for their time by using it wisely and efficiently.

Measure Your Work and Put Your Recommendations in Business Terms

Communicators need to be able to measure their work in a way that demonstrates value to the business – particularly if you are trying to secure support and resources. Measurement isn't about activities, it's about impact. For example, the number of social media posts generated about being a great place to work isn't a valuable measure. But, if talent attraction is a priority strategy, and you can correlate those posts to increases in viable job applications, you are demonstrating a return. To create meaningful measures, developing partnerships with others in the business may be critical (in this case, the recruiting team).

Embrace Diversity When Building Teams

Great communicators can come from uncommon places. Over the years, I've had colleagues from a variety of backgrounds; consulting; politics; another was a Ph.D. in communications; and another came from marketing and new product development. They all had excellent communications skills, and even more, they had a firm grounding in how business works. As a result, they were appreciated for being able to grasp the business implications of a challenge, see it from multiple angles, and bring communications to bear to shape and advance the strategy.

The world of business is looking to communicators increasingly as counselors. It's a big and rewarding opportunity, but an invitation that is only extended to those that have developed their own business acumen.

PART II

GUIDING APPROACHES TO BUSINESS

2

GROWTH, INNOVATION AND
TRANSFORMATION

Even disruptors worry about being disrupted.

Started some 50 years ago by Sam Walton, then a five-and-dime operator in rural Arkansas, Walmart has massively disrupted the retail landscape as its "every day low price" strategy has expanded across the United States and then around the world (L. Goldman, 2011; John, 2019). Whether viewed as a hero, a villain or somewhere in between, seemingly every-one agrees that Walmart significantly influences global business and society. Today, with annual revenue of more than $500 billion, more than 2 million employees and operations spanning the globe, Walmart is one of the world's largest and most closely watched corporations (*Fortune*, 2020b).

Doug McMillon, the chief executive officer (CEO) and president of Walmart, keeps an image on his cell phone, which he says reminds him to maintain a "healthy paranoia" to stay ahead of the company's rivals (L. Thomas, 2018, para. 3). The image lists the top 10 retailers in the United States by decade since the 1950s. Walmart assumed the top spot on this list for the first time in the 1990s. Major rival Amazon.com is now around the top of this list of retail giants, but wasn't even founded until 1994 (Stone, 2013b). According to McMillon, "businesses grow and they don't change enough and they decline over time. Retailers do that on a bit of a faster cycle" (L. Thomas, 2018, para. 2).

The retail graveyard in the United States is littered with retailers that went from fast-growing innovators to declining laggards and then out of business entirely. Borders Books and Music, Circuit City, Hollywood Video, K.B. Toys, Montgomery Ward and Woolworth are just some notable examples (Fidlin, 2011). The list McMillon keeps on his phone drives this point home.

A CONCERN OF CEOs: NAVIGATING DISRUPTIVE INNOVATIONS

The fear of McMillon and other CEOs about successfully navigating their businesses through disruptive innovations is not new. For example, some 20 years ago, Andy Grove, then the CEO and chair of Intel, the world's largest chip maker, wrote the best-selling book, *Only the Paranoid Survive.* Grove (1999) spoke of the challenges of successfully guiding a business through massive technological and societal changes and disruptions, which he called strategic inflection points.

Only the pace of change and innovation may be accelerating today. Name an industry and there are multiple market disruptors that are challenging long established market leaders and upturning industry practices (Rossman, 2019; Stone, 2017). Amazon is in seemingly every area of shopping. Apple in digital devices. Facebook and Google in all-things digital media and online advertising. Uber, Lyft and Tesla in transportation. Airbnb in hotels and hospitality. Netflix in television programming and films. Spotify in music. Salesforce.com in cloud-based enterprise software. Square and Venmo (PayPal) in digital payments and financial technology. The list goes on. The strategic communication agency world is no different, as it faces disruption from a host of new competitors, such as the big consulting and professional services firms, which are rapidly adding more creative and digital capabilities (Maheshwari, 2019). Some clients are also devoting more resources to building up their own in-house agencies and creative departments (Handley, 2019).

Moore's Law is well-known in technology circles. Coined in 1965 by Gordon Moore, an Intel founder, Moore's Law (also known as the law of exponential growth) has predicted an exponential growth in computing power in particular and the evolution of technology in general (Intel Corporation, n.d.; Kurzweil, 2006). For example, consider the time it has taken through the decades for new disruptive innovations to reach a critical mass in customer adoption (Ritholtz, 2017). The landline telephone took 75 years to reach 50 million users. Airplanes reportedly hit this milestone in 68 years. It took the automobile 62 years. Light bulbs hit 50 million in 46 years. Televisions reached this milestone in 22 years. Digital platforms and technologies have allowed for exponentially faster adoption rates. For example, YouTube, Facebook and Twitter obtained the 50 million user mark in just four, three and two years, respectively (Ritholtz, 2017).

While disruptive innovation is often associated with technology (Wessel & Christensen, 2012), innovations are not only driven by technological changes and developments. Importantly, innovations may also emerge through disruptive shifts in society, culture and/or geopolitics, such as major changes in stakeholder expectations and preferences (Arthur W. Page Society, 2019a; Drucker, 2002, 2014; McCorkindale, Hynes, & Kotcher, 2018). For example, the rise of consumer preferences for natural, organic, more sustainable and local products (and the associated focus on clean product ingredients and labeling) has upended entire industries, such as agriculture and farming, consumer packaged goods, restaurants and retailers. Many new innovators have emerged.

Just as there are corporate reputation rankings and best places to work lists, there are also lists of the most innovative companies. Simply put, stakeholders, whether employees, customers or investors, generally want to be associated with innovation. Management consulting firm Boston Consulting Group (BCG, 2020) produces a well-regarded annual list of the most innovative companies, based largely upon a survey of 2,500 global innovation executives. US-based companies typically associated with innovation dot this list, including Alphabet/Google, Amazon, Apple, Netflix and Tesla. Fast-growing innovative companies based in China like Alibaba, Huawei, Tencent and Xiaomi have also moved onto this list. See Table 2.1 for the complete list of the top 25 most innovative companies based upon this research by BCG.

Table 2.1:   The Top 25 Most Innovative Companies.

Rank	Company	Headquarters	Annual Revenue
1	Apple, Inc.	Cupertino, CA, USA	$260.2 billion
2	Alphabet/Google	Mountain View, CA, USA	$161.9 billion
3	Amazon.com	Seattle, WA, USA	$280.5 billion
4	Microsoft	Redmond, WA, USA	$143.0 billion
5	Samsung	Seoul, South Korea	$208.5 billion
6	Huawei	Shenzhen, China	CN¥858.8 billion
7	Alibaba Group	Hangzhou, China	CN¥509.7 billion
8	IBM	Armonk, NY, USA	$77.1 billion
9	SONY	Tokyo, Japan	¥8.259 trillion
10	Facebook	Menlo Park, CA, USA	$55.8 billion
11	Tesla	Palo Alto, CA, USA	$21.5 billion
12	Cisco Systems	San Jose, CA, USA	$49.3 billion
13	Walmart	Bentonville, AR, USA	$523.9 billion
14	Tencent Holdings	Shenzhen, China	CN¥377.3 billion
15	HP, Inc.	Palo Alto, CA, USA	$58.8 billion
16	NIKE, Inc.	Beaverton, OR, USA	$37.4 billion
17	Netflix	Los Gatos, CA, USA	$15.8 billion
18	LG Electronics	Seoul, South Korea	$54.4 billion
19	Intel	Santa Clara, CA, USA	$71.9 billion
20	Dell	Round Rock, TX, USA	$90.6 billion
21	SIEMENS	Munich, Germany	€83.0 billion
22	Target	Minneapolis, MN, USA	$75.4 billion
23	PHILIPS	Amsterdam, The Netherlands	€18.1 billion
24	Xiaomi	Beijing, China	CN¥205.8 billion
25	Oracle	Redwood City, CA, USA	$39.5 billion

Source: Adapted from 2020 BCG Global Innovation Survey (survey of 2,500 global innovation executives).
Note: Company annual revenue data are for 2019.

THE CEO IMPERATIVE: DRIVING ORGANIZATIONAL GROWTH

Reviews of surveys of the top priorities of CEOs drive home the corporate focus on innovation and growth, as well as the link between the two (e.g., Gartner, Inc., 2019; KPMG International, 2018; PwC, 2019a; Workday, Inc., 2016). Not surprisingly, CEOs and other business leaders want their organizations to become more innovative and to successfully navigate disruptive innovations (Wessel & Christensen, 2012). But this is a means to an end. The end goal for many CEOs is to *find ways to keep driving business growth on behalf of their organizations.* Often, growth means an increase in top-line performance: revenue (i.e., sales) and, in turn, a boost to bottom-line performance: profits. For example, the annual Gartner CEO and Senior Business Executive Survey finds that *growth* is the number one priority of these executives with over half (53%) mentioning this imperative (Gartner, Inc., 2019). This survey also found an increase in executives deeming financial priorities important (Gartner, Inc., 2019).

In many ways, growth is the lifeblood of an organization, whether a corporation, an educational institution or a non-profit organization (Christensen & Raynor, 2003). Good things tend to happen when an organization is experiencing growth in its overall revenue, whether through product/service sales, tuition or fundraising. Positive momentum tends to beget more positive momentum. In economics, this is called a *virtuous cycle* – a cycle of growth where success reinforces itself through a feedback loop, thereby driving further favorable results (Sowell, 2011). Conversely, when an organization is starved for growth and experiencing decline, it may fall into a *vicious cycle* – a cycle of decline that self-perpetuates and is difficult to reverse (Sowell, 2011). A negative growth organization may have less resources to work with and may face more difficult decisions, such as cost-cutting and re-organizations. Many CEOs would rather manage an organization that is growing, then to try and steer a turnaround.

Further, CEOs and other business leaders are often predisposed to seek out growth because they are often rewarded for delivering it (Christensen & Raynor, 2003; Ragas & Culp, 2014a, 2018b). Fame and fortune often go to growers *not decliners*. For example, executive compensation packages and bonus targets set by boards of directors often reward executives for achieving increases in revenue, profits and/or related financial growth measures

(Borneman, 2019; Lev, 2012; Tortoriello, 2018). Further, the news media often favorably feature executives and organizations that deliver impressive growth. For example, the cover of a *Crain's Chicago Business* "Fast 50" issue of the fastest-growing Chicago area businesses (as measured by annual revenue growth) was literally titled, "The Rockstars of Growth."

There are two major forms of revenue growth: *organic-driven growth* and *acquisition-driven growth*. Organic growth, on one hand, is exactly what it sounds like – "homegrown" revenue growth driven by the revenue performance of existing business operations. Acquisition-driven (or inorganic) growth, on the other hand, is revenue that comes from acquiring another company. Companies take different approaches to driving growth. For example, Amazon, on one hand, is known more for organic growth resulting from innovations it has developed largely in-house, such as Amazon Web Services (AWS) or Alexa products (Rossman, 2019). Salesforce.com, on the other hand, has been a frequent acquirer of other software companies (Moorhead, 2019). The agency holding companies, such as IPG, Omnicom, Publicis and WPP, have also relied in part on acquisitions over the years to fuel growth. Wall Street generally places a greater value on organic growth, since it is non-dependent on future mergers and acquisitions (and the successful integration of acquired firms) to keep fueling growth (Moorhead, 2019).

Chief communications officers (CCOs) indicate that the most important factor in driving high performance in the communications function within enterprises is that the function's work is aligned with business goals (Penning & Bain, 2018). While business goals will vary some by organizational leadership, a review of recent CEO surveys (Gartner, Inc, 2019; KPMG International, 2018; PwC, 2019a) indicates that an overall priority of these leaders is often to support business growth. Strategic communication professionals and teams that can help their organizations and clients deliver upon this innovation-fueled growth priority may be more highly valued and rewarded.

"As a person who has had the privilege of serving as both the CEO and CCO of business units at multiple large companies, I have seen this issue from both sides and strongly believe that a communication strategy that is not completely tied to the business growth strategy is a losing proposition," says David Albritton, vice president, Global Communications, AWS Public Sector & Vertical Industries for Amazon Web Services (personal communication, November 18, 2020). Albritton previously made the move from senior communication leader at General Motors to heading a business unit there. Before GM, Albritton was vice president and CCO for Exelis Inc., now part of Harris Corp. "In today's dynamic business environment, perceived leadership in critical areas, such as innovative technologies and/or differentiated offerings, disciplined financial management, operating efficiency, customer intimacy and corporate citizenship are key drivers of a positive corporate reputation."

Further evidence that organizational growth and innovation has become a strategic priority across the corporate and agency world is the rise of a new C-level position, the chief growth officer (CGO) (Hinds, Hayes, Sanderson, Sachar, & Samson, 2016). This new position first emerged at technology and software companies as a way to formalize strategic growth as an organizational imperative and to encourage better integration of marketing with other key business activities like innovation, analytics and strategy (Sternberg, 2019; Vista Equity Partners Management, LLC, 2020). In some companies, the chief marketing officer (CMO) position has been supplanted by the CGO position, while in other organizations, the reverse has occurred (Albanese, 2019). Still, in other organizations, there are both CMOs and CGOs. For example, in recent years, the Coca-Cola Co. has had only a CMO, then only a CGO, and then back to having a CMO. On the agency side, the CGO title has popped up across a growing number of agencies and is a high-profile, hot-seat position, with this executive responsible for delivering on C-suite and board-level growth targets (Sternberg, 2019).

INNOVATION AS A DRIVER OF ORGANIZATIONAL GROWTH

Innovation is not a new idea in the business world. Pun intended. Some business management consultants and scholars have long researched and talked about the art and science of innovation. For example, near the height of the dot com boom of the 1990s, Harvard Business School professor Clayton Christensen (1997) published the highly influential book, *The Innovator's Dilemma*. But one needs to re-wind decades earlier to the publication of the first edition of *Diffusion of Innovations* by Everett Rogers (1962), a communications theorists and sociologist, to more fully appreciate that the study of innovation has been going on for decades, if not longer. The actual term "innovation" reportedly appeared in print as early as the fifteenth century and has its roots in the Latin noun *innovatus*, meaning renewal or change (Kwoh, 2012).

What is different today is that references to innovation are everywhere. Businesspeople and policymakers have exuberantly embraced the term. From job descriptions to conference programs to business magazine covers, talk of "innovation" is rampant (Wessel & Christensen, 2012; Wladawsky-Berger, 2018). Some argue that this has diluted the term (Kwoh, 2012; O'Bryan, 2013; Sax, 2018). There is no one widely agreed upon definition of innovation. Many can agree that simply *any* new product, service, process or practice does *not* qualify as an innovation. Many can also agree that an innovation does not need to be an invention – something entirely new that did not exist before (Sax, 2018). For the purpose of this book, an innovation can be defined as a product, service, process or practice that offers significant new value in solving problems for adopters, whether they be customers, employees or other stakeholders.

What there is more agreement upon is there are many ways that organizations are fostering the development and adoption of successful innovations to drive growth. Corporations are establishing innovation centers, labs and associated facilities and programs in their headquarters and/or regional offices. Some companies are establishing satellite offices focused on innovation and collaboration inside of or in partnership with outside accelerators, incubators and co-working spaces. For example, Chicago-based incubator 1871, which has consistently been named among the best in the world among university-affiliated business incubators, houses numerous university, corporate and non-profit partners, early stage venture capital firms, specialized accelerator programs and startup companies – all under one physical and virtual roof (Tai, 2018).

There is also a renewal of interest by firms in corporate venture capital funds and programs to help finance, support and grow startups. Corporate communication professionals and agency partners are often involved in developing and promoting these programs to employees and other stakeholders. Examples of such programs include Kraft Heinz's Springboard Accelerator, General Mills' 301 INC Kellogg's eighteen94 Capital, Campbell Soup's Acre Venture Partners and Tyson Foods' Tyson New Ventures LLC. Even younger brands like Chobani and Chipotle have incubators (Bomkamp, 2018; CBINSIGHTS, 2018).

Communication agency and consultancy holding companies also are playing the role of incubators and accelerators as a way to drive growth and innovation. Some 20 years ago, Zeno Group was founded by Edelman founder Dan Edelman as a so-called "conflict shop" focused on tech sector accounts (Edelman, 2019). Over the years, DJE Holdings, the parent company of Edelman, has nurtured and supported Zeno as part of its portfolio of companies. Today Zeno is regularly recognized as among the best of the mid-sized strategic communication agencies (Edelman, 2019).

"'Fearless pursuit of the unexpected,' our North Star, speaks directly to the role and importance of innovation – to take risks, experiment and try new things. The greatest obstacle to innovation is not trying or saying it cannot be done," explains Barby K. Siegel, CEO of Zeno Group, who joined the agency when it had 55 team members (Sudhaman, 2018). Zeno now has more than 500 people, known as Zenoids.

Today, some of our best innovation comes from Zeno team members outside of the leadership team, people at various levels of experience who know they have the freedom to go off and build the plane – even if it fails. Innovate, fail; innovate, learn. Innovate and change the world. That's good for us and even better for our clients. (B. K. Siegel, personal communication, August 17, 2019)

BUSINESS TRANSFORMATIONS AND STRATEGIC COMMUNICATION

One constant today in business and society is change. As explained by Wladawsky-Berger (2018): "To survive in today's fast changing marketplace, every business – large or small, startup or long established – must be capable of a continual process of transformation and renewal" (para. 1). Research by KPMG International (2016) suggests that more than 9 in 10 organizations (96%) report that they are in some form of transformation, but less than half (47%) expect to realize sustainable value from these efforts. Examples of change management communication programs include rebranding efforts; changes in senior leadership, mergers or acquisitions; and downsizings and workforce reductions. Some report that more than two-thirds (70%) of change programs fail, in part due to lackluster strategic communications

(Daly, Teague, & Kitchen, 2003). Some communication professionals indicate that they deserve a more strategic role in developing such programs. Greater business acumen may help achieve this (Neill, 2019).

Change management communication and supporting business transformations is a growing practice area and focus for communications professionals, whether working on the agency side or in-house (Bowen, Rawlins, & Martin, 2019; Lambiase, 2018; Scott, 2019). Internal and organizational communications professionals often play a meaningful role in supporting change initiatives, working in collaboration with organizational leadership and colleagues from human resources, marketing, finance, IT and other departments (Men, 2019; Men & Bowen, 2017; Neill, 2018). As with innovation initiatives and programs, a frequent desired outcome of change management by the C-suite is revitalizing and/or accelerating organizational growth (Harrison & Mühlberg, 2015; Ramanujam, 2019).

Much like with "innovation," some argue that the term "transformation" is overused. Consultants at McKinsey & Co. posit that "any form of change, however minor or routine" is *not* a transformation (Bucy, Hall, & Yakola, 2016). This group (Bucy et al., 2016) notes that there are several types of transformations, including organizational transformations (re-drawing organizational roles and accountabilities), strategic transformations (changing a business model) and digital reinventions or transformations (an organization re-working how it is wired). They define transformation "with a capital *T*" as "an intense, organization-wide program to enhance performance (an earnings improvement of 25 percent or more, for example) and to boost organizational health" (Bucy et al., 2016, para. 5). As emphasized earlier in this chapter, CEOs want growth. Growth often gets measured in the business world in dollars and cents, such as a program or initiative contributing to an increase in revenue and/or profits (Ramanujam, 2019).

According to Kelly McGinnis, senior vice president and CCO for Levi Strauss & Co., in her experience, a business transformation can present an opportunity, not just for the organization, but for communications professionals, their communications departments and their teams (personal communication, July 16, 2019). "Transformations have moments that require you to be thoughtful, smart, proactive, innovative and aggressive," explains McGinnis, who prior to heading communications for Levi's held senior positions with Dell and FleishmanHillard.

"If you do so, you'll find yourself more visible and influential than you imagined. These are times when your leadership can impact and influence your businesses in ways that go well beyond the scope of traditional PR and communications."

AN OPPORTUNITY FOR STRATEGIC COMMUNICATION TO LEAD

Organizational growth, innovation and transformation are all interrelated. All deal with trying to successfully manage change and disruption. Effective strategic communication, particularly strong employee engagement and organizational communication, is critical to helping organizations, stakeholders and clients not just survive, but thrive in the eye of this swirling "change storm" (Lambiase, 2018; Men, 2019; Men & Bowen, 2017; Scott, 2019).

A decade or so ago, communication departments, teams and agency partners began taking leadership roles in advancing corporate social responsibility and sustainability initiatives both inside and outside of organizations (Coombs & Holladay, 2012; Ragas & Culp, 2014a, 2018b). Today, innovation and change programs and initiatives are emerging as critical additional opportunities for communication departments, teams and agency partners to create strategic value and help lead their organizations forward (Arthur W. Page Society, 2019a).

KEY TERMS

Accelerator	Invention
Acquisition-driven growth	Organic growth
Change management communication	Moore's Law
Corporate social responsibility	Transformation
Co-working space	Venture capital
Disruption	Vicious cycle
Incubator	Virtuous cycle
Innovation	

DISCUSSION QUESTIONS

(1) What are examples of disruptive innovations that you believe will specifically impact the strategic communication profession in the years ahead? Explain your reasoning.

(2) A top priority of CEOs is driving organizational growth, often meaning an increase in financial indicators like sales and profits. What do you think about this focus? Is it always good? Can it be bad?

(3) There are many different "most innovative company" lists. In your opinion, what are some of the most innovative organizations today? Write out your own list and share.

(4) What is an example of a larger, older organization that is impressively navigating through disruptive innovations and successfully transforming the organization?

(5) Do you think strategic communication professionals will play a bigger or smaller role in organizational innovation, change and transformations in the years ahead? Why?

By Maril MacDonald, Founder & CEO, Gagen MacDonald

In a highly disruptive environment, it's increasingly important to recognize the difference between change leadership and transformational leadership. While both are important, they are often confused.

From what I've observed, over the last 20 years, communicators have greatly improved our skills at introducing change. However, we lag further behind in leading transformations. This is our next frontier, and it requires both a skillset and mindset shift.

Specifically, it necessitates going from managing projects to sparking movements. What do I mean by this?

A project is a clearly defined initiative that has a start date, an end date and a scope. In a corporate context, it typically has executive sponsors, assigned budgets, specific and limited resources and clear milestones. Most changes are projects, and when a project is over, everyone goes back to their "day job."

Whereas change is about doing something differently to get a different result (e.g., a new procurement process), transformations are different. Transformations are comprised of multiple interdependent changes throughout an enterprise that together create something fundamentally different and new. Ongoing transformation is how Amazon has gone from an online book seller to a dominant player in ecommerce, logistics and cloud storage (among other things). And transformations are powered by movements.

Research shows that successful social movements share certain unique properties. They are leaderless and amorphous, enabled not by structures, but ignited by ideas. They invite diverse groups of people to sign up and join. They don't end but rather establish a "new normal." And they cannot be controlled.

To spark a movement, we need to resist the "project mindset" to "control the message," "mange information flow," and generally stuff everything on to spreadsheets, but focus instead on several fundamental areas where we can have tremendous impact.

First, *storytelling*.

From Civil Rights to #MeToo, every movement that has proven transformative has stemmed from imagination of a better future. Stories are powerful in both articulating a case for transformation, as well as illuminating what's possible. As communicators, we must tell stories that ...

- Possess drama.

- Build to an exciting but uncertain conclusion.

- Travel an emotional arc.

- Resonate with a diversity of individuals.

- Speak to a larger purpose.

Second, *leadership*.

Transformation occurs when a broad and deep group of leaders unite around a common idea, and then bring their respective organizations along in a shared journey. Communicators must coach, advise and equip leaders to support their efforts. In particular, communicators must help leaders ...

- Tell a clear and consistent story.

- Participate in dialogue.

- Model desired behaviors.

- Stay visible in many formats.

Finally, a *path forward*.

Research shows that movements take hold when diverse groups of people connect to build something new together. Often, these connections fail to occur not because of a lack of shared interest, but because the pathways between people are buried in clutter. Communicators have the skills to bring those pathways to light. Specifically, communicators can ...

- Gather and share insights on where roadblocks exist.

- Reiterate critical priorities so what's important doesn't get lost to what's urgent.

- Create feedback forums to allow for recalibration.

- Serve as the voice of employees to top leaders.

While transformations are hard and messy work, they can be the thrill of a career. As communicators, we have an essential skillset to bring to the table.

3

THE LEAN AND AGILE ENTERPRISE

The pace of disruptive change in business and society is accelerating. In turn, chief executive officers (CEOs) and their teams are racing to transform their organizations into more lean and agile enterprises.

The Standard and Poor's 500 index, better known as simply the S&P 500, is an influential and widely followed stock market index that measures the performance of 500 large corporations listed on stock exchanges in the United States. Research indicates that the average tenure of companies on the S&P 500 has declined significantly in recent decades (Anthony, Viguerie, Schwartz, & Van Landeghem, 2018). In 1964, the average tenure of a company on the S&P 500 was 33 years. By 2016, this life span had narrowed to 24 years. By 2027, this life span is forecasted to decline to just 12 years (Anthony et al., 2018). At the current churn rate, about half of S&P 500 companies will be replaced over the next decade. Companies drop off the S&P 500 list for a variety of reasons, such as being the subject of a merger or acquisition or being overtaken by a faster-growing company and falling below the market capitalization threshold. Larger, more mature companies are particularly in the crosshairs of this acceleration in disruptive technological, societal and economic changes; they can either adapt or decline (Schwartz, 2019).

Jeff Bezos, the founder and CEO of Amazon.com, one of the world's most powerful companies, believes that even Amazon will one day be disrupted and enter a period of decline. For example, Bezos has been quoted as saying at an all-hands staff meeting: "In fact, I predict one day Amazon will fail. Amazon will go bankrupt. If you look at large companies, their lifespans tend to be 30-plus years, not a hundred-plus years" (Kim, 2018, para. 3). According to this report, Bezos believes that a key to forestalling Amazon's demise is for it to "obsess over customers" (Hamilton, 2019, para. 4). As such, he has tried to establish a company culture in which failure is an acceptable – and even necessary – part of rapidly developing and launching customer-focused innovations (Green, 2019). Given Amazon's dominance across multiple industries, it is hard to imagine a future in which it declines significantly or outright fails, but Bezos's message is clear: change is the constant today. No company can rest on its laurels.

More CEOs, C-suites and boardrooms are getting this message loud and clear. A global survey of more than a thousand CEOs of some of the world's largest organizations found that two-thirds (67%) of these leaders believe that *acting with agility* is the new currency of business (KPMG International, 2019). Being too slow risks bankruptcy. In the words of KPMG International (2019), the international professional services firm that authored this survey, "a successful CEO is an agile CEO" and "if they fail to adapt to a constantly changing world, their business will become irrelevant" (para. 1). Another global CEO survey conducted by The Conference Board (2019), a well-regarded business think tank, tells a similar story. The number one internal hot-button issue for CEOs is the attraction and retention of top talent, followed by creating new business models because of disruptive technologies (The Conference Board, 2019). Finally, research by global management consultant McKinsey & Co. (Aghina, De Smet, Lackey, Lurie, & Murarka, 2018) indicates that agile organizations may achieve superior business performance, including greater customer-centricity, faster time to market, higher revenue growth, lower costs and a more engaged workforce.

Strategic communications professionals are increasingly on the front lines of helping their organizations and clients become more lean and agile (Feldman, 2019; Korn Ferry, 2020c). Senior communication leaders rate agility as the top attribute of a high performing corporate culture (Arthur W. Page Society, 2019a). More communication professionals are also using Agile techniques and approaches for campaign and program management (Budd & Cooper, 2004; van Ruler, 2014, 2015, 2018). This chapter converges in many ways with the prior chapter's focus on organizational growth, innovation and transformation. Lean and agile methods, approaches and thinking have their roots in the product manufacturing and software development worlds, respectively (J. Martin, 2017; Rose, 2015). In recent years, the general DNA underlying lean and agile has increasingly been adopted across the enterprise – all the way up to the C-suite and the boardroom (Cappelli &

Tavis, 2018; Garton & Noble, 2017; Rigby, Elk, & Berez, 2020), ushering in a new business management and leadership paradigm that is more customer-centric, employee team-focused, market responsive and adaptive to change (Denning, 2017, 2019; Rigby, Sutherland, & Takeuchi, 2016; Rigby et al., 2020; Rigby, Sutherland, & Noble, 2018).

THE LEAN AND AGILE DNA

There is a paradigm shift underway in organizational management, leadership, design and strategy. The traditional scientific management paradigm has been one of "top-down" organizational hierarchies with variations of "command and control" leadership styles. Such an organizational structure has typically been built around functional specializations and silos (Morgan, 1986). Organizations operating under this traditional paradigm can be thought of as hierarchical and linear "machines"; they are generally stable and efficient, but are not particularly nimble or dynamic around change (Aghina et al., 2018; Aghina, Handscomb, Ludolph, West, & Yip, 2019). This is problematic as the pace of change accelerates.

In comparison, the new enterprise management paradigm reduces the emphasis on "boxes and lines" reporting, with leadership instead showing direction and enabling action, such as providing flexible resources to empowered cross-functional teams built around end-to-end accountability. These agile organizations can be thought of as "living organisms" rather than "machines." Organizations operating under the new paradigm balance stability with dynamism, allowing them to better adapt to new challenges and opportunities (Aghina et al., 2018, 2019).

This new paradigm is infused with the DNA of lean and agile. Lean has its roots in the product manufacturing world. The ideas and tools developed in lean manufacturing led in part to the creation of lean software development (Rose, 2015). Lean manufacturing is closely associated with Toyota and the Toyota production system, which helped propel Toyota in recent decades to become one of the largest and most profitable automotive manufacturers in the world (Liker, 2004). Lean thinking and related approaches, such as the Kanban method, include focusing on delivering customer value, continuous improvement, adapting to change, respect for people, being transparent and the elimination of waste (Project Management Institute, Inc., 2017a, 2017b). Lean manufacturing is associated with the Six Sigma method of process improvement that has been pioneered by GE and others (Rose, 2015). Lean thinking and concepts have been popularized within the technology start-up company community and beyond by best-selling business books, such as *The Lean Startup* by Eric Ries (2011).

In recent decades, lean thinking from the world of *physical* product manu-facturing has inspired new and improved methods and approaches to *digital* manufacturing: software development. In 2001, 17 software developers and software project managers met at a ski resort in Snowbird, Utah to dis-cuss what was then being called "lightweight" software development (Rose, 2015). A critical result of this meeting was the publication of an influential document called *The Agile Manifesto* (*Agilemanifesto.org*, 2001), which cre-ated a list of 4 core shared values and 12 supporting principles for agile software development projects.

These four core shared values are at the core of the agile mindset and agile thinking, regardless of the specific agile approach, method or framework employed:

- Individuals and interactions over processes and tools.

- Working software over comprehensive documentation.

- Customer collaboration over contract negotiation.

- Responding to change over following a plan.

The values and principles outlined in *The Agile Manifesto* provide the foundation for the agile mindset. See Fig. 3.1 for the progression of an agile mindset, which is manifested by many different practices and frame-works. Common agile frameworks include Scrum, Extreme Programming, the Scaled Agile Framework and DevOps (Rose, 2015). Fig. 3.2 shows the relationships between lean, agile and Kanban. The various agile frameworks may be thought of as descendants of lean thinking, while Kanban straddles the two worlds, as Kanban is a method used for knowledge work that was inspired by the original lean manufacturing system.

Since the publication of *The Agile Manifesto*, the agile approach to soft-ware development has taken off in information technology (IT) departments and project management offices in companies and organizations of all sizes

Fig. 3.1:   The Progression of an Agile Mindset.

The progression of an agile mindset.

Agile is a mindset.	Described by 4 values.	Defined by 12 principles.	And manifested by many different practices.

Described by 4 values.

Individuals and interactions over processes and tools.

Working software over comprehensive documentation.

Customer collaboration over contract negotiation.

Responding to change over following a plan.

Defined by 12 principles.

Creating value through continuous delivery.

Working with changing requirements.

Delivering working software frequently.

Working with businesspeople.

Creating results.

Communicating face-to-face.

Building working software.

Providing manageable environments.

Paying attention to details.

Keeping things simple.

Relying on self-led teams.

Adjusting the project practices.

Sources: Adapted from Project Management Institute, Inc. (2017a) and Phillips (2019).

Fig. 3.2:   The Relationship between Lean, Agile and Kanban Approaches.

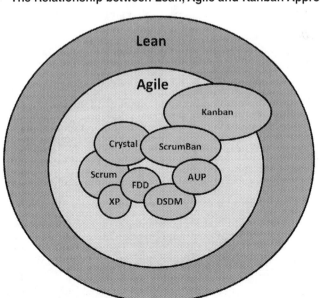

Lean

Agile

Kanban

Crystal   ScrumBan

Scrum

FDD   AUP

XP   DSDM

Source: Adapted from Project Management Institute, Inc. (2017a).

around the world (Denning, 2017, 2019; Miller, 2017). Agile frameworks emphasize project adaptation and flexibility in short development cycles (called "sprints"), in contrast to the traditional predictive engineering approach to project development and management, which is known as the "waterfall" methodology. As the name implies, a waterfall approach breaks a project down into flowing sequential phases and works best when a project is lower in uncertainty. Research shows that many developers and project managers use a mix of *both* approaches (PM Solutions, 2018).

ORGANIZATIONAL AGILITY: A CEO AND C-SUITE PRIORITY

Technology is often at the core of innovation, disruption and change within and outside of organizations today. Perhaps then it is not surprising that lean and agile approaches and thinking started in IT departments and affiliated disciplines before spreading outward to other departments and functional areas within the enterprise (Capelli & Tavis, 2018; J. Martin, 2017; Rigby et al., 2016, 2020; Rodrigues, 2018; van Ruler, 2014, 2015, 2018). As discussed earlier in this chapter, business leaders are eager to successfully transform their organizations into more lean and agile enterprises that are better suited to adapt to the demands of a constantly changing world (Aghina et al., 2018; Anthony et al., 2018; The Conference Board, 2019; KPMG International, 2019). As explained by Rigby et al. (2020):

> *Agile leadership demands that executives create a carefully balanced system that delivers both stability and agility – a system that runs the business efficiently, changes the business effectively and merges the two activities without destroying both elements. (p. 73)*

Executives often talk about their teams, functions and/or organizations as "doing agile," "being agile" or "becoming agile." But what does this really mean? In short, agile management and leadership can mean different things to different people. This can breed noise and confusion. In 2017, a group of large organizations, all members of the SD Learning Consortium (SDLC), came together in New York City to discuss and reach consensus on what Agile management stood for in their own organizations, following two years of site visits to fellow member organizations (Denning, 2017).

SDLC members at the time of the meeting collectively represented many billions of dollars in total market value with tens of thousands of employees (SD Learning Consortium, 2017). The member firms converged on four elements of the agile mindset that they saw as representing the essence of agility in the business world:

- Delighting customers.

- Descaling work.

- Enterprise-wide agility.

- Nurturing culture.

According to the SD Learning Consortium (2017), "as a result of globalization, deregulation, knowledge work and new technology, power in the marketplace has shifted from seller to buyer" (p. 3). The group calls this "a veritable Copernican revolution in management" (p. 3) with firms now revolving around users/customers – the new center of the solar system – versus the old way in which users/customers were supposed to revolve around the firm (SD Learning Consortium, 2017, p. 3). A key conclusion of the group's work is that

> achieving continuous innovation is dependent on an entrepreneurial mindset pervading the organization. Where the management tools and processes of Agile, Lean or Kanban are implemented without the requisite mindset, few, if any benefits were observed. (SD Learning Consortium, 2016, p. 4)

Interest in lean and agile by the corner office and the boardroom seemingly reached a tipping point in 2018 and has expanded further in the years since (Rigby et al., 2020). Discussion of lean and agile management increased at business conferences, in business publications and among management consultants – far beyond the realms of IT and project management. For example, the May–June 2018 cover story of *Harvard Business Review* was titled, "Agile at Scale: How to Create a Truly Flexible Organization" (Rigby et al., 2018). Agile management was once again the cover story for the May–June 2020 of *HBR*: "The Agile C-Suite" (Ribgy et al., 2020).

In an annual letter to shareholders, Jamie Dimon, the CEO and chair of JPMorgan Chase, and one of the most closely followed business executives in the world, specifically highlighted efforts to make the global financial services giant more agile as an organization:

Agile technology generally means using new forms of technology – think cloud computing, for example – to enable small teams of programmers to build and properly execute new programs and products rapidly and effectively. The concept of agile management goes hand in hand with this approach. Small teams of people responsible for products and services work with technologists to improve the customer experience. To do this, they must be given the necessary authority and resources. It is also important they understand they can make mistakes without punishment. (Dimon, 2018, p. 27)

Dimon has become friendly over the years with Jeff Bezos, the founder and CEO of Amazon, which even back in its early years was embracing agile-like concepts (Glazer, Stevens, & Andriotis, 2019; Rossman, 2019). Early in Amazon's history, Bezos even tried to hire Dimon to become the then upstart company's president (Glazer et al., 2019). Dimon and his leadership team have reportedly adopted elements of Bezos's "customer obsession" mantra, which says that employees should start by identifying customer problems, and then by developing products and services that help solve these customer problems. For example, Amazon's very convenient one-click purchase capability for its customers encouraged Chase, the retail arm of JPMorgan Chase, to reduce the number of steps at its ATMs (Kandell, 2018). A cash withdrawal used to take six steps. Now it can be done in just three.

STRATEGIC COMMUNICATIONS AND ORGANIZATIONAL AGILITY

Digital technology innovations and insights are the lifeblood of many organizations today. Whether an organization has a chief information officer (CIO), a chief technology officer (CTO) and/or a chief digital officer (CDO), the roles, responsibilities and budgets of these critical business leaders and their technology teams are likely to grow in the years ahead (Aghina et al., 2018; Feldman, 2019). At a minimum, communication professionals, whether working in-house or at agencies or consultancies, should gain basic proficiency in lean and agile terminology, concepts and tools. In many ways, lean, agile and its derivatives are becoming a predominant language and mindset of developers, project and product managers and data scientists (Friess, 2018).

Communication professionals who gain fluency in this language will be able to work more effectively with IT and project management teams and serve as better translators and integrators of technology-driven initiatives, innovations and digital engagement systems across the enterprise (Arthur W. Page Society, 2016a, 2016b, 2017, 2019a). Recognizing the growing importance of agile to the future of the strategic communication profession, the *International Journal of Strategic Communication*, a top academic journal published by Taylor & Francis Group, produced a special issue on agile communications. One of the co-authors of this book contributed an article to this special issue (see M. W. Ragas & T. H. Ragas, forthcoming).

Korn Ferry is one of the world's top executive search and organizational consulting firms. Based on a Korn Ferry assessment of its recent work with clients and industry leaders, chief communications officers (CCOs) are increasingly expected to have a skillset that goes beyond communication and prepares them to potentially lead business operations or even become CEOs. Topping Korn Ferry's (2020c) list of critical skills and traits for successful CCOs to develop is *agility* since "on any given day, CCOs are faced with a range of disparate issues that required deft management" (p. 5). The other critical skills and traits that Korn Ferry (2020c) feels CCOs and other senior communication leaders should develop mastery of is strategic thinking, risk management, holistic insight and stakeholder relationship building skills.

An area where communications professionals can have a significant impact is in helping their organizations and clients embrace – and reward – lean and agile thinking, policies and work methods by employees, partners and other internal stakeholders. Communicators can play an essential role in helping organizations and clients (re)define, activate and align organizational mission, purpose and values around organizational cultures that (1) empower and respect employees and (2) are customer-focused – two core ingredients of lean and agile organizations and the agile mindset (Arthur W. Page Society, 2019a; KPMG International, 2019; Rigby et al., 2016, 2018). The next chapter will address the rise of corporate mission, vision, purpose, values and culture as sources of sustainable competitive advantage for organizations. As may be more evident by now, each of the guiding approach to business chapters have key interrelationships.

Purpose-driven organizations do not need to be young or small to nurture an agile mindset. Larger, more mature organizations can demonstrate agile characteristics too. Mayo Clinic is an excellent case in point. Founded more than 150 years ago, the not-for-profit organization is widely regarded as one of the top health systems in the world (Berry & Seltman, 2014). Each year, more than 1.3 million people from all 50 states and 138 countries come to Mayo Foundation for Medical Education and Research for care (Mayo Clinic, 2019a). Core to the enduring success of Mayo is what the organization calls its "Mayo Clinic Model of Care." The primary value is "the needs of the patient come first" (Mayo Clinic, 2019b). Mayo's supporting values are encapsulated by the acronym RICH TIES (Respect, Integrity, Compassion, Healing, Teamwork, Innovation, Excellence and Stewardship). Long before "patient-centered health care" and "medical teamwork" – intraorganizational medical teams converging to serve the needs of patients – became familiar concepts in the healthcare world, Mayo was practicing this agile-like approach (Berry & Seltman, 2014).

"When we began doing more storytelling about our patients' experience at Mayo Clinic around 20 years ago, we surveyed every patient who participated to ensure they didn't feel we compromised their privacy," says Chris Gade, chief public affairs officer at Mayo Clinic (personal communication, September 29, 2019). "Not long after, we stopped the survey. Universally, patients expressed enthusiasm to share their story so other patients could benefit. The act of being intentional to survey each patient reflects Mayo Clinic's firm commitment to its primary value, the needs of the patient come first."

"Of equal importance at Mayo Clinic is the principle of working in teams," says Gade. "We accomplish so much more by working together, rather than separately. In our clinical practice and in public affairs, we surround whatever is in front of us, whether a complex medical diagnosis or equally complex public issue, with the best minds, working together to overcome whatever challenging obstacle is in front of us."

Founded almost 60 years ago, Padilla is a mid-sized brand strategy and strategic communication agency with offices across the United States. It was an employee-owned agency for most of its history prior to joining AVENIR Global, a Canadian agency holding company with more than 1,000 staff and offices around the world. Inspired in part by the "team approach" of long-time client Mayo Clinic and the changing dynamics of agency work, Padilla is implementing "ensemble team" training for employees across the organization. As a foundation platform, Padilla has a defined set of shared values, known as Padilla Beliefs, which it developed with significant input from its employees. The Padilla Beliefs are:

- Walk in their world.

- Wonder and wander.

- Think as many.

- Work brave.

- Build trust.

- Own it and act on it.

"The changes in our field mean that work has to be done differently. Back when clients primarily relied on agencies for media relations and crisis management, you could serve their needs with a small, focused account team doing the majority of the work," says Matt Kucharski, president of Padilla (personal communication, August 29, 2019). "Now that same client requires experts in a wide range of disciplines – multiple channels, multiple content types, multiple stakeholders – all with more sophisticated insights, data and analytics at the core. That calls for an ensemble team approach – one that brings forth the best possible talent in a nimble and agile way while still retaining continuity, quality and consistency. That's what we're striving for."

Some of the most successful and enduring communication agencies and consultancies have been grounded since their founding in organizational cultures that encourage agile thinking and risk tasking. A pioneering agency entrepreneur, Margi Booth founded her eponymous firm called M Booth in 1983 with a goal of developing innovative communication campaigns for consumer, lifestyle and corporate brands (*PRWeek*, 2016). According to M Booth (2019), "culture is everything" (para. 1). Its employees strive to be courageous in their thinking, accountable to their clients and find ways to have fun every day (M Booth, 2019). Now part of the Next 15 Communications family of marketing businesses, M Booth boasts a history of agency of the year and best places to work awards to go along with a roster of blue-chip clients.

"The most forward-thinking agencies boast agile workplaces that aren't dictated. They rise up from the bottom and are supported from the top with leaders who know too much precision often kills creativity and innovation," says Margi Booth, a member of the *PRWeek* Hall of Fame (personal communication, September 9, 2019). "Their client partnerships thrive on inspired cultures, alive with courage and invention. They are fast moving, fleet of foot, and always with permission to fail-forward."

ORGANIZATIONAL AGILITY IN A VUCA WORLD

The managerial acronym VUCA – volatility, uncertainty, complexity and ambiguity – sums up much of what the future likely holds for business and society (Bennett & Lemoine, 2014). A VUCA world will likely favor those organizations and business leaders that can continuously adapt – quickly, smartly and effectively – to the changing environment around them. In short, lean and agile organizations are likely to survive and thrive in the years ahead, while lumbering behemoths may find themselves endangered, if not outright extinct (Aghina et al., 2018, 2019).

Many organizations are either in the middle of transformation initiatives or have plans to undergo transformations to help them better navigate change and deliver more value added innovations for customers and other stakeholders (Bucy, Hall, & Yakola, 2016; KPMG International, 2016; Scott, 2019). Strategic communication professionals and teams that embrace lean and agile thinking and management approaches (McGinnis, 2018; van Ruler, 2014, 2015, 2018) – and who can operate within the accelerating speed of change – will be well positioned to create longer-term strategic value for their organizations, clients and their own careers.

KEY TERMS

Agile	Project management
Agile management	Project management office
Agile Manifesto	S&P 500
Chief digital officer	Scrum
Chief information officer	Six Sigma
Chief technology officer	Sprints
Kanban	Transformation
Lean	VUCA

DISCUSSION QUESTIONS

(1) Why do you think CEOs and C-suites are making organizational agility a top priority for their organizations? What are the factors driving this embrace of a more agile mindset?

(2) If you were writing your own *Agile Manifesto* specifically for strategic communicators, what would be your four core shared values that would be at the heart of agile?

(3) What is an example of a larger organization that, in your experience, is well positioned for a VUCA world? What about an organization that you feel is *not* well positioned?

(4) Research suggests that the pace of disruptive change is accelerating and that the lifecycle of successful companies is shortening. What have you found in your own experiences?

(5) Which approach – agile or waterfall – do you think is better for communication campaign or program planning and management? Or does it depend? Explain your thinking.

By Bob Feldman,
Vice Chair, and **Grant Toups,**
Managing Partner and Chief
Client Officer, ICF Next

Agility is a hot topic and it's clear why: constant, unyielding change is the new normal and success requires the ability to adapt quickly, efficiently and effectively again and again.

So, what is an agile organization? Working with global companies across industries, a clear set of characteristics has emerged that mark an agile function, whether marketing, communications, government affairs or human resources. The good news is, with some focus and effort, it's easily attainable.

Nine Characteristics of an Agile Organization

(1) *North Star:*

Every company has a corporate mission, but it's often big and difficult to connect to daily activities. Supplement it with a clear, documented and widely understood functional mission that captures what the function is there to do, how it will advance the corporate mission and functional core competencies. It becomes a guidebook to help navigate the changing terrain of everyday work.

(2) *Operating model:*

With a new functional North Star in place, define what work the function is going to do, who it will do it for and, equally importantly, what it *won't* do.

(3) *Structure and skills:*

Most org charts are relics of the function's history. To be agile, functions require a continuous org refresh to efficiently and effectively adapt to the needs of a changing landscape. Build a structure that can flex instead of break under pressure, then populate it with the right talent in the right roles.

(4) *Tools and tech:*

Technology has altered the modern workplace for everyone. Few experience this as acutely as communicators. Define a CommTech suite (e.g., collaboration, CRM, data visualization, etc.) based on needs and deploy it with a healthy focus on behavior change.

(5) *Process and governance:*
It's critical to define the way(s) of working, interdependencies, accountabilities and how work flows. It may not be exciting, but getting it wrong dramatically slows a function's ability to adapt. Document processes and governance. Improve them regularly.

(6) *Strategy and execution:*
The annual plan is dead. Strategic planning must be a living, evolving idea. Agile organizations efficiently flex to the market instead of being disrupted by it. Evolve as external stakeholder needs and wants change.

(7) *Change empowerment:*
Agile organizations value and reward adaptability and creative problem-solving. They no longer think about *change management.* Today, change is to be leveraged, not managed.

(8) *Data and measurement:*
Leaders have long seen the value in using data to drive decision-making. Today that means real-time, visualized data used to make near real-time decisions about content, outreach, even issue escalation. Don't suffer under the burden of the large, quarterly metrics reports. Prioritize and measure what you can act upon.

(9) *Continuous improvement:*
The power of data is the power to adapt in real-time: continuously improve process, strategy and how you empower change.

These characteristics are a good blueprint to position a communications function for success in a rapidly changing world.

4

THE PURPOSE-DRIVEN ENTERPRISE

Profit and purpose should be like two peas in a pod.

That is essentially the message that financial executive and philanthropist Larry Fink has shared in his closely followed annual letters to chief executive officers (CEOs) in recent years (Fink, 2018, 2019, 2020). Fink's message that companies must do more than simply generate profits for investors, but rather strive to create purpose-driven value for *all* stakeholders and society, has sent shockwaves through corporate boardrooms (Sorkin, 2018, 2019a). Fink can't easily be ignored by his peers. He is the founder, CEO and chair of BlackRock, the largest money-management firm in the world with more than $7 trillion in assets under management (Lim, 2020).

In his 2018 letter to CEOs, known among investors as simply "Larry's Letter," Fink (2018) argued that "to prosper over time, every company must not only deliver financial performance, but also show how it makes a positive contribution to society" (para. 4). In Fink's view: "without a sense of purpose, no company, either public or private, can achieve its full potential" and it will lose the support of key stakeholders, thereby generating subpar long-term returns (Fink, 2018, para. 5). Fink has implored CEOs and their boards of directors to publicly articulate their strategy for long-term value creation, including their corporate purpose.

In his 2019 letter, Fink clarified and elucidated further on his perspective that companies need not choose between profit or purpose, but rather the two should be inextricably linked and at the core of management and board decision-making. According to Fink (2019), "purpose is not the sole pursuit of profits but the animating force for achieving them" (para. 4). In his view, "companies that fulfill their purpose and responsibilities to stakeholders reap rewards over the long-term," while "companies that ignore them stumble and fail" (Fink, 2019, para. 9). Finally, in his 2020 letter, Fink reiterated that, "ultimately, purpose is the engine of long-term profitability" (para. 14).

SHIFTING EXPECTATIONS FOR BUSINESS BY SOCIETY

Fink's focus on profit and purpose mirrors the very rapid rise in recent years in investment dollars flowing into sustainable, responsible and impact (SRI) investing funds and other vehicles (National Investor Relations Institute, 2019). US investment assets following SRI strategies have grown 25-fold since 1996 and by 43% just between 2018 and 2020 (US SIF Foundation, 2020). US investors now consider environmental, social and governance factors across $17 trillion in professionally managed assets or one in every three dollars invested (US SIF Foundation, 2020).

In many ways, the investment world is simply "playing catch up" to the majority views already held by other stakeholder groups, such as consumers and employees, about the expanded expectations of business in society today (Salter, 2019; Tahmincioglu, 2019). Surveys tend to show that Americans are increasingly willing to support purpose-driven companies through purchase, engagement and even advocacy (Edelman, 2018a, 2019, 2020; McTavish, 2018; Porter Novelli, 2018, 2019). For example, more than 7 out of 10 Americans (72%) say they feel it is more important than ever that the brands they buy from reflect their values (Porter Novelli, 2019). Conversely, less than 4 out of 10 Millennials (37%) – the future leaders in society – believe that business leaders are making a positive impact on the world (Deloitte, 2019b).

More CEOs, board members and other business leaders are sitting up, taking notice and taking action (Nooyi, 2019). But there is still much work to be done. For example, a national survey of business leaders across industries found that a strong majority (79%) of these leaders believe purpose is central to business success and an organization's existence (PwC, 2016). However, only a little more than a third (34%) of these same leaders agree that purpose is currently a guidepost for leadership decision-making (PwC, 2016). Helping the management of organizations close this gap and consistently demonstrate purpose-driven leadership and decision-making will likely be a top priority in the years ahead for chief communications officers

(CCOs), their communication teams and their agency partners (Bolton, Stacks, & Mizrachi, 2018; Bowen, Hardage, & Strong, 2018; Hynes, 2017; Mackey, McIntosh, & Phipps, 2020; Mackey & Sisodia, 2014; Ragas & Culp, 2014b, 2018a).

PURPOSE AND PROFITS: INSIDE THE TWO PEAS IN A POD

The choice of purpose *or* profit is a false one. Even trying to find a so-called "balance" between purpose and profits may be at least somewhat misguided. Purpose-driven enterprises are not allergic to profits (Nooyi, 2019; Salter, 2019). Far from it. But a purpose-driven enterprise acknowledges that it does not exist simply to *maximize short-term profits* for investors at the possible detriment of other stakeholder groups and society (The Aspen Institute, 2014; Cohen, 2011; Mackey et al., 2020; Mackey & Sisodia, 2014). As argued by BlackRock's Fink and others, blatantly privileging investors in the *short-term* can lead to *longer-term* negative effects on the business and its financial performance (Bowen et al., 2018; Fink, 2018, 2019, 2020; Salter, 2019; Tahmincioglu, 2019). Generating profits is essential; profits help an organization have the resources to invest in successfully accomplishing its mission and pursuing its vision.

John Mackey, the co-founder of Whole Foods Market, has helped spark discussion of corporate purpose in corner officers and boardrooms through the publication of his books *Conscious Capitalism* (2014) with Raj Sisodia and *Conscious Leadership* (2020) with Steve McIntosh and Carter Phipps. Whole Foods was acquired by Amazon.com in 2017 for nearly $14 billion (Clifford, 2018). Mackey appropriately uses a food analogy to explain how he views the relationship between purpose and profits:

> *Making high profits is the means to the ends of fulfilling Whole Foods' core business mission. We want to improve the health and well-being of everyone on the planet through higher-quality foods and better nutrition, and we can't fulfill this mission unless we are highly profitable. High profits are necessary to fuel our growth across the United States and the world. Just as people cannot live without eating, so a business cannot live without profits. But most people don't live to eat, and neither must a business live just to make profits. (Friedman, Mackey, & Rodgers, 2005, para. 54)*

Legendary business management scholar Peter Drucker reportedly used to provide a similar analogy to his students in explaining that the goal of business should not be profit maximization (Blakey, 2016; Cohen, 2011). According to a former student (Cohen, 2011), Drucker equated profits to be like oxygen for the human body. Without oxygen, the body cannot survive for long. Without profit, an organization can typically not survive for very long either. But if one thinks that acquiring oxygen is the purpose of their life, then they are missing something. Similarly, according to Drucker, a leader who thinks the *sole purpose* of their business is to generate higher profits is missing something. As argued by Cohen (2011), "profit maximization can cause organizational toxicity in the same way that oxygen toxicity can damage the body" (para. 5).

"Purpose is a 'competitive advantage' in business and life," says Patrice Tanaka, chief joy officer, Joyful Planet, LLC and a serial entrepreneur, having co-founded three award-winning public relations and marketing agencies, including serving as chief counselor and creative strategist for PadillaCRT (personal communication, July 23, 2019). "Discovering and actively living our life purpose or operationalizing our business purpose is the single most efficient and powerful way to unleash leadership potential and greater success, fulfillment and joy in our personal lives, our workplaces and our communities."

Costco Wholesale Corporation, one of the country's largest retailers and a perennial member of "best places to work" and "best corporate reputation" lists, has a clearly stated and straightforward mission posted on its website: "to continually provide our members with quality goods and services at the lowest possible prices" (Costco Wholesale Corporation, 2020, para. 1).

"We have never been a company that puts the shareholder on top," according to a speech Costco CEO and president W. Craig Jelinek gave about the history and growth of the company (Matthews, 2018, para. 6). "You have a responsibility to a shareholder – you do – but if you take the shareholder first, you are going to be in it for the short-term."

Not coincidentally, Costco's Code of Ethics places its members near the top of the list only behind always obeying the laws, rules and regulations of the land:

- Obey the law.

- Take care of our members.

- Take care of our employees.

- Respect our suppliers.

Costco Wholesale Corporation (2020) concludes its code by saying: "if we do these four things throughout our organization, then we will achieve our ultimate goal, which is to reward our shareholders" (para. 4). Costco commits to paying its employees living wages with health benefits and has some of the lowest employee turnover among large retailers (Stone, 2013a). Such investment in Costco's people has not come at the expense of impressive long-term financial performance and stock market returns. Some argue that it has helped fuel it. For example, over a 10-year period (2008–2018), Costco's shares rose in value by 240%, far outperforming the 131% gain of the Standard & Poor's 500, an index of 500, large publicly traded companies, during this same period.

MISSION, VISION, VALUES AND ETHICS

Concepts often associated with corporate or organizational purpose include organizational mission, vision, values and ethics. While these are interrelated concepts, there are also important differences (Bowen, 2005). Mackey and Sisodia (2014) define purpose as "the difference you're trying to make in the world" as an organization, while Fink (2018) says that purpose is "a company's fundamental reason for being – what it does every day to create value for its stakeholders" (para. 4). Bowen et al. (2018) explain that

> an enterprise's mission serves to clarify its purpose: why it exists and what its goals are. A mission is often based on a competitive advantage and communicated through a mission statement. (p. 58)

An enterprise's vision is "longer term, broader, and more aspirational in nature" (Bowen et al., 2018) and "spells out a target for change and the desired long-term goal state" (Bowen, 2005, p. 535). This vision may be formally stated in a vision statement. Finally, core values are "the ethical beliefs, norms, and standards that are held by an enterprise and the people in it" (Bowen et al., 2018).

The idea of vision, mission, purpose and values statements is not new, but has gained renewed interest and importance in recent years in guiding company decision-making. Some 75 years ago, Robert Wood Johnson, then the chair of Johnson & Johnson (J&J), crafted J&J's corporate credo, long before the term corporate social responsibility (CSR) had been coined (Johnson & Johnson Services, Inc., 2020). The credo outlines that J&J's first responsibility is to the patients, doctors, nurses and all others who use its products; its next responsibility is to its employees who work with the company throughout the world; its third responsibility is to the communities in which it operates and the world community; and its final responsibility is to its stockholders (Johnson & Johnson Services, Inc., 2020). In the estimation of Johnson & Johnson Services, Inc. (2020), "when we operate according to these principles, the stockholders should realize a fair return" (para. 6).

Some organizations do a better job than others in clearly and explicitly defining and sharing their organizational purpose, mission, vision and values with stakeholders and the public. Co-founded in 1967 by Herb Kelleher, as a low-cost commuter airline in Texas (J. J. Russell, 1989), Southwest Airlines is widely admired for its values-driven corporate culture (Uysal, 2016). Southwest has grown from a scrappy upstart into the largest domestic airline in the United States and the only domestic airline that remained for more than four decades in a row (Southwest Airlines Co., 2020a). The Southwest website clearly and distinctly states the company's purpose, vision, values and mission – all in one place. Southwest's stated purpose is to "connect people to what's important in their lives through friendly, reliable, and low-cost air travel" (Southwest Airlines, 2020a, para. 1). See Fig. 4.1 for "The Southwest Way," which articulates the company's purpose, vision, promise and values, and Fig. 4.2, which shows how "The Southwest Way" comes to life through team member behaviors.

Strategic communication professionals can play a critical role in helping an organization align with and live its stated purpose and values. For example, Lenovo, the world's largest PC and tablet manufacturer, has a stated corporate philosophy that "Different is Better," which includes supporting diversity and inclusion among its workforce, customers and company partners (Lenovo, 2020; Neptune, 2020). There are 20 different nationalities represented among Lenovo's top 100 executives (Lenovo, 2020). As such, as part of its communications agency review process, Lenovo has required

Fig. 4.1: The Southwest Way: Purpose, Vision, Promise and Values.

Our Purpose
Connect People to what's important in their lives through friendly, reliable, and low-cost air travel

Our Vision
Be the world's most loved, most efficient, and most profitable airline

The Southwest Way
Company Promise Southwest will provide a stable work environment with equal opportunity for learning and personal growth. Employees will be provided the same concern, respect, and caring attitude within the organization that they are expected to share externally with every Southwest Customer.
Employee Promise I will demonstrate my Warrior Spirit by striving to be my best and never giving up. I will show my Servant's Heart by delivering Legendary Customer Service and treating others with respect. I will express my Fun-LUVing Attitude by not taking myself too seriously and embracing my Southwest Family.

Our Values		
Me How I Show Up	**We** How We Treat Each Other	**Southwest** How Southwest Succeeds
Pride Have a strong work ethic, take initiative, and be accountable	**Teamwork** Practice civility, embrace Team over self, and be inclusive	**Efficiency** Don't make the easy hard, keep costs low, and stay agile
Integrity Act like an owner, choose to do right, and be courageous	**Honesty** Speak up, be transparent, and tell the truth	**Discipline** Be safe, focused, and reliable
Humility Don't take yourself too seriously, keep perspective, and don't be a jerk	**Service with LUV** Practice Hospitality, live by The Golden Rule, and don't be rude	**Excellence** Get results, win the right way, and kick tail

Source: Southwest Airlines.

agencies to demonstrate their commitment to diversity and inclusion, including providing agency-wide diversity staffing data (Bradley, 2019; Neptune, 2020; Sudhaman, 2017).

"At Lenovo, our brand purpose – Smarter Technology for All – reflects our belief in the value of technology that is not just available and accessible for every consumer throughout the world, but also that is truly inclusive in its design and development," says Torod Neptune, the former worldwide group vice president and chief communications officer (CCO) for Lenovo

Fig. 4.2:   Our Behaviors: How the Southwest Way Comes to Life.

Our Behaviors		
How The Southwest Way Comes to Life		
Me	**We**	**Southwest**
How I Show Up	How We Treat Each Other	How Southwest Succeeds
Pride Have a strong work ethic, take initiative, and be accountable	**Teamwork** Practice civility, embrace Team over self, and be inclusive	**Efficiency** Don't make the easy hard, keep costs low, and stay agile
• I am dependable and engaged • I put my Heart into my work • I do not blame others	• I assume positive intent • I appreciate the strengths of my Cohearts • I avoid tribalism	• I embrace simplicity • I look for ways to improve • I am flexible and open to change
Integrity Act like an owner, choose to do right, and be courageous	**Honesty** Speak up, be transparent, and tell the truth	**Discipline** Be safe, focused, and reliable
• I do not walk past problems • I spend Company money wisely • I do not sacrifice my integrity for results	• I handle issues proactively • I seek the truth and do not gossip • I am straightforward and sincere	• I comply with policies, procedures, and regulations • I consistently produce high-quality work • I do not get distracted from my work
Humility Don't take yourself too seriously, keep perspective, and don't be a jerk	**Service with LUV** Practice Hospitality, live by The Golden Rule, and don't be rude	**Excellence** Get results, win the right way, and kick tail
• I keep my ego in check • I understand it's not all about me • I bring a sense of fun to hard work	• I make others feel welcomed, cared for, and appreciated • I treat my Customers with respect • I embrace and support our communities	• I do my best every day • I am not complacent • I know what it takes to win

Source: Southwest Airlines.

(personal communication, July 31, 2019). Neptune, who joined Medtronic in 2021 as a senior vice president and its CCO, is a recipient of the PRSA Foundation's Paladin Award, recognizing his work on advancing diversity, equity and inclusion within the profession. "It is this commitment to walking the talk, and expecting our partners to share our commitment to becoming more diverse and inclusive along with us that is at the heart of what we believe to be perhaps one the most pressing issues facing businesses today – balancing the crucial commitment to delivering positive shareholder returns against the equally important priority of mattering in the world."

PURPOSE: PROVING IT WITH ACTION

Trust in institutions by the public is generally mixed (Edelman, 2019, 2020). Skepticism among the public, particularly younger generations, in the motives of big business and capitalism is higher than many CEOs and businesspeople would care or like to admit (Salmon, 2019; Sorkin, 2019a). For example, some surveys suggest that GenZ, the post-Millennial generation, prefers the term "socialism" to "capitalism" (Salmon, 2019). Writing lofty purpose, mission and vision statements and plastering them all over websites, annual reports, job postings and in the lobbies of headquarters – but then not living out these values through management and front-line employee decision-making – can be seen as virtue signaling at its worst (Hengeveld, 2019). To earn (and keep) the trust of stakeholders and the public, organizations need to not just "talk to the talk," but consistently "walk the walk" when it comes to organizational purpose (Hynes, 2018; Ragas & Culp, 2014b, 2018a). Words and deeds must be aligned and consistent (Soriano, 2019).

To re-visit the second Page Principle, which was discussed in the first chapter: "prove it with action" (Arthur W. Page Society, 2019b, para. 4). This second principle goes on to say that "public perception of an enterprise is determined 90 percent by what it does and 10 percent by what it says" (Arthur W. Page Society, 2019b, para. 5). While the actual percentage is debatable, the message is very clear: the strongest and most powerful form of communication is often *communicative action*, such as observable organizational policies, behaviors and actions. Aedhmar Hynes, the 2018–2019 chair of the board of trustees of Page and the former CEO of digital communication agency Text100 (now known as Archetype) says that communicators are at their best "when [they] create and shape action, not just words" (Hynes, 2017, para. 4). According to Hynes (2017), the combination of action and communication is at the core of purpose-driven brands:

> If it seems counter-intuitive that we should counsel that clients not communicate, consider that almost everything about how stakeholders perceive a brand is related to how a company behaves and lives up to its purpose. It doesn't matter whether that client is marketing a new product or dealing with a crisis: If a company doesn't act in alignment with its values and purpose, what it says won't matter. (para. 4)

The stated purpose of CVS Health, the operator of the largest pharmacy chain in the United States by number of locations and a provider of health services and plans, is "helping people on their path to better health" (CVS Health, 2020b, para. 2). In a highly visible and landmark example of "proving it with action," CVS Health announced in 2014 that it would no longer sell tobacco products in its stores because doing so conflicted with its corporate purpose (CVS Health, 2015). With this decision, CVS gave up $2 billion in revenue from tobacco sales, but gained a longer-term boost in corporate reputation, stakeholder engagement and trust (Christ, Sandor, & Tonne, 2015). CVS has repeatedly doubled down in the years since this announcement with investments in smoking prevention and cessation programs for people of all ages, including an effort to create the first tobacco-free generation. For example, in 2019, CVS became the first major corporate brand to sign the Quit Big Tobacco campaign, pledging to not work with advertising or public relations agencies that work with tobacco and e-cigarette companies (CVS Health, 2019).

"We are truly committed to our purpose of helping people on their path to better health. Every action we take, every decision we make, is viewed through our purpose – it guides everything we do," explains Eileen Boone, senior vice president of CSR and philanthropy, and chief sustainability officer for CVS Health, a Fortune 10 company with nearly 300,000 employees across the United States (personal communication, September 12, 2019). "But, as we homed in on our purpose, we immediately saw an inconsistency. We were selling tobacco in our stores. Once we made the decision to stop selling tobacco products, we used our purpose to explore other areas of opportunity for meaningful social impact."

Additional expressions of CVS Health's purpose include company decisions to eliminate trans fats from its store brand foods, to remove chemicals of concern from its store brand beauty and personal products and to launch its Beauty Mark – a commitment to never digitally alter the beauty images in its stores and in its advertising content (CVS Health, 2020a).

STRATEGIC COMMUNICATION AS CORPORATE CONSCIENCE

Public scrutiny of the purpose and values of organizations of all sizes and types is not a passing fad. Corporations must particularly demonstrate that they have a corporate character (Arthur W. Page Society, 2012, 2013, 2019a) worthy of earning (and keeping) public trust (Edelman, 2018a, 2019; Porter Novelli, 2018, 2019). Millennials are already the largest generation in the workplace (Fry, 2018) and these rising leaders tend to support organizations they feel are making a positive difference in the world (Christ & Sandor, 2015; Deloitte, 2019b; PwC, 2016). Some research suggests that even business school students seem less interested in the traditional "profit maximization" gospel (Haski-Leventhal, Pournader, & McKinnon, 2017).

An organization's culture must consistently reinforce and reflect the stated purpose, values and principles of the organization, its leadership and its employees (H. Shelton, personal communication, August 14, 2020). "Young communications pros are far more interested than 'in just the job' and the regularity that comes with it. They are seeking purpose- and values-driven firms that live by their principles as evidenced in the culture and in the services they provide to clients," says Helen C. Shelton, a senior partner at Finn Partners, a fast-growing, independent global marketing communication agency with offices on three continents. In the estimate of Shelton, there's "a direct correlation" between organizations that successfully attract, retain and develop younger talent and that have strong values and principles-driven organizational cultures.

For CCOs, their strategic communication teams and their agency and consultancy partners, the need to serve as the corporate conscience and ethics counsel of organizations has perhaps never been more pressing (Bowen, 2008; Bowen et al., 2018; Hynes, 2018). Strategic communicators must help advise organizational management and other team members that *alignment between an organization's stated principles and values and its actual actions and words* is at the core of successful purpose-driven enterprises (Bolton et al., 2018; Hynes, 2017; Ragas & Culp, 2014b, 2018a). Those brands steeped in purpose that courageously and consistently demonstrate through their behaviors that they are committed to creating both business and social value are likely to not just endure, but to thrive in the years ahead.

KEY TERMS

Board of directors	Corporate purpose
Capitalism	Corporate social responsibility (CSR)
Corporate character	Environmental, social, and governance
Corporate conscience	Ethics

Mission   Values
Socialism   Vision
Sustainable, responsible, and   Virtue signaling
    impact (SRI) investing

DISCUSSION QUESTIONS

(1) What do you think of the claim by Larry Fink, CEO and chair of BlackRock, that "purpose is not the sole pursuit of profits but the animating force for achieving them?"

(2) The authors argue that "the choice of purpose *or* profit is a false one." What do *you think*? Can an organization effectively act with purpose *and* generate healthy profits?

(3) Visit the "About Us" section of the website of a large organization that you admire and respect. What is this organization's stated purpose, mission, vision and values?

(4) In your opinion, what is an example of a large organization that does not simply "talk the talk" but meaningfully "walks the walk" thereby demonstrating that it is purpose-driven?

(5) Do you think strategic communication professionals will play a larger or smaller role in the future in helping define, activate and align organizational purpose and values? Why?

By Carol Cone, CEO and Founder, Carol Cone on PURPOSE

Purpose is here to stay.

A series of watershed statements, reports, and initiatives from some of the world's most well-known capitalists is heralding a new zeitgeist, during which businesses are expected to *exist* to benefit society – not just shareholders.

We call this approach purpose: a company's reason for being beyond profits, grounded in humanity. Purpose is no longer nice-to-have, but must-have. It's long-term, embedded in operations, results-driven, and people-first. That's historic change.

We first connected business with social impact in the 1980s, linking Rockport with walking, Reebok with human rights, and Avon with breast cancer. All during a time when business was rooted in Milton Friedman's profit-above-all ethos.

Now, a growing chorus of voices is calling for companies to embed social purpose into their operating models. It's not a request. It's a demand to boost societal impact in lockstep with bottom line growth.

This is heralded by Larry Fink's (2018, 2019) letters, the Just Capital JUST 100, EY's Business Case for Purpose, Millennial demands, the Imperative Global Purpose Index, and others. Capitalism is changing. Dramatically.

EY's Business Case for Purpose report (2015) affirms Fink's theory that companies with a clear reason for being, supported by social purpose, can accelerate top-line growth. Around 58% of companies that *prioritize* purpose say they generated more than 10% growth in revenues over the past three years (EY Beacon Institute, 2015).

Millennials: Business Must be Accountable to Society

More than 75 million-strong, Millennials continue to shape consumer and societal trends in a profound way. They are consumers, professionals, community members, and activists. By 2020 they will make up half of the world's work force (Fry, 2018).

Businesses of all sectors need Millennial talent, and one of the best ways to attract them is through a values-based culture that emphasizes the confluence of business and society as 76% of Millennials consider a company's social commitments when deciding where to work (Cone Communications, 2016).

What the New Zeitgeist Will Look Like

Creating a business that operates *for* society and *with* society demands long-term vision and a flexible framework to support it. To do this, I believe companies must embrace the following critical principles:

(i) *Lead from the C-suite* to set the social purpose vision as organizational business strategy. This leadership is critical to embed a company's reason for being, beyond profits, into culture and behaviors.

(ii) *Operationalize and embed social purpose* to align with the competencies and priorities of the business and its employees. This is more scalable and sustainable as stated by Peter F. Drucker, "Every single social and global issue of our day is a business opportunity in disguise" (Cooperrider, 2008, para. 3).

(iii) *Put employees front, center, and first* in the development and delivery of social purpose. This engenders trust and affirms authenticity internally and externally.

I've made the advancement of social purpose as my mission for more than three decades and have never seen such a seismic shift. The more companies serve society, the more society will respond and business can grow. Purpose's time has come.

PART III

THE PEOPLE

5

STAKEHOLDERS AND SOCIETY

There are spirited debates taking place in corner offices and boardrooms around the world about the roles and responsibilities of business in society today. In the most heated moments, these debates might even be called battles for the future soul of capitalism (Benioff & Langley; 2019; Collier, 2018; Edelman, 2020; George, 2017, 2019; Salmon, 2019; Sorkin, 2019b).

On one side of this debate are business leaders, often including chief communications officers (CCOs), who advocate for taking a more holistic, purpose-driven approach to organizational management and decision-making, with a focus on creating both business *and* social value (Arthur W. Page Society, 2019a; Cone, 2019). This multi-stakeholder view of the enterprise goes by many names, including stakeholder capitalism, conscious capitalism, responsible capitalism and sustainable capitalism (Murray, 2019; Tett, 2019). Entrenched on the other side of this debate are the business leaders who view investors as the rightful "owners" of a business. In this view, which may be called shareholder capitalism or shareholder primacy, organizational decision-making should prioritize investors, such as shareholders, and the lawful pursuit of maximizing profits. This latter group is not opposed to corporate social responsibility (CSR) and environmental, social, governance (ESG) initiatives, *if* such efforts can be linked back to improving business profits (Murray, 2019; Tett, 2019).

The unsolicited $143 billion-dollar attempted takeover of Unilever by Kraft Heinz in 2017 provides a vivid example of when these two opposing business management philosophies collide (Daneshkhu & Barber, 2017; Finkbeiner, Lecher, Sowa, & Ohm, 2018). On one side was Kraft Heinz, in which company management was known for zero-based budgeting, cost containment and a seemingly shareholder-first approach to maximizing profits (George, 2017, 2019). On the other side was Unilever, a rival global consumers goods company well known for its Unilever Sustainable Living Plan, which aimed to double the company's revenue by halving its environmental impact (Daneshkhu & Barber, 2017; Finkbeiner et al., 2018; Gelles, 2019). In the sharp words of then Unilever chief executive officer (CEO) Paul Polman, Kraft Heinz's bid for Unilever allegedly represented "a clash between people who think about billions of people in the world and some people that think about a few billionaires" (Edgecliffe-Johnson, 2018, para. 6).

Polman and other Unilever senior leaders were able to quickly build support among Unilever shareholders that more long-term value could be created by rejecting the hostile offer and keeping the company independent. This included convincing Warren Buffett, a major Kraft Heinz shareholder, to withdraw support for the bid. Ultimately, in the weeks and months that followed, both sides adjusted their business management philosophy, at least to some extent, to the approach of the other side. For example, Unilever made new commitments to improving its profit margins and better rewarding its shareholders, while Kraft Heinz announced a series of enhanced commitments to CSR and sustainability initiatives (Finkbeiner et al., 2018).

Through year-end 2019, nearly three years after this failed bid, Unilever's stock price had risen by about +35%, slightly underperforming the overall stock market's rise during this time (+37%), while Kraft Heinz shares had declined by more than –60%, as it struggled to re-invent its business amidst continued cost-cutting and an investigation into its accounting practices (Gelles, 2019). In this case study, "doing well by doing good" was more than just a pithy phrase. The future of business in some ways may be summed up by Unilever and Kraft Heinz: neither side's approach to business may be "fully right" or "fully wrong." Finding a balance between purpose and profits that fuels sustainable, longer-term value creation – for *all of an organization's stakeholders* – may become the new normal in the years ahead (Ragas & Culp, 2014a, 2018b).

Strategic communication professionals have long been expected to have an expertise in environmental scanning – bringing the perspectives of "the world outside" inside the organization and vice versa (Place, 2019). The difference now is that making sure the voices of internal and external stakeholder groups are represented and understood by the C-suite, the board and other senior leaders is increasingly a *strategic imperative* for organizations (Benioff & Langley, 2019). As such, more leaders are welcoming the unique stakeholder mosaic insights that communicators can provide as a result of organizational listening and scanning efforts.

With the rise of digital media-empowered stakeholders, particularly the more socially conscious younger generations as consumers and employees (Freberg, 2019; Luttrell, 2019), all business leaders are under pressure to adopt more of a multi-stakeholder view of the world in making strategic business decisions (Dodd, 2018; McCorkindale, Hynes, & Kotcher, 2018). This significant shift represents yet another important opportunity for CCOs, the communication function and their agency and consultancy partners to help lead and serve in more of a trusted advisor/counselor capacity (Bolton, Stacks, & Mizrachi, 2018; Ragas, 2019a; Ragas & Culp, 2014a, 2018b).

SHAREHOLDER THEORY VERSUS STAKEHOLDER THEORY

Over the last 40 years, there have been at least two dominant perspectives within American business on the role and responsibility of business in society: shareholder theory and stakeholder theory (Benioff & Langley, 2019; Collier, 2018; May, 2016; Rawlins, 2005).

Shareholder theory is closely associated with free market economist and Nobel Prize-winning professor Milton Friedman (1965, 1970). The core perspective of shareholder theory (sometimes even called the "Friedman doctrine") is succinctly stated in the title of Friedman's classic essay in *The New York Times Magazine*: "The Social Responsibility of Business is to Increase its Profits" (Friedman, 1970). Importantly, Friedman says that businesspeople must still conform to the basic rules and regulations of society in the pursuit of maximizing shareholder profits. On the 50th anniversary of Friedman's essay, *The New York Times Magazine* and *DealBook* published a special section in which business leaders and economists debated the enduring influence of their perspective on business and society today (Sorkin, 2020).

According to shareholder theorists, a primary focus on growing "single bottom line" profits creates business and societal value through making products and services that solve customer problems, by creating jobs for employees and by producing profits for investors (Altman & Berman, 2011; Machan, 2011). Under this view, since investors provide the financial capital, they are viewed as the true "owners of the business." As such, investors should be able to choose to do as they please with company profits, such as to engage (or not) in individual philanthropy with such profits (Friedman, 1970). Importantly, shareholder theorists may feel it is appropriate for a business to directly engage in CSR and ESG initiatives, but *only* if such efforts *improve the long-term financial performance of the organization* (Friedman, Mackey, & Rodgers, 2005).

Embedded within shareholder theory is the concept of shareholder primacy. Shareholder primacy views corporate executives as "agents" or "employees" of shareholders (Jensen & Chew, 2000; Jensen & Meckling, 1976). Shareholders are seen as the "principals" or rightful "employers" of the business. In essence, under this perspective, the board of directors and the C-suite should represent – first and foremost – the interests and perspectives of a company's shareholders. Under a shareholder primacy approach to business management, shareholders are typically prioritized over other stakeholder groups in organizational decision-making. This is not to say that the views and interests of other stakeholders *do not matter* under shareholder primacy, but only as much as satisfying such other groups can be seen as helping to ultimately boost profits and maximize shareholder value (Jensen & Chew, 2000; Jensen & Meckling, 1976).

On the opposite end of the spectrum regarding the role and responsibility of business in society is stakeholder theory. This perspective is closely associated with business ethicist professor R. Edward Freeman and his colleagues (Freeman, 2010; Freeman, Harrison, & Wicks, 2007; Freeman, Harrison, Wicks, Parmar, & de Colle, 2010; Freeman, Harrison, & Zyglidopoulos, 2018). Stakeholders are those groups that have a shared interest or "stake" in the performance of an organization. The term *stakeholder* is now a common part of the business vernacular. According to stakeholder theorists, customers, employees, suppliers, communities and other stakeholder groups are all rightful "owners" of a business. Stakeholder theorists generally believe that businesspeople, including company managers and boards, have an ethical and moral obligation to try and create value for *all* stakeholder groups and contribute to the broader public good; simply privileging one group – shareholders – is unacceptable (Freeman, 2010; Freeman et al., 2007, 2010, 2018). Strong business ethics is paramount (Bowen, 2008; Bowen, Hardage, & Strong, 2018). Stakeholder theory advocates generally adopt a "triple bottom line" approach to evaluating business impact across three broad areas: people, planet and profits (Elkington, 2018).

Some would argue that a stakeholder capitalism approach to business is not just "the right thing to do" but is simply "smart business" today (Aguinis & Glavas, 2012; Porter & Kramer, 2006). Business leaders, such as Whole Foods co-founder John Mackey and Salesforce.com founder Marc Benioff, have argued that a stakeholder-centric approach to managing a business increasingly leads to superior long-term business results, including better financial performance (Benioff & Langley, 2019; Mackey & Sisodia, 2014). Of course, a multi-stakeholder approach to managing a business and creating "wins" for all stakeholders can be challenging to implement in practice. At least over the short term, there may be times when the interests of stakeholder groups may be in conflict (Cahill, 2019). At times, business managers must choose to prioritize various stakeholder group's interests when making decisions (Rawlins, 2006). Such challenging decisions may be guided in part by the stated mission, purpose and values of the organization.

On the continuum between shareholder theory and stakeholder theory, more US business leaders are moving in the direction of embracing a multi-stakeholder approach and stakeholder capitalism. In August 2019, the Business Roundtable (2019a), a powerful trade group whose membership is exclusively comprised of CEOs, announced a re-defined purpose of the corporation statement. The statement, signed by 181 CEOs, moved away from shareholder primacy and stated a commitment by these business leaders to leading their companies for the benefit of *all* stakeholders. Prior versions of this document since 1997 had endorsed principles of shareholder primacy (Business Roundtable, 2019a).

The Business Roundtable (2019a) statement says that these CEOs and their firms commit to delivering value to their customers, investing in their employees, dealing fairly and ethically with their suppliers, supporting the communities in which they work and the environment and generating long-term value for shareholders. See Fig. 5.1 for the group's complete statement, which has sparked intense discussion among businesspeople, strategic communication professionals and the general public.

While praised by many, the Business Roundtable statement also has been met with some criticism. For example, the Council of Institutional Investors, an influential association for institutional investment managers, expressed concern with the statement, arguing that "it is critical to respect stakeholders, but also to have clear accountability to company owners" (para. 3). In the view of the Council of Institutional Investors (2019), "accountability to

Fig. 5.1:   Business Roundtable: Statement on the Purpose of a Corporation.

STATEMENT ON THE PURPOSE OF A CORPORATION

Americans deserve an economy that allows each person to succeed through hard work and creativity and to lead a life of meaning and dignity. We believe the free market system is the best means of generating good jobs, a strong and sustainable economy, innovation, a healthy environment and economic opportunity for all.

Businesses play a vital role in the economy by creating jobs, fostering innovation and providing essential goods and services. Businesses make and sell consumer products; manufacture equipment and vehicles; support the national defense; grow and produce food; provide healthcare; generate and deliver energy; and offer financial, communications and other services that underpin economic growth.

WHILE EACH OF OUR INDIVIDUAL COMPANIES SERVES ITS OWN CORPORATE PURPOSE, WE SHARE A FUNDAMENTAL COMMITMENT TO ALL OF OUR STAKEHOLDERS. WE COMMIT TO:

DELIVERING VALUE TO OUR CUSTOMERS. We will further the tradition of American companies leading the way in meeting or exceeding customer expectations.

INVESTING IN OUR EMPLOYEES. This starts with compensating them fairly and providing important benefits. It also includes supporting them through training and education that help develop new skills for a rapidly changing world. We foster diversity and inclusion, dignity and respect.

DEALING FAIRLY AND ETHICALLY WITH OUR SUPPLIERS. We are dedicated to serving as good partners to the other companies, large and small, that help us meet our missions.

SUPPORTING THE COMMUNITIES IN WHICH WE WORK. We respect the people in our communities and protect the environment by embracing sustainable practices across our businesses.

GENERATING LONG-TERM VALUE FOR SHAREHOLDERS, WHO PROVIDE THE CAPITAL THAT ALLOWS COMPANIES TO INVEST, GROW AND INNOVATE. We are committed to transparency and effective engagement with shareholders.

EACH OF OUR STAKEHOLDERS IS ESSENTIAL. WE COMMIT TO DELIVER VALUE TO ALL OF THEM, FOR THE FUTURE SUCCESS OF OUR COMPANIES, OUR COMMUNITIES AND OUR COUNTRY.

BRT.org/OurCommitment   BR) Business Roundtable

Source: Business Roundtable.

everyone means accountability to no one" (para. 4). Stephen Schwarzman, the CEO and co-founder of Blackstone Group, one of the world's largest investment firms, was one of the handful of Business Roundtable members who declined to sign on to the document. According to Schwarzman, he objected to the statement's notion that generating profits should be treated as equal to the other four issues (Sorkin, 2019c).

The CEOs who signed the Business Roundtable statement will be judged in the years and decades ahead by the actual *actions* they take in managing their businesses (Grothaus, 2019; Whitaker, 2019). Signing on to this statement is one thing; consistently behaving this way when it comes to "walking the talk" is another. To revisit one of the Page Principles of the Arthur W. Page Society (2019b), the professional association for senior communication leaders, organizations and their leaders must regularly "prove it with action."

"Especially in this era of radical transparency and hyper-connectivity, the true character of an institution – which is demonstrated by its actions, not its words – will shine through," says Roger Bolton, president of Page (personal communication, December 9, 2019). Previously, Bolton served in a variety of corporate communication leadership roles, including as senior vice president of communications at Aetna, now a subsidiary of CVS Health. "The key here is for enterprises to genuinely dedicate themselves to societal value creation, to set concrete goals, and to hold themselves accountable to achieving them."

THE EVOLUTION OF CSR

That business should contribute meaningfully to the public good is hardly a new idea. More than a century ago, Andrew Carnegie (1889) wrote "The Gospel of Wealth" imploring his fellow business leaders and entrepreneurs to be philanthropic. In the words of Carnegie, the funder of several thousand public libraries across the United States: "The man who dies rich thus dies disgraced" (Carnegie, 1889, p. 18). Carnegie's philosophy inspired the creation of "The Giving Pledge" in 2010 by Warren Buffett and Bill and Melinda Gates (Kolbert, 2018). This pledge encourages billionaires to publicly promise to give away at least half of their wealth. More than 200 individuals, couples and families in nearly two dozen countries have signed on to the pledge.

Recent years have seen growing distrust toward the capitalist system under which much of this wealth has been built (Salmon, 2019; Sorkin, 2019b). The public wants to see that business is more of a solution to societal and environmental issues and less of the cause of such problems. Some would argue that businesses' very "license to operate" – granted by the trust and approval of the public – is at risk (Collier, 2018; Dodd, 2018). Conversely, trust among the public in other institutions, such as government, is low (Edelman, 2019, 2020). This has resulted in an evolution of the social responsibility of business (Cone, 2019). Decades ago, businesses pioneered corporate philanthropy, the giving of gifts to charitable and cultural organizations, and cause marketing, the donating of a portion of product or service sales to a particular cause.

Modern CSR takes a broader and more encompassing view of the roles and responsibility of business in society, which goes beyond the traditional philanthropic domains of check-writing and even employee volunteering programs (Pompper, 2015). CSR may be defined as "the voluntary actions that a corporation implements as it pursues its mission and fulfills its perceived obligations to stakeholders, including employees, communities, the environment, and society as a whole" (Coombs & Holladay, 2012, p. 8).

Former PepsiCo CEO Indra Nooyi is credited with developing a new governing and operating philosophy for the global food, snack and beverage giant called "Performance with Purpose" (Boston Consulting Group, 2010). In the words of Nooyi (2019), this mantra "is about changing the way PepsiCo makes money, not just what it does with the money it makes" (para. 9). This quote also smartly sums up the evolution of CSR and ESG programs and initiatives over the past decade. Increasingly, stakeholders don't just care about corporate giving and volunteering programs (i.e., what a firm does with the money it has made), but the inner workings, values and principles of companies (i.e., how it made that money in the first place and how it treats the environment and its stakeholders). As such, subjects such as diversity, equity and inclusion among an organization's employees, suppliers and other stakeholders has become a major strategic focus area for organizations and those who advise them, such as the communication profession (Mundy, 2019; S. Spector & Spector, 2018).

"A company's value cannot be assessed solely on its financial performance. There are attributes, such as innovation, client focus, community involvement and a diverse, inclusive, equitable, and engaged culture for all employees that are critical components of our success," says Sheryl Battles, vice president of global diversity, inclusion and engagement for Pitney Bowes, a more than 100-year-old Fortune 1000 company named by *Forbes* as a best employer for women and diversity (personal communication, August 16, 2020). "The needs of the organization and those around it are intertwined and the only way to deliver sustainable value is through a foundation that works in the interests for all, starting with employees."

In an effort to boost transparency and keep stakeholders and the public better informed, Pitney Bowes, like many corporations, particularly large, publicly traded firms, releases CSR reports on a regular basis (Coombs & Holladay, 2012; May, 2016; Pompper, 2015). Pitney Bowes, for example, posts CSR reports from 2008 to present on its website. Such reports may go by a variety of names, including using terms such as social responsibility, ESG, corporate citizenship and/or sustainability. Some companies have also started issuing diversity and inclusion reports.

Research indicates that, as of 2019, 9 out of 10 (90%) S&P 500 companies, which is an index of 500 large companies listed on US stock exchanges, released corporate responsibility or sustainability reports (Governance & Accountability Institute, Inc., 2020). By comparison, in 2011, just under 20% of S&P 500 companies were issuing such reports. Smaller publicly traded companies have been slower to join the CSR reporting trend. Looking at the smallest 500 companies included in the Russell 1000, an index made up of the 1,000 largest publicly traded companies in the United States, only a little more than one out of three (34%) of these companies published such a report in 2018 (Governance & Accountability Institute, Inc., 2019).

Fortune 500 supplemental health and life insurance company Aflac, home of the iconic Aflac Duck, is widely recognized as a leader in CSR and ESG. Aflac has repeatedly been named each year to *Fortune's* list of the World's Most Admired Companies and one of the 100 Best Companies to Work for in America, as well as by Ethisphere as one of the World's Most Ethical Companies (Aflac Incorporated, 2020). A recent award-winning initiative is My Special Aflac Duck, a robotic device that helps children cope with cancer treatment (Kulp, 2019; Sudhaman, 2019). Every year, Aflac invests more than $3 million in its My Special Aflac Duck program having delivered more than 8,000 robotic ducks free of charge to children battling cancer (Aflac Incorporated, 2020; C. Hernandez-Blades, personal communication, November 18, 2019). Over the past 25 years, Aflac has donated more than $140 million to pediatric cancer research efforts (Aflac Incorporated, 2020; Kulp, 2019; Sudhaman, 2019).

"The company pivoted the look and voice of its brand icon – a recognized pop culture icon – the Aflac Duck, bringing it to life as a robotic companion for children with cancer," says Catherine Hernandez-Blades, former senior vice president, chief ESG and communications officer, Aflac (personal communication, November 18, 2019). "Aflac's market cap is about $40 billion, with the brand representing almost half that figure. To take a $20 billion brand asset and transition part of its mission and purpose is not without risk. However, the company strongly believed that this would be the only way to do it because it so authentically and strongly reflects Aflac's values."

CORPORATE SOCIAL ADVOCACY ON THE RISE

There is growing interest among the public in better understanding what an organization stands for, specifically its stated purpose, principles and values (Fink, 2018, 2019; Whitaker, 2019). More stakeholders – from customers to employees and even investors – are interested in aligning their time, talents and treasure with organizations that share and reflect their values and beliefs – and steering clear of or even actively opposing those that do not (Edelman, 2018a, 2020; JUST Capital, 2017, 2019; Porter Novelli, 2018,

2019). Further, a growing percentage of the public, driven by the rise of younger generations in the workplace and the marketplace (Cone Communications, 2016; Deloitte, 2019b; Fry, 2018), feel that business leaders should speak up and take action on social and/or political issues that conflict with a company's stated purpose, principles and values (APCO Worldwide, 2018; Weber Shandwick, 2017, 2018, 2019a).

Corporations and CEOs have traditionally steered away from publicly commenting on controversial political and/or social issues, particularly if the subject is viewed as being not directly related to the business (Chatterji & Toffel, 2018; Gelles, 2017; Weber Shandwick, 2019a). But societal expectations are rapidly shifting on this front. For example, by some measures, a clear majority of Americans (59%) now feel that the CEOs of large companies have a responsibility to take a public stand on important social issues (JUST Capital, 2019).

The COVID-19 global pandemic and Black Lives Matter protests following the death of George Floyd seem to have further buttressed the public's view that businesses should more fully embrace stakeholder capitalism. A national poll by JUST Capital and The Harris Poll (2020) found that 9 out of 10 Americans (80%) viewed the pandemic as an opportunity for large companies to hit "reset" and focus on doing right by their workers, customers, communities and the environment. A separate JUST Capital poll indicated that the majority of the American public believed that companies should implement workplace policies that dismantle racism and advance equity, and that CEOs and business leaders should speak up and speak out against systematic racism (Adesina & Mizell, 2020).

More stakeholders, driven in part by the rise of internal employee activism (Gaines-Ross, 2019; Weber Shandwick, 2019b), are pushing organizational leadership to engage in what can be termed corporate social advocacy (CSA). Melissa Dodd and Dustin Supa (2015) define CSA as the public relations (PR) function in which firms and/or their CEOs intentionally or even unintentionally "align themselves with a controversial social-political issue outside their normal sphere or CSR interest" (p. 288). Related terms sometimes associated with CSA include corporate activism, CEO activism, social issues management and political CSR (Chatterji & Toffel, 2018; Coombs & Holladay, 2018; Dodd, 2018; Dodd & Supa, 2014, 2015).

In recent years, CEOs of major companies have publicly spoken out – and, in some cases, also flexed their firms' economic muscles – on a wide range of social-political issues, including climate change, immigration, LGBTQ rights, gun control and gun violence, gender and pay equality, systematic racism and police brutality (Chatterji & Toffel, 2018, 2019; Gelles, 2017). Such corporate advocacy efforts can have a positive or negative effect on an organization's reputation and future performance. But in an increasingly politicized environment, silence and *inaction* on major social-political issues may also not be a viable longer-term strategy (Dodd, 2018).

Weber Shandwick, one of the world's largest PR and strategic communication agencies, has conducted a series of in-depth research studies over a multi-year period on the rise of corporate advocacy and the so-called CEO activism (see Weber Shandwick, 2018, 2019a, 2019b). According to Leslie Gaines-Ross, chief reputation strategist for Weber Shandwick, this research has found that, in many ways, corporate and CEO advocacy is now "mainstream" and "the new normal" (personal communication, November 9, 2019).

"CEO and companies can no longer afford to be bystanders. They must stand up for their corporate and employee values, particularly if those values are aligned with their core business," says Gaines-Ross, one of the world's most recognized experts on CEO and corporate reputation (personal communication, November 9, 2019). "In addition to taking a position on hot button societal issues, if they choose to, they must also take action. Words are no longer enough."

STAKEHOLDER CAPITALISM AND STRATEGIC COMMUNICATIONS

There is a trust gap between business and the rest of society. Strategic communication professionals can help their organizations and clients close this critical gap (Gaines-Ross, 2019). A strengthening majority of the American public (e.g., Edelman, 2018a, 2020; JUST Capital, 2019; Weber Shandwick, 2018) believe that corporations should make meaningful contributions to the public good and their efforts should benefit *all stakeholders* – not just investors (Whitaker, 2019). However, by some measures (JUST Capital, 2019), less than half of the public feel that companies are actually fulfilling this mandate for a stakeholder capitalism approach to business.

Lofty statements on re-defining the purpose of business are not enough (Business Roundtable, 2019a, 2019b; Gilbert, Kassoy, & Houlahan, 2019). Such words must be driven by *meaningful and consistent actions* in the years ahead by CEOs and other business leaders that show a dedication to creating both business and societal value (Adesina & Mizell, 2020; Bolton et al., 2018; Grothaus, 2019; JUST Capital & The Harris Poll, 2020). With the further ascendance of values-driven, digital media-empowered GenZ's and millennials across the stakeholder landscape, CSR, ESG and CSA are likely to stay near the top of corporate agendas in the future.

KEY TERMS

Capitalism	Environmental, social, governance
Cause marketing	(ESG)
CEO activism	Socialism
Corporate philanthropy	Shareholder theory
Corporate social advocacy (CSA)	Shareholder primacy
Corporate social responsibility (CSR)	Stakeholder
Diversity, equity and inclusion	Stakeholder theory
Employee activism	Zero-based budgeting
Environmental scanning	

DISCUSSION QUESTIONS

(1) Where do you side in the debate between operating businesses under shareholder theory (and shareholder primacy) versus under stakeholder theory? Explain your reasoning.

(2) What is an example of a company that you think does a *very good job* at CSR and ESG? What is an example of a company that you think does *poorly* at CSR and ESG?

(3) Carefully review the Business Roundtable's vaunted statement on "The Purpose of the Corporation" signed by many top CEOs. What is your opinion of this statement?

(4) Do you think businesses should engage in CSA? Yes or no? If, yes, under what conditions do you think companies should engage in CSA?

(5) Do you think the rise of millennials and GenZ as key stakeholders and rising leaders in organizations will change how corporations behave in the years ahead? Why or why not?

By Catherine Hernandez-Blades,
former SVP, Chief ESG & Communications Officer

As a corporate communications professional, I never thought I would directly oversee electronic manufacturing or manage a supply chain.

Enter My Special Aflac Duck, a social robot that serves as a companion for children undergoing cancer treatment. With RFID technology, this special duck has feeling cards in the form of electronic emoji that allow it to act out a range of emotions on the child's behalf. There are protocols for medical play, letting children take back power by treating their ducks in the same way caregivers treat them. Additionally, there are companion features, such as a soothing heartbeat, a nuzzling ability and a deep breathing exercise capability, so that child life specials can further support patients throughout treatment. And, yes, there is an app for that. The app allows children to bathe and feed their ducks and provides escape mechanisms, letting kids virtually visit farms, carnivals, gardens and even outer space. The most powerful feature of all is that the duck also has a port, just like the young patients. For fun, My Special Aflac Ducks dance when music is played and communicate with each other. How? By quacking of course!

Lesson: Be innovative! "But it has never been done before!" are my favorite words because I love to make the impossible become the possible. In order to do this successfully, curate your career carefully to include all aspects of business acumen throughout your work, including the items well beyond functional scope. Most important of all: develop your financial acumen. The numbers are critical. Know them and understand how they are generated!

Since its prototype launch at CES in January 2018, My Special Aflac Duck has received many awards, including Tech for a Better World, two Cannes Lions, a People's Choice at SXSW and has been included on Time's list of the World's 100 Best Inventions of the Year. As a reflection of the power of public relations, after over 500 interviews and six months into the program, research demonstrated that 15% of Americans had heard of the initiative and 100% of those were more likely to buy Aflac insurance as a result.

My Special Aflac Duck is the culmination of a three-year corporate social responsibility (CSR) campaign. I implemented the CSR campaign because Aflac has a brilliant social good story that had never been told. What led me in this direction was the Reputation Institute, now known as The RepTrak Company. The RepTrak model reflects seven dimensions of reputation, with 23 attributes behind those dimensions, weighted by industry. In financial services, Governance, Workplace and Citizenship account for almost 50% of the model. When I brief the board of directors quarterly, I overlay the RepTrak data with our employee engagement scores, social and editorial media sentiment, stock price and sales, accounting for the open enrollment anomaly. We don't isolate the metric enough to prove causation, but correlation is obvious.

Lesson: It's all about the results. Always measure, but don't measure tactics. Measure outcomes.

The program works because it is authentic. Without Aflac's 25-year commitment to childhood cancer, the program would not have been as effective. More importantly, My Special Aflac Duck tangibly demonstrates the power of corporations for both purpose and profit.

Lesson: Companies are in the business of making money. If they don't, there are no resources with which to go out and do good work. It's about purpose AND profit.

6

THE BOARD OF DIRECTORS AND THE C-SUITE

Even company founders and chief executive officers (CEOs) have bosses. They are called the board of directors. Just ask Sir Martin Sorrell, the founder and former CEO of WPP plc, one of the world's largest marketing, advertising and public relations (PR) agency holding companies (Garrahan, 2018).

Over three decades, Sorrell transformed an obscure UK-based wire-basket maker, Wire & Plastic Products, into the owner of more than 300 agencies (WPP plc, 2020), including many top global firms, such as Burson Cohn & Wolfe (BCW), GroupM, J. Walter Thompson, Mindshare, and Ogilvy, totaling more than 130,000 employees and clients in more than 110 countries (Fildes, 2019; Kostov & Vranica, 2019). Described by *The Financial Times* as "the ad land Sun King," Sorrell was consistently among the highest-paid British CEOs (Marriage & Garrahan, 2018, para. 21). By 2017, though, Sorrell was under increasing pressure from both WPP shareholders and his board of directors, as WPP had missed its financial projections, reduced its financial outlook and the company's stock price had declined by roughly a third in value (Kostov & Vranica, 2019). The year also marked the rise of the #MeToo movement, which created public awareness around sexual harassment and sexual assault in the workplace by powerful men, including some top business leaders (Zacharek, Dockterman, & Sweetland Edwards, 2017).

Against this backdrop, in early 2018, a WPP employee made a whistleblower complaint against Sorrell alleging personal misconduct and potential misuse of company funds. A decision was made to take the allegation to Roberto Quarta, the then chair of WPP's board (Marriage & Garrahan, 2018). The board decided to set up a subcommittee and hire an external law firm to conduct an independent investigation. Neither side disclosed the investigation's findings, but details of the allegations leaked to the news media (Kostov & Vranica, 2019). Sorrell rejected the allegations of misconduct (Fildes, 2019), but following the media reports, decided to resign as CEO from the company he had spent 33 years building (Garrahan, 2018). Such a stunning turn of events for Sorrell, a titan of the agency world, provides a vivid example of the high-stakes potential outcomes resulting from corner office and corporate boardroom deliberations. Sorrell has since founded S4 Capital, a digital marketing services holding company (Fildes, 2019).

To serve as trusted business advisors and counselors (Penning & Bain, 2018; Ragas, 2019a, 2019b), strategic communication professionals should have at least an intermediate understanding of the roles and responsibilities of the board of directors and the C-suite; the current issues at the intersection of corporate governance and strategic communication; and the institutionalized influence of shareholders on boards and C-suites (Pettigrew & Reber, 2013). Boards of directors, in particular, are powerful forces within corporations and society as a whole, but they have often operated largely "behind the curtains" (Deloitte, 2016; Monks & Minow, 2011).

Perhaps to their own detriment, C-suites are also sometimes out of sight and cloaked in mystery for many stakeholders and the general public (Clarke & Branson, 2012; Ragas & Culp, 2014a, 2018b). In an era of rising stakeholder activism (Edelman, 2020; Ragas, 2018; Uysal & Tsetsura, 2015) – ranging from shareholder activism to employee activism – there is increasing public interest and scrutiny on the CEO, the C-suite and the board of directors, including on such salient issues as executive compensation and pay inequality among corporate executives and workers, as well as C-suite and boardroom diversity, equity and inclusion (DE&I).

INSIDE THE BOARDROOM

The board of directors is critical to the overall governance of an organization, including providing oversight of the organization's senior leadership and strategy. The board is expected to hold management accountable on organizational performance and decision-making (Deloitte, 2016; Lev, 2012). This typically includes hiring (and firing) decisions regarding company officers, such as the CEO. Under classic agency theory (Fama, 1980;

Fama & Jensen, 1983), shareholders are viewed as the "absentee owners" of a company. The members of the board may be viewed as "agents" that act on behalf of shareholders, the "principals" of the firm.

Board members at corporations are typically elected by the firm's shareholders at the annual meeting or a special meeting (Strine, 2016, 2017). There is a chair of the board. The CEO often holds a seat on the board. Increasingly, the board chair position is not also held by the CEO with the argument being that separating these roles helps give the board greater independence (Monks & Minow, 2011). At corporations there are typically several standing committees of the board, such as the audit, compensation, finance and nominating and governance committees. Special committees may be formed as needed, such as to evaluate a merger or an acquisition. Many public company directors have prior experience as CEOs, chief financial officers (CFOs) and/or as company founders (Spencer Stuart, 2018a). As corporate purpose, brand stewardship and innovation become more critical to business performance (Arthur W. Page Society, 2019a), there is a need for more business-savvy strategic communications executives to serve on company boards (Spencer Stuart, 2018b).

"In a world in which companies are hungry for innovation, marketing and communications executives can bring a unique perspective on customers and other stakeholders to boardroom discussions, but this perspective must be grounded in business acumen," says Beth Comstock, who serves on the board of directors of NIKE, Inc. and is a trustee of The National Geographic Society (personal communication, April 23, 2020). Comstock previously held a series of increasingly senior roles at General Electric (GE), including VP, corporate communications and SVP, chief marketing and commercial officer, rising all the way to become vice chair of GE. To start learning about how boards think and operate, Comstock recommends that communication professionals seek out board service early in their careers, such as looking to serve on the boards of local non-profit organizations.

There is not just one generally accepted definition of corporate governance, but there is similarity around how this key concept is defined (Clarke & Branson, 2012). For example, the U.S. Securities and Exchange Commission (2012) defines corporate governance as

> *the framework of rules and practices that reflect and define the responsibilities and the appropriate level of accountability of a company's decision makers – both the directors elected by shareholders and the managers selected by directors. (para. 9)*

On the contrary, Carolyn Kay Brancato and Christian Plath (2005) of The Conference Board, a well-regarded member-driven think tank, define corporate governance as "a system of checks and balances between the board, management, and investors that should produce an efficiently functioning corporation, ideally geared to produce long-term value" (p. 8). Organizational governance is codified in an organization's charter, bylaws, policies and principles, such as company ethics and privacy statements, and in its culture and customs (Ragas & Culp, 2014a). With public companies, some of this information is available under the corporate governance section of the company's website.

Board members at corporations have certain responsibilities, which are known as fiduciary duties or obligations (Lincoln, n.d.). An individual owes others fiduciary duties when that individual has influence over the financial interests of another (Cooley LLP, 2019). A board member of a company owes shareholders of the firm fiduciary duties because the decisions of the board can influence the value of a company's stock. Directors who do not properly fulfill their fiduciary obligations may be open to personal liability. Specifically, directors have a *duty of loyalty* and a *duty of care* to the company and its stockholders.

Directors should avoid perceived or real conflicts of interest. In essence, a company's board and its individual board members should put the interests of the company and its stockholders ahead of their own personal interests, and should make decisions that are in the best interests of the firm and its stockholders (Lincoln, n.d.). This does not mean that directors can simply ignore the interests and perspectives of other stakeholder groups (Stout, 2012), but US general corporate law has traditionally privileged *shareholder* interests (Strine, 2016, 2017, 2019). A board of advisors is typically less formal and does not have the same fiduciary obligations as a corporate board of directors.

DE&I ON BOARDS

US corporate boardrooms have been derisively described as "pale, male and stale." While there have been some changes in recent years, this pithy description is still fairly accurate. While the percentages of women and minorities on corporate boards are rising, board seats are still dominated by older, white men (an average age of nearly 61 years old) (Deloitte, 2019a). A global study of boardrooms by Deloitte (2019a) finds that only around 1 out of 6 (17%) board seats are held by women and that men hold around 19 out of every 20

(95%) board chair positions (Deloitte, 2019a). A milestone was reached in July 2019 within the S&P 500 index, when all company boards had at least one female board member (Society for Human Resource Management, 2019). By some estimates, it is projected that women and minorities will hold 40% of Fortune 500 board seats by 2024 (Deloitte & Alliance for Board Diversity, 2019). As of 2018, minority men and women held around one out of every six board seats (16%) within Fortune 500 company boardrooms. Women and people of color (POC) together made up a little over a third (34%) of Fortune 500 board seats in total (Deloitte & Alliance for Board Diversity, 2019).

In an effort to increase boardroom diversity, European countries have passed legislation in recent years mandating quotas requiring women on corporate boards (Gupta, 2019). In September 2018, California became the first state to require public companies based there to include female representation on boards (Gupta, 2019). Since this mandate went into effect, the number of smaller public companies in the state with no women on the board has dropped sharply. By one estimate, at year-end 2019, the number of all-male boards at smaller public companies in California had plummeted from 91 companies to just 6 (Prang, 2020).

In 2020, California law makers passed landmark additional legislation to require a minimum number of POC on the boards of firms based there (Kishan, 2020). More specifically, boards must include at least one board member from an underrepresented community (Black, African-American, Hispanic, Latinx, Asian, Pacific Islander, Native American, Native Hawaiian and Alaska Native). Investment banks are also pushing firms to have more diverse boards. For example, Goldman Sachs Group said that, starting in July 2020, it would no longer take companies public in the United States or Europe if their boards did not have at least one female or non-white director (Prang, 2020). Exchanges are also placing a great emphasis on diversity with the NASDAQ proposing board diversity requirements for listed companies (Osipovich, 2020).

The accumulating research often indicates that more diverse boards may be associated with higher corporate performance; diversity of board backgrounds, thoughts and perspectives may be a source of competitive advantage (see Catalyst, 2018). More large investment managers are using their voting power as shareholders to help achieve greater boardroom diversity (US SIF Foundation, 2020). For example, State Street Global Advisors, one of the world's largest asset managers, has received a mix of praise and criticism for its award-winning Fearless Girl campaign, which has pushed for improving women's representation on corporate boards (Baer, 2019). According to State Street Global Advisors (2020), since the launch of the Fearless Girl campaign on the eve of International Women's Day in March 2017, nearly half (681) of the 1,384 firms identified by State Street as having no women on their boards have responded to its call to action by adding at least one female director.

"Research studies have increasingly showed the value of having more gender diverse boards, but the issue was rarely covered in the mainstream media. Almost overnight that changed with the Fearless Girl campaign. After literally billions of impressions on social and earned media, a number of other very large investors joined our call to have more diverse boards because it matters to company performance," says John Brockelman, Global Head of Brand Marketing and Communications at State Street Global Advisors (personal communication, February, 5, 2020). "Bottom line, with many large shareholders now making diversity a priority, marketers and communications professionals can add real value on this issue by helping their leadership teams articulate where their company stands."

Greater DE&I in the boardroom is a strategic priority not only for many companies, but also for a growing number of non-profit organizations, including foundations, endowments, cultural institutions, associations and colleges and universities (BoardSource, 2017; E. A. Castillo, 2018). Within non-profit settings, the board may go by different names, such as a board of trustees, a board of governors or a board of regents. Such board positions may be appointed or elected and may be a paid position or the director may serve on a voluntary basis. The overreaching purpose, though, of such boards remains similar: to help provide oversight of the organizational strategy, leadership and performance.

The Institute for Public Relations (IPR, n.d.) is a US-based non-profit foundation with a more than 60-year heritage of fostering research and research-based knowledge in PR and corporate communication practice. In the words of IPR, its research efforts help fuel *the science beneath the art of public relations*. IPR is supported by a board of trustees, made up of senior strategic communication and PR leaders.

"The IPR board of trustees is charged with overseeing the strategic direction of the organization, while the CEO implements it," says Dr. Tina McCorkindale, the president and CEO of IPR (personal communication, January 25, 2020). "The IPR trustees, with their strong business acumen, provide much needed checks and balances, especially from a fiduciary and governance standpoint." To start gaining board-level experience and perspective early in one's career, McCorkindale recommends that college students seek leadership opportunities in pre-professional organizations and that younger professionals should volunteer in non-profits, community organizations or industry associations.

INSIDE THE CORNER OFFICE

The C-suite, particularly the company CEO and president, is generally more visible to stakeholders, such as employees, customers and investors, than the board of directors. At large companies, though, even employees may have limited to no direct interaction with the CEO and other members of the senior leadership team. The term C-suite refers to those corporate officers that have "chief" in their job title and/or are considered part of the senior management team, such as the CEO, the CFO, chief operating officer, chief legal officer and general counsel, chief human resources officer (CHRO) and chief information officer (CIO) or chief technology officer (CTO). Note that in some organizations the human resources (HR) function is now being called people operations or people teams.

The heads of operating and functional business divisions, units and/or departments at companies may also be considered part of the C-suite (Neatby, 2016). Traditionally, the most senior leaders of an organization have often held the corner offices. This is less so now in the era of open office space designs and more remote work, but the phrase "the corner office" is still often used to collectively refer to the corporate officers and the executive team.

In addition to the C-suite and the board of directors, most corporations have an executive committee. This committee is comprised of a broader group of the most senior executives across the company (Neatby, 2016). The executive committee is typically headed by the CEO. In larger companies, the chief marketing officer (CMO) and/or the chief communications officer (CCO) is often a member of the executive committee. For example, Jay Carney, the public policy and communications chief for Amazon and a former White House press secretary, is reportedly a member of the company's senior leadership team, which is known internally as the "S-team" (Kim, 2019). This team of around 20 Amazon executives regularly meets with Amazon founder and CEO Jeff Bezos to discuss critical business decisions (Kim, 2019; Nickelsburg, 2019).

The overall profile of the executives that make up the C-suites in the United States today is not all that different than the profiles found in many corporate boardrooms. For the most part, while there is a shift toward more women and POC assuming leadership roles, the executive teams of US companies are still largely made up of older, white males with backgrounds in business or engineering (CristKolder Associates, 2019; Korn Ferry, 2019). Research by Korn Ferry (2019), an executive search firm, of the top 1,000 US companies by revenue finds that three quarters (75%) of the most prominent C-suite titles (i.e., CEO, CFO, CIO/CTO and CHRO) are held by men. Looking across these positions, the smallest percentage of women holding a specific position title is at CEO (at just 6%). In comparison, women hold considerably higher percentages of the CMO (36%) and CHRO (55%) roles (Korn Ferry, 2019).

According to Korn Ferry (2020b), when analyzed in the aggregate, the average age for a C-suite member among this sample is 56 and the average tenure in the C-suite is 4.9 years. CEOs are the oldest on average of any C-suite role, while CFOs and CMOs are tied for the youngest in age (Korn Ferry, 2020b). Analysis by CristKolder Associates (2019), another executive search firm, tells a similar story. More specifically, CristKolder (2019) finds that the average age of sitting CEOs at large US companies tends to be in their mid-to-late fifties, while CFOs tend to be around their early fifties. This same research indicates that POC hold less than one out of every 10 CEO (around 9%) and CFO positions (around 8%) (CristKolder Associates, 2019).

By some indications, the level of executive turnover in the C-suite is around record levels (CristKolder Associates, 2019). Such turnover arguably pressures executives to potentially prioritize trying to achieve visible short-term results over focusing on longer-term strategic planning and investments that take time to pay off (Ives, 2019). For example, research by Spencer Stuart (2020), a top executive search and advisory services firm, finds that for 2019 the median tenure for CMOs at 100 of the most advertised US brands was around 2.5 years on the job (30 months). This compares to a median tenure of 36 months on the job for CMOs in 2011, when Spencer Stuart (2020) first started tracking this metric. By comparison, the median tenure of CEOs is considerably longer at approximately five years (Marcec, 2017).

While executive turnover is high (CristKolder Associates, 2019), senior leaders are being very richly compensated for serving in these positions, particularly as the CEO (AFL-CIO, 2019). For 2019, median annual compensation for CEOs at 400 large US companies reached a new record level of at least $13 million (Francis, 2020). The AFL-CIO (2019) estimates that the CEOs of S&P 500 companies received, on average, total compensation of $14.5 million for 2018. By some estimates, total CEO compensation has grown 940% over a 30-year period (1978–2018), outpacing the gain of the S&P 500 stock index (707%) over this period and exponentially surpassing the gain in typical worker compensation (12%) during this time (Mishel & Wolfe, 2019). As of 2018, by some estimates, the average S&P 500 CEO-to-worker pay ratio had swelled to 287-to-1. In contrast, this ratio was around 20-to-1 in 1965 (Mishel & Wolfe, 2019). Before it was acquired by Amazon, Whole Foods Market had in place a novel executive pay cap of no more than 19 times the average worker's salary (Gandel, 2017).

The COVID-19 global pandemic had the indirect effect of shining a spotlight on executive compensation with not just investors, but among employees and the public. In response to the severe business disruptions and revenue shortfalls caused by the pandemic, many companies announced various cost-cutting plans, including partial or full furloughs and/or layoffs of employees (Trentmann & Broughton, 2020). More than 300 large, public US companies announced reductions in executive salaries as a show of solidarity with their employees, although some companies were criticized for not making deeper cuts to C-suite compensation packages (Trentmann & Broughton, 2020). As a condition of receiving $25 billion in grants and loans from the US federal government to help revitalize the slumping airline industry as a result of COVID-19, all airline companies receiving this financial support were required to agree to limits on executive pay until late March 2022 (Rappeport & Chokshi, 2020).

THE INSTITUTIONALIZED INFLUENCE OF SHAREHOLDERS ON GOVERNANCE

In recent years, a growing number of CEOs and business leaders have made public commitments to embracing stakeholder capitalism and redefining the purpose of the corporation (Business Roundtable, 2019a, 2019b). While more CEOs and boards seem committed to contributing meaningfully to the public good and trying to balance the interests of *all stakeholders* (Fink, 2018, 2019) – and not simply the sometimes shorter-term demands of investors – there is an institutionalized influence of shareholders on corporate governance that cannot be ignored (Cahill, 2019; Stout, 2012; Strine, 2016, 2017, 2019). Especially since communication professionals are often tasked with helping lead corporate social responsibility and corporate purpose-related initiatives, they should understand that a variety of factors in the corporate world still converge to potentially privilege the interests of investors, such as shareholders, over other stakeholder groups, such as employees, customers, communities and suppliers (Brancato & Plath, 2005; Monks & Minow, 2011; Tonello & Brancato, 2007).

The "maximization of shareholder value" approach to business management still wields considerable influence in C-suites and corporate boardrooms for a variety of reasons (Lev, 2012). For one thing, top executives like CEOs and board members are often partially compensated in company stock options and restricted stock awards (Mishel & Wolfe, 2019). Bonuses may also be tied to the achievement of financial targets. In essence, compensation schemes usually reward the achievement of greater profits and higher stock prices (Stoll, 2019). Second, at least within corporations, only shareholders typically have the right to vote in corporate elections and elect board members (U.S. Securities and Exchange Commission, n.d.-b. 2012b). As such, a corporate board is more likely to reflect the investor perspective. Third, if shareholders are unhappy with the performance of a board and its C-suite, they may engage in shareholder activism (Ragas, 2018). This can include holding a proxy contest, in which shareholders nominate alternate candidates for the board, threaten to vote out part or all of the existing board and perhaps even replace the current management team. Finally, while directors do have some latitude in their decision-making, traditional US corporate law generally pressures board of directors into making and supporting decisions through the narrower lens of shareholder value maximization (Strine, 2016, 2017, 2019).

Several efforts are underway that help counterbalance the institutionalized influence of shareholders in corporate boardrooms and corner offices. Many large corporations are incorporated under a legal structure called a C Corporation (or a C Corp). Smaller businesses have traditionally used legal structures such as the S Corporation (or an S Corp) or the limited liability company (or LLC). As Leo Strine (2016), the former chief justice of the Delaware Supreme Court, explains:

> a clear-eyed look at the law of corporations in Delaware reveals that, within the limits of their discretion, directors must make stockholder welfare their sole end, and that other interests may be taken into consideration only as a means of promoting stockholder welfare. (p. 10)

A new legal entity called a Benefit corporation (or a public benefit corporation) is a for-profit incorporating structure, similar to a C or S Corp, but the benefit company bylaws explicitly allow directors to legally consider the welfare of *all* stakeholders when making business decisions; this negates shareholder primacy (Buerkle, Change, & Storto, 2018).

In a related vein, more companies (whether structured as a Benefit corporation, a C Corp or some other legal structure) are opting to seek B Corp certification. The B Corp certification is managed by a non-profit called B Lab and is bestowed on companies that meet standards of social and environmental performance, accountability and transparency (Buerkle et al., 2018). According to the founders of the B Corp movement, there are now more than 10,000 certified B Corps and Benefit corporations combined, spanning 150 industries and 60 countries (Gilbert, Kassoy, & Houlahan, 2019). See Table 6.1 for a breakdown of the overlap in requirements between Benefit Corporation status and B Corp certification.

The B Lab website provides a searchable database of B Corp companies. Examples of B Corp businesses include Amalgamated Bank, Ben & Jerry's, Danone North America, Eileen Fisher, Kickstarter, Natura, Patagonia and Stonyfield Organic (Grothaus, 2019). In response to the Business

Table 6.1:   Benefit Corps versus Certified B Corps.

Issue	Benefit Corporations	Certified B Corporations
Accountability	Directors required to consider impact on *all* stakeholders	Directors required to consider impact on *all* stakeholders
Transparency	Must publish public report of overall social and environmental performance assessed against a third party standard[a]	Must publish public report of overall social and environmental performance assessed against a third party standard[a]
Performance	Self-reported	Recertification required every three years against evolving standard
Availability	Available for corporations only in around 30 US states and DC[b]	Available to every business regardless of corporate structure, state or country of inception
Cost	State filing fees from $70 to $200	B Lab certification fees from $500 to $50,000 per year, based on revenues
Role of B Lab	Developed model legislation; works for its passage and use; offers free reporting tool to meet transparency requirement; no role in oversight	Certifying body and supporting 501c(3) offering access to Certified B Corporation logo, portfolio of services and a vibrant community of practice among B Corps

Source: Adapted from B Lab, benefitcorp.net (2020).
[a]Delaware benefit corps are not required to report publicly or against a third party standard.
[b]Oregon and Maryland offer benefit LLC options.

Fig. 6.1: B Lab Advertisement: "Let's Get to Work."

LET'S GET TO WORK

Dear Business Roundtable CEOs,

We are part of a community of Certified B Corporations who are walking the walk of stakeholder capitalism. We are successful businesses that meet the highest standards of verified positive impact for our workers, customers, suppliers, communities and the environment.

We operate with a better model of corporate governance – benefit corporation governance – which gives us, and could give you, a way to combat short-termism and the freedom to make decisions to balance profit and purpose.

As you know, with continued resistance from investors on this new definition of business, we've got work to do to help them see that stakeholder governance builds trust and builds value.

More importantly, it also ensures that the purpose of capitalism is to work for everyone and for the long term.

Let's work together to make real change happen.

Source: B Lab.

Roundtable's (2019a, 2019b) statement re-defining the purpose of a corporation, B Lab took out a full page ad in the Sunday edition of *The New York Times* in which B Corp leaders implored big company CEOs to put their words into action. See Fig. 6.1 for this advertisement.

CORPORATE GOVERNANCE AND STRATEGIC COMMUNICATIONS

Corporate governance – who leads organizations, why and what are the goals, values and behaviors of those in the corner office and the boardroom – is of increasing interest to company stakeholders, the news media and the public (Mishel & Wolfe, 2019; Pettigrew & Reber, 2013). Whether a public or a private company, greater transparency into the policies and decision-making of the C-suite and the board of directors, including corporate purpose and strategy, is the new normal (McCorkindale, Hynes, & Kotcher, 2018; Neill, 2018; Rutherford, 2018). As such, strategic communication professionals, whether working as external counselors to clients or on in-house communication teams, will almost certainly find themselves encountering more governance-related issues and subjects in the years ahead. This means communicators will need to be able to take often complex governance and leadership matters and distill them down into understandable and accessible messages for both internal and external stakeholders, as well as other audiences.

Adam Bryant is a bestselling author, consultant and expert on executive leadership, having interviewed more than 600 CEOs and other senior executives for *The New York Times* Corner Office column and now for outlets including CNBC and LinkedIn. According to Bryant, one of the great challenges facing leadership teams is "simplifying complexity" for employees and other stakeholders (personal communication, December 6, 2019). "The challenge is to hone all communications so that they are simple, but not simplistic, and so that they pass the most important test of all – people inside the company can remember them off the top of their heads," says Bryant, managing director and partner at Merryck & Co., a global leadership development firm. "CCOs and senior PR professionals can play a crucial role in helping refine the core pillars of a company into memorable and meaningful messages."

C-suites and boards of directors must continually demonstrate that they are transparent and ethical stewards of organizational assets that are worthy of public trust and respect (Arthur W. Page Society, 2012, 2013, 2019a; Penning & Bain, 2018; Ragas, 2019a; Ragas & Culp, 2014a, 2018a). Organizational leaders must rapidly move from conducting business seemingly in the dark at times and more fully embrace the light. Strategic communication professionals steeped in business acumen (and with the ear of the C-suite and boards) can help ensure that in the years ahead, through consistent, admirable company leadership behaviors, the analogy of "the smoke-filled back room" (Safire, 1968) will join the scrap heap of time – where it belongs.

KEY TERMS

Agency theory

B Corp certification

Benefit corporation

Boardroom

Board of advisors

Board of directors

Chief executive officer (CEO)

Corner office

Corporate governance

Corporate officer

C Corporation (C Corp)

C-suite

Diversity, equity, and inclusion

  (DE&I)

Employee activism

Executive committee

Fiduciary

Fiduciary duties

Pay ratio rule

Proxy contest

S Corporation (S Corp)

U.S. Securities and Exchange

  Commission

Shareholder activism

DISCUSSION QUESTIONS

(1) Visit the website of a large public company you are interested in and look up its leadership team bios. What do you find noteworthy about the backgrounds of this C-suite team?

(2) Repeat this same exercise, but this time look up the bios for the company's board of directors. What do you find noteworthy about the backgrounds of this board?

(3) If you were a CCO, how would you make the case to the CEO that greater DE&I is needed within your organization?

(4) Keep on your CCO hat for a while longer. Your CEO wants your opinion on whether your company should pursue B Corp certification? What do you say?

(5) Do you think corporate governance will become a more important subject for strategic communication professionals in the future? Why or why not? Explain your rationale.

By Shelly Lazarus, Chairman Emeritus, Ogilvy & Mather

I vividly recall the first time I was invited to present at a corporate board meeting. Since I was the only woman in the room and younger than most board members, I admit to being a bit terrified. But I also was confident since I was passionate about the work I was presenting and, importantly, I fully understood the company's business model and goals.

While there has been considerable progress since that meeting nearly 40 years ago, women and people of color remain underrepresented on corporate boards and in the C-suite. The communications industry, specifically advertising and public relations, is perhaps the least represented major profession in these corporate corridors. As of 2019, roughly 35% of Fortune 500 board seats were held by women and minorities, and only 32 women and 11 people of color were chief executive officers (Deloitte & Alliance for Board Diversity, 2019; Zillman, 2019). And it's safe to say that only a few advertising and public relation executives have made it to corner offices.

That's why, when given the opportunity, up-and-coming communications professionals must understand what it takes to succeed in the C-suite. It takes more than being in the right place at the right time; it requires a clear understanding of how businesses succeed and fail in today's complex marketplace.

You'll be dealing with a market that is truly global, which was not true for most of history. For instance, Ogilvy recently acquired a global account in China that has one headquarters location in Beijing and one in North Carolina, and decided to move its marketing center to India. Constant changes and shifts in business strategy is the nature of business in the world today.

The rate of change also has accelerated. Just when you think you've figured out an industry, all of a sudden there is a technological change, organizational change, new competitors from countries that weren't previously in the field and new ways of doing business that were unthinkable before. To cope with and advance your career during this exciting time for the global economy, here's my advice for young professionals:

(1) *Embrace change:* Don't be frightened of change. Beyond accepting change, enjoy it, and remain completely open-minded.

(2) *Become a problem solver:* A client might ask me, "How do I build a brand?" or "How can I establish a communications program?" But I start farther back. I say, "Give me the business problem you're trying to solve, and then we can talk about what marketing can do within the context of the problem."

(3) *Start with internal communications:* Often, the most overlooked segment of potential brand building is the internal audience – all the employees of the organization. They're out in the world interacting with people every day. Help them understand your strategy and goals.

(4) *Understand business basics:* Before entering the business world, young professionals should become comfortable with business basics. How do you read a profit and loss statement? How do you assess a balance sheet? What are the principles of marketing, such as how to get consumer insights? And of course, what are key ethics and corporate governance issues?

(5) *Be authentic:* Be yourself and love what you do. If you don't like what you're doing professionally, your life will never be in balance.

PART IV

THE MONEY AND THE NUMBERS

7

FINANCE AND THE CAPITAL MARKETS

Before there was "Netflix and chill," many Americans would choose to "make it a Blockbuster night" (Randolph, 2019). Of course, for many, this entailed getting in the car and driving to a Blockbuster store, hoping a copy of the movie you wanted to rent was in stock, waiting in line to check out and then driving back home to watch it. Then there were the annoying late fees if you didn't physically return the VHS tape or DVD on time to the store.

Serial entrepreneurs Reed Hastings and Marc Randolph identified these problems and launched a possible solution when they founded Netflix in 1997, the same year that DVDs were first introduced in the United States (Hastings & Meyer, 2020; Keating, 2013; Randolph, 2019). Originally self-funded by Hastings and Randolph, Netflix started as the world's first online DVD rental store (Gallo, 2019). After several years of trial and error, Netflix smartly adapted its business model to a monthly subscription with flat-fee unlimited DVD rentals that were mailed to customers in its now iconic red envelopes (M. Castillo, 2017). In 1999, a still money-losing Netflix received a critical $30 million venture capital investment from Group Arnault, which believed in the potential of this industry disruptor (Keating, 2013). In 2000, as Netflix was growing, but still losing money and in need of additional capital, the company approached Blockbuster about potentially making an investment or even an outright acquisition. Blockbuster executives report-edly laughed at the pitch and instead launched competitor Blockbuster Online (Gallo, 2019).

Two years later, as Netflix was posting impressive subscriber growth, but still losing money and in need of additional capital, the upstart company held its initial public offering (IPO) (*The New York Times*, 2002). In July 2002, the lead underwriter, investment bank Merrill Lynch, helped Netflix sell 5.5 million shares of stock at a price of $15 a share, raising $82.5 million. At the time of the IPO, Netflix had more than 600,000 subscribers, annual revenue of around $76 million and was still a DVD-by-mail company that didn't produce any of its own content (Owens, 2017). Some 20 years later, Netflix is one of the most powerful media and entertainment companies in the world with more than 193 million paid memberships in over 190 countries and $20 billion in annual revenue (Hastings & Meyer, 2020; Netflix, Inc., 2020). While there is still a DVD rental component to Netflix, its online streaming service, which first launched in 2007, now dominates. Netflix is also known today for its award-winning original programming.

Less than a decade after the Netflix IPO, the tables had turned drastically for Netflix and its competitors. By 2010, one-time Netflix rivals Blockbuster Video, Hollywood Video and Movie Gallery had all filed for bankruptcy and were on their way to disappearing entirely (Owens, 2017; Satell, 2014). Early stock market investors in Netflix, on the contrary, were richly rewarded for believing in the company's prospects. By one estimate, an investment of just $990 in Netflix's stock back in 2002 at its IPO price (and after stock splits) would by early 2020 be worth approximately $340,000, a staggeringly successful financial return (*Investopedia*, 2020).

Without continued investor support in its early years through to today, Netflix might not have survived or have been nearly as successful. A winning business idea and sound execution of that idea is critical, but so is having access to capital and understanding how the capital markets work. Financial considerations and implications are often on the minds of the C-suite and business leaders as they assess recommended courses of action and evaluate programs and plans. As such, to be more effective as counselors and advisors, strategic communication professionals do not need to have the financial proficiency level of a Wall Street analyst or even of an investor relations (IR) professional, but they should gain at least a working knowledge of the world of finance and the capital markets. This includes, but is not limited to, understanding the role and purpose of finance and the capital markets; the basics of how the stock market works; familiarity with the key players that make up the financial community; and the process of "going public."

"In my personal experience, as the founder and operator of a company and as a communicator, it is often my business and financial experience drawn from academic and in-the-trenches learning, that allows me to form strategic advice that is both listened to and implemented by business leaders and CEOs," says Jennifer Prosek, founder, chief executive officer (CEO) and a managing partner of Prosek Partners, a leading independent public relations (PR) and financial communications consultancy with a focus on financial and professional services clients (personal communication, May 11, 2020). Prosek explains that CEOs "will most definitely have finance and operations acumen" so those chief communications officers (CCO) and their teams that demonstrate financial and business acumen will have "an edge" when dealing with the C-suite.

FINANCE AND THE CAPITAL MARKETS

Finance is essentially about the management of money, more formally called capital. Every organization, whether a start-up company like Netflix in its early years or the multinational entertainment media corporation that it is today, needs readily available access to capital to help sustain and grow its operations. Corporate finance is specifically focused on the raising and managing of funds (i.e., capital) to help meet the goal of creating value for stakeholders through solving customer problems (Stern & Chew, 2003). In plain terms, finance is about "getting money" and effectively "managing money" to "make money." Investors typically provide capital to organizations with the expectation of generating a return (Appleby, 2011).

A company management team and board of directors may access capital and grow a business through a variety of financing options (Ragas & Culp, 2014a). Such options include, but are not limited to: (1) re-investing retained profits, called earnings, back into the operations of the business, (2) pursuing grants and gifts, such as crowdfunding (e.g., Kickstarter and Indiegogo campaigns), (3) borrowing money and getting lines of credit from banks and other lenders, (4) taking on debt by selling bonds to investors or (5) through raising capital by selling stock to investors. When someone buys stock (i.e., equity) in a company, they become an owner, a shareholder, in the underlying business, whereas a bond is a form of debt. When a company issues bonds, it borrows money from investors at an agreed upon interest rate and terms, and the company must pay back the borrowed funds at an agreed upon future date. Stocks and bonds are both examples of securities, a financial instrument that holds some type of monetary value.

The capital markets are where organizations go to raise capital and it is where buyers and sellers engage in the trading of securities, such as stocks and bonds (*Investopedia*, 2019). In 2018, the securities industry in the United States raised $2.4 trillion in capital for organizations through debt and equity issuances (Kolchin & Podziemska, 2019). While the stock market typically receives more attention from the media and the public, the bond market is somewhat larger in size. The collective value of global equity markets is around $75 trillion, while the collective global value of the bond markets is more than $100 trillion (Kolchin & Podziemska, 2019). Many large companies issue a mix of both stocks and bonds as sources of financing. Often, larger and more established companies will choose to meet the requirements needed to list their stock for trading on a stock exchange, as a stock listing makes company shares considerably easier for a wider range of investors to buy and sell. Anyone with cash in a brokerage account may buy shares in a public company, whereas with private companies the shares are typically closely held; the company usually controls who does or does not become a shareholder.

Very broadly speaking, younger and smaller companies tend to be privately held, whereas older and more mature companies, such as Fortune 500 corporations, tend to be publicly traded, meaning their stock is listed on an exchange. Within the United States in recent decades, due to various factors, including greater availability of private capital and rising regulatory and compliance costs for public companies, there has been a *decline* in the total number of publicly listed companies (Benham & Obregon, 2019). There are around 4,000 public companies in the United States (J. M. Thomas, 2017). By comparison, there are many thousands more privately held firms. Some very large, successful corporations choose to stay private. Some of the largest privately held companies in the United States include Bechtel, Cargill, Deloitte, Ernst & Young, Koch Industries, Mars, Meijer, Pricewaterhouse-Coopers, Publix, SC Johnson and Wegmans (*Forbes*, 2019).

From a strategic communication perspective, private companies may choose to disclose fairly limited information about the inner workings of their business and financial performance, whereas public companies must submit quarterly and annual financial reports, as well as periodic reports as needed, with the US Securities and Exchange Commission (SEC). Such reports are available to the general public. As such, public companies are required to continually demonstrate a much higher level of transparency than private companies. However, it is important to note that in recent years more private companies are voluntarily choosing to become more transparent with stakeholders and the public about their business performance and plans.

Family owned for more than a century, Mars Incorporated is one of the largest privately held companies and biggest employers in the United States. With $35 billion in annual revenue and more than 125,000 associates – lovingly known as Martians among some Mars associates (Kaplan, 2013) – in 80 countries around the world, Mars has four operating segments: Mars Food, Mars Wrigley, Mars Petcare and Mars Edge (Mars, Incorporated, 2020). In recent years, Mars has made visible strides in becoming more transparent with the public, including becoming more outspoken about what Mars stands for as a company and providing more information about its sustainability commitments (Edgecliffe-Johnson, 2019; Kaplan, 2013; Staley, 2017).

"At Mars we have a saying that the consumer is our boss – we know consumers build their trust in brands through transparent communication. Plus, we know our current and future associates want to know the company they are working for, which is another reason to communicate internally and externally – to retain and attract great people," says Allyson Park, global vice president, corporate affairs, Mars Wrigley (personal communication, April 6, 2020). "For Mars, over the past several years, we have made our leaders more visible externally. They have talked openly about our Five Principles and culture, the combination of purpose plus performance, and important topics like climate change and long-term investments we have made – like in wind energy."

HOW THE STOCK MARKET WORKS

At its core, a stock exchange serves as a venue that matches buyers and sellers of a company's stock, thereby facilitating more efficient trading and capital raising for firms (Beattie, 2019). The so-called "bid" is the price someone is willing to pay for shares, while the "ask" is the price at which sellers are willing to sell shares. In many ways, a stock exchange is like eBay or a more specialized auction platform like Stubhub or StockX, only the products being bought or sold typically five days a week during regular trading hours, except for major holidays, are shares in public companies, rather than event tickets or sneakers (Sundaram, 2019).

Each company listed on an exchange is given its own ticker symbol, a series of letters which uniquely identify the company. This is similar to how airports are given unique codes, such as ORD for Chicago O'Hare International Airport or ATL for Hartfield-Jackson Atlanta International Airport. Stock ticker symbols often bear some relation to the name of the company and/or its products. For example, the ticker symbol for Microsoft is MSFT and for Apple, Inc. is AAPL.

The two largest stock exchanges in the United States – and the entire world – are The New York Stock Exchange (NYSE), also nicknamed "the Big Board," and the NASDAQ (Haqqi, 2020; The World Federation of Exchanges, 2019). Both the NYSE and the NASDAQ are based in New York City, which is a global hub for the financial markets. Other major financial hubs around the world include Amsterdam, London, Hong Kong, Mumbai, Shanghai, Shenzhen, Tokyo and Toronto. See Table 7.1 for a list of the world's largest stock exchanges based on the combined market capitalizations of the companies listed on these exchanges.

Founded in 1792 and today owned by Intercontinental Exchange, the NYSE is much older and larger than the NASDAQ (Beattie, 2019). The famous NYSE trading floor and the ringing of the opening bell from the balcony overlooking the trading floor is often included as part of company marketing plans, as well as featured in news reports and even in television shows and movies. Floor trading by humans still plays a role at the NYSE, but the majority of daily trading volume is now conducted electronically (Detrixhe, 2017). On March 23, 2020, due to public health concerns around the COVID-19 pandemic, the NYSE opened for trading *without* floor trading and human traders for the first time in its more than 225-year history (Detrixhe, 2020). About two months later, limited human trading resumed.

The NASDAQ, founded in 1971, has always been an all-electronic exchange and was traditionally known for attracting the listings of up-and-coming technology companies. This has changed in recent decades, as the NYSE and NASDAQ both compete for a broader range of company stock listings. Located in Times Square, the exterior of the NASDAQ MarketSite includes an iconic seven-story LED video display, which is widely photographed (Nasdaq, Inc., 2020). More speculative and higher risk public companies that *do not* meet the listing requirements of the exchanges may be traded via quotation services maintained by OTC Markets, informally dubbed the OTC bulletin board (OTC Markets Group, Inc., 2020).

The stock market and the financial community are often referred to as "Wall Street" or simply "the street." Wall Street is the name of the iconic

Table 7.1: The World's 20 Largest Stock Exchanges.

Rank	Stock Exchange	Headquarters	Market Capitalization
1	The New York Stock Exchange (NYSE)	New York, NY, USA	$28.5 trillion
2	The NASDAQ Stock Exchange	New York, NY, USA	$10 trillion
3	The Tokyo Stock Exchange	Tokyo, Japan	$5.1 trillion
4	The Shanghai Stock Exchange	Shanghai, China	$4.9 trillion
5	The Euronext Stock Exchange	Amsterdam, The Netherlands	$4.82 trillion
6	The LSE (London Stock Exchange)	London, UK	$4.59 trillion
7	The Hong Kong Stock Exchange	Hong Kong, China	$4.23 trillion
8	The Shenzhen Stock Exchange	Shenzhen, China	$3.28 trillion
9	The TSX (Toronto Stock Exchange)	Toronto, Canada	$3.0 trillion
10	The Bombay Stock Exchange	Mumbai, India	$2.19 trillion
11	The NSE (National Stock Exchange of India	Palo Alto, CA, USA	$2.1 trillion
12	The ASX (Australian Securities Exchange)	Sydney, Australia	$1.6 trillion
13	The Deutsch Börse Exchange	Bentonville, AR, USA	$1.56 trillion
14	The Swiss Exchange	Zurich, Switzerland	$1.5 trillion
15	The Korea Exchange	Busan, South Korea	$1.46 trillion
16	The NASDAQ Nordic Exchange	Stockholm, Sweden	$1.37 trillion
17	The Taiwan Stock Exchange	Taipei, Taiwan	$966 billion
18	Brasil Bolsa Balcão Exchange	Sao Paulo, Brazil	$938 billion
19	Johannesburg Stock Exchange (JSE)	Johannesburg, South Africa	$894 billion
20	Bolsas Mercados Exchange (BME)	Madrid, Spain	$764 billion

Source: Adapted from Insider Monkey.
Note: Rankings as of August 2020.

street in the financial district of lower Manhattan in New York, which has historically been the home of many brokerage houses and investment firms, including the location of the NYSE. By some estimates, a little more than half of American households invest directly or indirectly (through various types of retirement accounts) in the stock market (Kolchin, 2019). As such, business news has grown in popularity in recent decades (Roush, 2016).

Daily news reports will often include an update on the performance of major stock market indices. An index tracks the performance of a collection of stocks. In the United States, the most widely followed stock market indices are the Dow Jones Industrial Average, often just called "the Dow," the Standard & Poor's 500 index, often just called "the S&P" and the NASDAQ Composite, often just referred to as "the NASDAQ."

There are variety of seismic shifts taking place on Wall Street and within the global financial markets that strategic communication professionals should know about, as these changes may have ramifications for their organizations and clients in the years ahead (National Investor Relations Institute, 2019). For starters, the ownership of many public companies today is increasingly dominated by large professional investment funds (e.g., mutual funds, pension funds and hedge funds), known as institutional investors, rather than by many smaller, non-professional investors, known as individual investors. In addition, there has been rapid growth in low-cost passive investment products called index funds, which track the composition of various indexes. At many public companies, this has resulted in the largest company stockholders being a handful of very large asset management firms, such as Blackrock, Vanguard and State Street, which are the major index fund providers (McLaughlin & Massa, 2020). Finally, the rise of algorithmic electronic trading could be leading to greater volatility in the stock market and more fluctuations in stock prices (Lewis, 2015).

TAKING A WALK DOWN WALL STREET

A wide range of players make up the Wall Street financial community. Unless a strategic communication professional specializes in financial communications, they likely won't *directly* interact with many of these players, but the *indirect* impact of these individuals is likely to still be felt (Ragas, 2019b). For example, the views and actions of finance-related decision-makers and stakeholders may influence everything from news coverage and analyst reports of one's organization or client to questions at employee town halls and forums to the contents of executive communications, such as CEO letters and annual reports. Communications professionals with at least a working understanding of the names and roles of these various players are better positioned to provide more effective counsel to executives on finance-influenced business and communication issues (Ragas & Culp, 2018b).

The financial community is comprised of a mix of players that are internal or external to the company. A corporation is referred to as "the issuer" in the parlance of Wall Street. This is because public companies *issue* or sell securities, such as stocks and bonds. Inside of corporations, the chief financial officer (CFO) typically works closely with the CEO on all strategic financial matters. Often the CFO is the primary point of contact with external players on Wall Street, such as major shareholders and investment analysts.

IR is the corporate function that is responsible for building relationships with current or prospective investors (Laskin, 2018). Typically, the investor relations officer (IRO) reports to the CFO or, less frequently, to the CEO (Laskin, 2014). The IRO and the IR department often collaborate to at least some degree on strategic communication messaging and positioning with the corporate communication and marketing departments (Ragas, Laskin, & Brusch, 2014). Within large companies, the communications team often has at least one professional that specializes in financial communications. This individual will often be the primary point of contact for business journalists and the news media (Ragas, 2016a).

"For communications professionals working in PR and marketing for a company, there is additional coordination required with the finance team when the company is public or is private and pursuing an IPO," says Steve Collins, a former public company CFO and current private and public company board member, including at Sprout Social and Instructure (personal communication, March 31, 2020). "When a company pursues an IPO or is already public, the CFO and the finance team are also conveying external messages to shareholders, prospective investors, Wall Street analysts and regulators, so it's important that these investor-related communications are consistent with the company's marketing and sales messages." Collins adds that, in one company where he was CFO, the company chose to have its director of marketing communications also lead the IR function to "assure this consistency in all of the company's external communications."

Investment professionals are typically defined as being part of the "buyside" or the "sellside." On the buyside are portfolio managers and support staff that work for investment funds that manage and invest capital. On the sellside are the investment analysts that work for brokerage firms and issue ratings and reports that may influence the trading behavior of buyside firms. Notable types of investment firms include hedge funds, which may invest in private or public companies; venture capital firms, which tend to invest in fast-growing private companies; and private equity firms, which tend to invest in more mature companies that may need to be restructured and transformed. Typical external advisors on financial matters to corporations include accounting firms and auditors, corporate law firms, investment banks and sometimes management consulting firms. Companies specifically hire firms called proxy solicitors to help them build support for or against matters going up for shareholder votes. There are also specialized financial communications agencies and IR consultancies that advise companies.

Very influential external players within the financial community are the federal and state policy-makers and regulators on investment matters, most notably, the SEC (Remund & Kuttis, 2018). The Financial Industry Regulatory Authority is the self-regulatory organization of the US securities industry. The NYSE and the NASDAQ are also influential in setting corporate finance standards as companies listed on their exchanges must comply with their listing requirements and procedures. Within established capital markets outside of the United States, there are often a similar mix of government and industry regulators.

Often little known, but very influential, external players on Wall Street are the proxy advisor firms. Proxy advisors are specialized firms that issue voting recommendations on shareholder proposals and voting matters, including on board of directors elections and mergers and acquisitions. Perhaps the most well-known proxy advisory firm is Institutional Shareholder Services, better known as ISS. Additional third-party external players are the business news media, ranging from traditional elite media at newspapers and broadcast outlets to bloggers and other opinion leaders.

THE PROCESS OF GOING PUBLIC AND RINGING THE BELL

An IPO is a high-profile, transformative event for a company that is typically several years in the planning. An IPO marks the first time a company sells stock to the public and lists its stock for trading on a stock exchange (U.S. Securities and Exchange Commission, 2019). In the United States, this typically means listing on either the NYSE or the NASDAQ. To initiate the IPO process, a company hires an investment bank to estimate the firm's valuation and assess investor interest in its stock. In preparation for the IPO, the company strengthens its internal financial controls and reporting systems to meet the regulatory requirements of being a public company.

In gearing up for an IPO, the company may also make changes to its board of directors and leadership team, such as adding directors and key executives, such as the CFO and/or CEO, with prior public company experience. The hiring of an IRO is another sign that a company may be planning to go public. If an IPO is well received by investors, a company may choose to sell additional shares and raise additional capital at a future date through what is called a secondary offering.

For US-based IPOs, the official unveiling of a company's plan to go public has traditionally been made through the filing of an initial S-1 registration statement, called a prospectus, with the SEC and its Electronic Data Gathering, Analysis, and Retrieval (EDGAR) online system (U.S. Securities and Exchange Commission, 2019). A team of outside consultants, such as investment bankers and lawyers, work closely with the company, including its finance, accounting, legal and communications teams, to craft the prospectus. This extensive document contains critical information about the company, including explaining its business model, its financial statements, competitors, risk factors and what it intends to do with any capital raised from the offering. With an eye on protecting investors, the SEC carefully reviews a firm's prospectus, asks for changes and must ultimately approve the prospectus *before* the company can proceed with its IPO plans.

Companies have traditionally received a burst of media coverage and public scrutiny when the initial S-1 is filed. For example, in 2019, high-profile shared workspace company WeWork postponed its planned IPO in part due to concerns revealed in the company's prospectus about its business model, corporate governance and possible conflicts of interest. Some current and former WeWork employees reportedly felt that the IPO prospectus was poorly written and delivered an unclear message about the business strategy (Eaglesham & Brown, 2019). See Fig. 7.1 for the first summary page from the now infamous prospectus for The We Company, the parent of WeWork.

In recent years, the SEC has extended a confidential filing option that was previously made available only to smaller companies to larger companies as well. The confidential filing route delays the public filing of the prospectus until much closer to the actual IPO date, and a firm even gains the option to withdraw a draft registration statement without having alerted the public.

The time from when a company files its initial prospectus with the SEC and before it has been approved (i.e., "declared effective") by the SEC is

Fig. 7.1:   Prospectus Summary First Page of WeWork S-1 Filing.

Source: US Securities and Exchange Commission, SEC.gov. https://www.sec.gov/edgar/searchedgar/companysearch.html; https://www.sec.gov/Archives/edgar/data/1533523/000119312519244329/d804478ds1a.htm.

known as the quiet period (U.S. Securities and Exchange Commission, 2017). A company must be careful about what it says during the quiet period, so as not to be seen as potentially hyping its stock. Once the prospectus is approved, the company's top executives go on what is called a road show with its underwriters (Henderson, 2019). The road show consists of a series of in-person and virtual presentations made to investment fund managers to drum up interest in the IPO. The COVID-19 global pandemic showed that road show presentations via video conferencing can be efficient and effective (L. Hodgson, 2020; Human, 2020).

IR and corporate communication professionals are often tasked with helping to prepare the presentation contents and helping the management team to articulate the company story in these meetings. These meeting materials are made available through the SEC's EDGAR filing system. In meetings with prospective investors, employees, the media or anyone else, company executives must be careful to only disclose material information that has already been made available in the prospectus and in the supplemental information the company has filed with EDGAR.

The big day of the IPO is not just a capital raising event, but also a media and marketing event. The company management team often celebrates at the stock exchange with the ringing of the opening bell. There may also be a celebration at the company headquarters with employees. Other stakeholders may also get involved in the IPO process. For example, when ride-sharing companies Uber and Lyft when public in 2019, they gave some long-time drivers a small cash award with an option to put it toward buying stock in the IPOs (Conger, 2019; Farrell, 2019).

An emerging alternative to the long-established IPO method is called a direct listing. In a direct listing, a company does not go on a road show or seek to raise any additional capital, but rather simply lists its existing shares on a stock exchange for trading (Coren, 2019). Within the US markets, venture capital-backed Palantir Technologies, Slack Technologies and Spotify Technology are examples of companies that have used the direct listing method in recent years to go public (Henderson, 2019; Nivedita, Franklin, & Hussain, 2020).

THE FUTURE OF FINANCE AND THE OPPORTUNITY FOR COMMUNICATORS

There is a groundswell of interest around the world in socially responsible and sustainable investing (US SIF Foundation, 2020). Investment dollars are rapidly flowing into investment funds that take into account corporate purpose (Business Roundtable, 2019a, 2019b) and company environmental, social and governance (ESG) performance when making investment decisions and allocating capital (Fink, 2018, 2019, 2020). By some estimates, by as soon as 2025, as much as half of all professionally managed investment assets in the United States could have an ESG mandate (Deloitte Development LLC,

2020). This increasing expectation that businesses create both economic *and* social value is transforming corporate finance and the capital markets. This transformation creates a significant opportunity for savvy corporate communication and strategic communication professionals to flex their muscles as advisors and counselors.

Corporate communication and strategic communication departments and teams have long been seen by business leaders as experts on corporate social responsibility (Coombs & Holladay, 2012; Pompper, 2015) and now on corporate social advocacy matters as well (Dodd & Supa, 2014, 2015). By extension, communication departments and agencies may also gain the opportunity to advise executives on ESG matters. But this will likely only happen in organizations and with clients where communicators can demonstrate at least an intermediate level of proficiency in understanding finance and the capital markets – the home of ESG policymaking. Put simply, if communicators choose to take the view that learning about finance and the investment world "does not apply to them," they are less likely to have their opinions on ESG be heard and valued by those sitting at the leadership table. Embrace learning about finance.

KEY TERMS

Bond
Capital markets
Corporate finance
Crowdfunding
Debt
Direct listing
EDGAR
Equity
Financial communications
Index fund
Individual investors
Initial Public Offering (IPO)

Institutional investors
Investor relations (IR)
Hedge fund
Private equity
Quiet period
Road show
Securities
Stock
Stock exchange
Ticker symbol
Venture capital
Wall Street

DISCUSSION QUESTIONS

(1) Think of one of your favorite companies. Now visit a financial website like Yahoo! Finance or MarketWatch and type in the name of the company. Is this favorite company privately held or publicly traded?

(2) Next, visit the corporate website of the company. What sort of information can you find on the corporate website about the financial and social performance of the firm?

(3) Assuming you have selected a publicly traded company, there should be an IR section to the corporate website. What information do you find in this section?

(4) Run a news search on a site like Google News for "IPOs." What are the names of companies that have recently gone public or plan to go public? What does the media coverage say about these companies?

(5) Do you think that *all* strategic communication professionals should learn at least the basics of the world of finance and the capital markets? Why or why not? Make your case.

By Joe Cohen,
Chief Marketing and
Communications Officer, AXIS

"I went into communications because I hate math."

This statement, and comments like it, are made all too often by communications professionals. And comments like this are among the most diminishing and career-limiting things you can say to a CEO, CFO, CMO or CCO.

A commonality among the top communications leaders in the field is that they aren't just experts in their craft; they are business leaders. These leaders often run their own teams like a business – putting forward strategies, programs and initiatives that are geared specifically to advancing *business* objectives, and their plans and actions are guided by data-driven insights.

Whether you are new to the field or a seasoned professional, below are several best practices worth embracing:

• *Deeply understand the business* – an often-used phrase in communications is "story-telling" – crafting messages, grounded in truth, that bring the narratives surrounding you or your clients' organization to life in a powerful, memorable way. Early in my career, I was fortunate to have mentors who taught me that this cannot be done properly without fully understanding the mechanics of a given business: business goals, how and why the company makes and loses money; and – at any given time – its overall fiscal health and why performance is strong or suffering.

• *Get comfortable with the financials* – it should go without saying that CEOs, CFOs and other business leaders talk numbers. Throughout my career, I've observed that the communications leaders who earn a "seat at the table" tend to be fluent in the financials. With that comes the importance of being adept at helping your CEO or partners/clients boil down complex concepts into easy to understand narratives. There is also the importance of your own budget management. Even if you choose to not directly manage the budget yourself, communications leaders need to oversee the budget and be able to understand where they are spending, why they are spending and where they are (or aren't) getting the most value.

- *Tether your programs to business objectives* – this is a comms cliché but one that I've consistently found to be true: any good communications strategy or program should ladder back directly to relevant business objectives. An initiative is only a good initiative if it can help deliver value back to the organization. It is imperative that communications professionals can easily and clearly explain the business rationale for any program or recommendation they propose – and how it can potentially help "move the needle." And, as taught in any good introductory communications course, every communications objective should be highly measurable.

- *Adopt a data-driven mindset* – I've often found that, just like many CEOs and others in the C-suite, some of the strongest communications leaders are obsessed with data. Gathering and assessing data are part of their daily routine. As such, one of the best investments a communications leader can make is in creating a strong measurement program, with needed tools and platforms, to help gauge the efficacy and impact of their work. And the data need to be put to good use – boiled down into actionable insights to help inform decision-making – and clearly illustrate not just the outputs (e.g., media impressions and social media engagement) but the outcomes (e.g., impacting purchasing decisions and influencing behaviors/perceptions).

- *Own the role and enrich your perspective* – self-perception matters. It begins with thinking about oneself as a businessperson – and embracing the role. In addition to delivering on your day-to-day duties, this requires added work. Investing time and energy in developing relationships with partners throughout the business and/or your clients' organizations is invaluable. It is also important to make time to stay current on trends, research and best practices, and expand your perspective beyond the bubble that is your direct circle of relationships. Broadening your view and taking classes in business management and becoming active in organizations like PRSA and Page can be extremely valuable. And adopting a diverse mindset and supporting and connecting with professionals of diverse backgrounds will both help them and enrich your perspective.

I hope these observations that I have picked up during my career experiences are helpful to you as you begin or continue your own professional journey. And, who knows, along the way you may even wind up realizing that you love math.

8

FINANCIAL STATEMENTS AND VALUATION ESSENTIALS

Accounting and finance are two of the leading languages of business (Piper, 2013; Ragas, 2019a, 2019b; Ragas & Culp, 2014a; Skonieczny, 2012; Taparia, 2004). Through the debits and credits, revenues and expenses and assets and liabilities found on financial statements and in financial reports, organizations communicate their financial performance to stakeholders and the public. Decision-makers in the corner office and in the boardroom use financials when setting strategies, making plans and allocating future resources.

In many ways, financial statements and reports serve as periodic performance scorecards for management teams and those throughout the organization, as well as for outside partners. These scorecards are of particular interest to financially incentivized current or prospective stakeholders, such as managers, investors, creditors, banks and other lenders. But investors are not the only groups that are interested in learning about an organization's financial performance and "making sense of the dollars and cents." Employees, suppliers, customers and communities all have a vested interest in understanding an organization's financial health, stability and future growth prospects, as this can impact the stakeholder's future relationship with the organization.

In recent decades, the chief financial officer (CFO) has emerged as one of the most powerful senior leaders in not just corporations, but also in many non-profit organizations (McCann, 2018). CFOs in many organizations today are not just responsible for overseeing financial planning, budgeting and management, but may also take on strategy, deal-making and operational responsibilities (Karaian, 2014). This is likely one of the reasons there has been a decline in recent years in the chief operating officer (COO) position across the corporate world (CristKolder Associates, 2019).

Ruth Porat is a great case in point. A fixture on "most powerful women in business" lists (Forbes & McGrath, 2019; *Fortune*, 2019b). Porat has served as the CFO of Alphabet, Inc., the parent company of Google and one of the world's most valuable companies, since 2015. Besides leading the finance function, Alphabet's business operations, people operations, real estate and workplace services teams all report in to Porat (D'Onfro, 2016; Farr & Elias, 2019). The former CFO of investment bank Morgan Stanley, Porat has served as a vice chair of Stanford University's board of trustees and as a member of the board of directors of the Stanford Management Company. Quarterly earnings conference calls for Alphabet are typically headed by two senior executives at Alphabet: chief executive officer (CEO) Sundar Pichai and Porat (Farr & Elias, 2019).

Unfortunately, far too many strategic communication professionals are uncomfortable with, unprepared for, or even disinterested in discussing the basics of accounting and finance with the Ruth Porats of the world. Many communicators major in liberal arts or social sciences in college and have a passion for creativity, words and images – not numbers (Feldman, 2016; Roush, 2006). But unless more communication professionals learn to "lean in" when it comes to accounting and finance, the communication profession may be limited in its aspirations to evolve into a bonafide strategic management function and C-suite advisor (Korn Ferry, 2020b). The communicator who learns how to speak finance and accounting as a second (or even third) language is at a strategic advantage (Duhé, 2013). Further, for communicators with their eyes set on leadership positions, they often need to become conversant with budgets and financial reports.

As such, this chapter provides communicators with an important grounding in some of the basics of accounting and finance, with an emphasis on corporate and financial communications. This includes learning about the referees that set the rules for financial reporting and disclosures; the three major types of financial statements, including how to read an income statement and a balance sheet; the importance of profit margins and how to calculate them; what is earnings per share (EPS) and how to calculate EPS; and what are several key financial valuation concepts and how to calculate each of them. Reading this chapter won't turn you into the next Ruth Porat, but it may mean you are more conversant with her colleagues in the future.

RULE SETTERS AND REFEREES FOR FINANCIAL REPORTING AND DISCLOSURES

As required by the Securities and Exchange Commission (SEC) and the stock exchanges, US public companies must report their financial and business performance on a quarterly basis. For US public companies, such reports are filed with the SEC's freely accessible Electronic Data Gathering, Analysis, and Retrieval (EDGAR) system. As explained by the U.S. Securities and Exchange Commission (2020), EDGAR helps increase "the efficiency, transparency and fairness of the securities markets" (para. 2). Included as part of these quarterly EDGAR filings, as well as typically in quarterly earnings news releases, are the company's quarterly financial statements. If a public company does not report its quarterly results with the SEC on a timely basis, its stock can be delisted from the stock exchange for not meeting the exchange's listing requirements (Gallant, 2019). Corporate disclosure laws, rules and regulations are discussed in much more detail in the next chapter.

There are several entities that play important roles as rule setters and referees when it comes to establishing financial reporting and accounting standards, and providing oversight of these standards. Such standards help bring greater consistency and transparency to financial reports across companies and industries. Granted authority by the SEC, the US-based Financial Accounting Standards Board (FASB) is a non-profit organization whose mission is to develop and improve the standards used in US financial reporting and accounting (Taparia, 2004). These standards are known as generally accepted accounting principles (GAAP). When a public company reports a non-GAAP financial measure, the company is required to provide a reconciliation between the adjusted and regular figure (Asper, McCoy, & Taylor, 2019). Two popular non-GAAP financial measures are earnings before interest and taxes (EBIT) and earnings before interest, taxes, depreciation, and amortization (EBITDA) (U.S. Securities and Exchange Commission, 2018).

Another entity granted authority by the SEC is the Public Company Accounting Oversight Board (PCAOB), which was formed in the early 2000s in the wake of the major corporate accounting scandals, such as Enron, World-Com and Tyco. The PCAOB oversees the audits of public companies in order to protect investors and the general public from potentially fraudulent behaviors (Public Company Accounting Oversight Board, 2020). The London-based International Accounting Standards Boards (IASB) is responsible for developing and promoting International Financial Reporting Standards (IFRS). The IASB has long worked with FASB to try to improve and converge GAAP and IFRS accounting standards (Financial Accounting Standards Board, n.d.).

There is a growing focus by the world's largest investment managers, such as BlackRock, State Street Global Advisors and others, on the environmental, social and governance (ESG) performance of corporations, particularly on ESG issues and measures that are material to a company's economic performance (Fink, 2020; Kramer, 2020; Wigglesworth, 2020). San Francisco-based non-profit Sustainability Accounting Standards Board (SASB) provides an ESG disclosure framework for how companies may report financially material ESG concerns for 77 different industries. Another major initiative is the Task Force on Climate-related Financial Disclosures (TFCD), which has developed a voluntary reporting framework on climate-related risks.

Looking beyond the investment world and into the broader domain of corporate social responsibility (CSR), Amsterdam-based Global Reporting Initiative (GRI) is a widely used reporting framework. SASB and GRI have announced a collaborative work plan designed to help companies learn how to use both sets of standards together (Sustainability Accounting Standards Board, 2020). These ESG standardization efforts are likely to significantly shape the future of finance, accounting and company financial reporting in the years ahead.

Concomitant with the rise of ESG and CSR, the role of the strategic communicator has been "significantly elevated" in recent years with stakeholders showing more interest in how companies conduct business than ever before, according to Tom Johnson, the CEO of Abernathy MacGregor Group, a top strategic communication advisory firm (personal communication, April 24, 2020). "It is no longer acceptable to just say a business is here to maximize profits for its investors," says Johnson, who majored in mass communication and started his career in business journalism before transitioning into financial communications. "Business strategies and performance must now be communicated across various stakeholder groups, and that is very hard to do unless you have a solid grounding in how money is flowing across the organization."

THE THREE MAJOR TYPES OF FINANCIAL STATEMENTS

Financial statements provide a snapshot in time look at an organization's business performance and the financial health of an organization. In an effort to keep investors and other stakeholders informed, US public companies are required to prepare and release their financial statements on a *quarterly basis*. It is important to keep in mind that the financial picture for a company can fluctuate and shift – sometimes substantially – in the 90 days in between these quarterly financial reports. Many companies choose to release supplemental financial and non-financial information and commentary to help contextualize the numbers found in the financial statements. This information is used by stakeholders to help determine the current or projected economic worth of a business and to understand the financial story (Lev, 2012, Lev & Gu, 2016).

"All numbers need a storyteller who can bring them to life with context and color," says Kathryn Beiser, vice president, global communications for Eli Lilly and Company, one of the world's largest pharmaceutical companies. Beiser previously served as the CCO for Kaiser Permanente, Hilton Hotels and Discover Financial Services, as well as in senior agency positions.

> *Working closely with the office of the CFO, communicators can help ensure the financial story supports the company narrative, investment thesis and other important objectives like employee recruiting and retention. (K. Beiser, personal communication, July 10, 2020)*

Financial statements will generally show the financial performance of an organization for at least two periods in time, with each time period represented by a column in the statement. For example, the first quarter performance of an organization for the current fiscal year will be compared with the first quarter performance of an organization for the prior fiscal year to assess the changes across numbers in the statement. This is referred to as a standard year-over-year (YoY) annual comparison of performance. Fast-growing startup companies and some more mature businesses may also choose to make sequential comparisons, where, for example, the first quarter performance from the current year is compared to the second quarter performance of the same year and so forth. This is referred to as a quarter-over-quarter comparison.

There are three major types of financial statements that all US public companies are required to prepare and publicly release to investors and other stakeholders on a quarterly basis:

(1) *Income statement:* This statement is also known as the profit and loss statement or simply the "P&L." As the name implies, this statement tracks the sales an organization generated, its expenses and whether it generated a profit or loss for a specific time period.

(2) *Balance sheet:* This statement tracks an organization's assets (what it owns), liabilities (what it owes) and shareholders' equity (retained earnings) for a specific point in time. The name "balance sheet" comes from that fact that the assets on one side of the balance sheet and the liabilities plus shareholders' equity on the other side must balance out.

(3) *Cash flow statement:* This statement summarizes the amount of cash and cash equivalents entering and leaving a company for a specific time period. The "flow" of cash from operating activities, investing activities and financing activities is tracked.

For many communication professionals, they are most likely to encounter income statements and/or balance sheets as part of their work, particularly as they gain budgetary and leadership responsibilities and/or move more into strategic advisor roles (Kolberg, 2014; Ragas & Culp, 2018a). Therefore, this chapter concentrates on exploring how to read income statements and balance sheets in more detail. For those communicators working in a more finance-intensive specialization, such as financial communication or investor relations, they need to gain a more advanced ability to interpret all three types of financial statements, plus a deeper grounding in a broader range of accounting and finance terminology (Ragas, 2019b).

Business and financial acumen are "enablers of career advancement" for communications professionals, according to Clarkson Hine, senior vice president of corporate communications and public affairs for Beam Suntory, one of the world's largest premium spirits companies (personal communication, May 27, 2020). Hine majored in history in college and spent his early career in politics, before joining a publicly traded company to lead its communications.

"Even though I had no experience in finance and accounting, much of my job depended on financial communications," says Hine (personal communication, May 27, 2020). "I was surrounded by a lot of people with MBAs, which could be intimidating. But I drew confidence from the fact that I knew a lot more about communications than they did, and I had a passion to make the numbers talk in a way that was easily understandable to all stakeholders." Hine recommends that communication professionals ask questions of colleagues in finance and accounting, while absorbing as many different business and financial information sources as possible, such as visits to operations, internal meetings and documents and business news media.

Publicly traded companies are not the only types of organizations that are required to regularly file financial statements and financial information that are then made available to the public (Roush, 2016). Within the United States, most federally tax-exempt organizations (e.g., non-profits) must disclose key financial and governance information on an *annual basis* with the Internal Revenue Service (IRS). This mandatory information is submitted to the IRS via a Form 990. Upon request, tax-exempt organizations are required to provide a copy of their three most recent years of Form 990s (Roush, 2016). Some non-profit organizations provide this information on their websites. Finally, there are third party sources, such as Guidestar, Charity Navigator and ProPublica, that provide searchable databases of these forms by organization and by other criteria.

READING AN INCOME STATEMENT

The income statement, also referred to as a profit and loss statement (P&L), shows how much revenue or sales an organization has generated over a certain time period and, after subtracting expenses or costs, shows whether the organization has made or lost money (i.e., produced net income or a net loss) for this time period, such as a quarter or a full year. Further, this statement shows whether these figures, such as profit or loss, have grown or declined compared to the prior comparison period included on the statement. Even with GAAP standards, the titles and terms included on an income statement may vary from organization to organization and industry to industry. This said, the major categories and general contents included within an income statement and other types of financial statements remain similar and fairly consistent.

To walk through how to read an income statement and a balance sheet, the annual financials of Alphabet, Inc., the parent company of Google, will be used. A Fortune 20 company, Alphabet is widely regarded as one of the world's most powerful corporations (*Fortune*, 2020a), controlling an estimated seven out of every ten dollars spent in the digital search advertising market in the United States (Ad Age Studio 360, 2019). Globally, there are estimates that Google has an approximately 40% market share of *all* online advertising dollars (Swartz, 2020).

Revenues

Revenues, also known as sales, is found at the top of the income statement. As such, revenue is often referred to as "the top line." As shown in Table 8.1, for fiscal 2019, Alphabet reported total revenues of nearly $162 billion, an increase of 18% from the prior year. Organizations may choose to break out revenue into multiple categories on the income statement and/or they may choose to provide supplemental financial information in another table.

In the case of Alphabet, to provide better visibility into the performance of its various revenue streams, in 2020 the company expanded its revenue disclosures. As shown in Table 8.2, while Alphabet is making progress in diversifying its revenue streams, nearly $135 billion of its fiscal 2019 revenue, or more than 83% of its total revenue, was associated with online ads in some form. Alphabet generated nearly $26 billion in non-advertising revenue during fiscal 2019 from its Google Cloud Platform, such as G Suite tools, and Google Other businesses segment, made up of hardware sales, Google Play app purchases

Table 8.1: Alphabet, Inc. Expanded Revenue Disclosures (2017–2019).

Alphabet, Inc.
EXPANDED REVENUE DISCLOSURES (2017–2019)

(Amounts in millions)	2017	2018	2019
Google Search & other	$69,811	$85,296	$98,115
YouTube ads[a]	8,150	11,155	15,149
Google properties	77,961	96,451	113,264
Google Network Members' properties	17,616	20,010	21,547
Google advertising	95,577	116,461	134,811
Google Cloud	4,056	5,838	8,918
Google other[a]	10,914	14,063	17,014
Google revenues	110,457	136,362	160,743
Other Bets revenues	477	595	659
Hedging gains (losses)[b]	(169)	(138)	455
Total revenues – Alphabet, Inc.	**$110,855**	**$136,819**	**$161,857**

[a]YouTube non-advertising revenues are included in Google other revenues.
[b]Hedging gains (losses) were previously included in Google revenues.

Table 8.2: Alphabet, Inc. Annual Income Statement (2017–2019).

Alphabet, Inc.

INCOME STATEMENT (2017–2019)

(Amounts in millions, except share amounts)	2017	2018	2019
Revenues	$110,855	$136,819	$161,857
Costs and expenses:			
Cost of revenues	45,583	59,549	71,896
Research and development	16,625	21,419	26,018
Sales and marketing	12,893	16,333	18,464
General and administrative	6,840	6,923	9,551
European Commission fines	2,736	5,071	1,697
Total costs and expenses, net	84,677	109,295	127,626
Income from operations	26,178	27,524	34,231
Other income (expense), net	1,015	7,389	5,394
Income before income taxes	27,193	34,913	39,625
Provision for income taxes	14,531	4,177	5,282
Net income – Alphabet, Inc.	$12,662	$30,736	$34,343
Basic net income per share of Classes A and B common stock, and Class C capital stock	$18.27	$44.22	$49.59
Average shares outstanding	693,049	695,070	692,596
Diluted earnings per common share	$18.00	$43.70	$49.16
Average shares outstanding	703,444	703,341	698,556

and non-advertising YouTube revenue. As a rule of thumb, financial executives and investors generally don't want to see an organization too overly reliant on a particular revenue stream, customer or operating segment.

Cost of Goods Sold

Cost of goods sold, also known as simply COGS, is a line or several lines found directly under the revenue line on the income statement. COGS lists the *direct* costs that go into producing an organization's products or services and generating the resulting revenues. For a business that produces physical products, the expenses related to labor and the raw materials used to manufacture a product would be found under COGS. For a more digital product based company like Alphabet, COGS include search traffic acquisition costs, content acquisition and licensing expenses, and expenses related to its data centers and other operations. COGS may be listed under a related term, such as cost of revenue, as is the case with Alphabet. Cost of revenue for Alphabet in fiscal 2019 totaled nearly $72 billion.

General and Administrative Expenses

General and administrative expenses, also known as G&A, is a line (or several lines) located below the COGS line (or lines) on the income statement. Sometimes this line or lines will be presented as sales, general and administrative (called "SG&A") on the income statement. Whichever label is used, G&A and SG&A encompass the costs that *indirectly* contribute to the production and sale of the product or service and the resulting revenue generation. Typical expenses included in G&A or SG&A include items like sales, marketing and public relations (PR) spending; research and development (R&D); compensation of headquarters personnel; and other associated "overhead" that does not go directly into producing the product or service.

In the case of Alphabet, to provide more granularity, the company chooses to break out expenses associated with G&A into four different lines on the income statement rather than just one. As shown in Table 8.1, for fiscal 2019, Alphabet spent $26 billion on R&D, more than $18 billion on sales and marketing, approximately $9.5 billion on G&A, and approximately $1.7 billion on European Commission fines. These expense lines totaled $55.7 billion. The G&A line for Alphabet specifically includes compensation and facilities-related expenses for some employees, depreciation expenses, equipment-related expenses, legal-related expenses and professional services related fees.

Operating Income

Operating income, which also may be labeled as income from operations or operating profit, is a line on the income statement that is found directly below the total costs and expenses line. The operating income line shows how much money the organization made or lost *after it takes into account* all direct costs (i.e., COGS) and indirect costs (i.e., G&A expenses) but *before* the organization pays any taxes and ~~before it pays any interest~~ expenses related to borrowings (and/or generates any non-operating income, such as from investment gains). For fiscal 2019, Alphabet reported income from operations of $34.2 billion, an increase of approximately 24% from the prior year.

Net Income

The literal "bottom line," the net income line is at the bottom of the income statement. The double underline in tables found under the net income figure signals a grand total. Net income may also be labeled as net earnings or a related term. This crucial line on the income statement shows how much money the organization made or lost after *every* revenue and expense item (both operating and non-operating items) have been taken into account. For fiscal 2019, Alphabet reported net income of $34.3 billion, an increase of nearly 12% from the prior year.

KEEPING AN EYE ON PROFIT MARGINS

Business leaders, such as CEOs and other members of the C-suite, boards of directors and other financially incentivized stakeholders, such as shareholders, generally have a keen interest in an organization's profit margins. Often, an organization's financial performance is gauged not only by its *absolute* net profits or earnings, but its *relative* level of profitability; in other words, what percentage of every dollar in revenue generated drops to the bottom line. C-suite leaders, boards and investors generally want to see an organization's profit margins hold steady or expand from one year to the next, rather than decline. Publicly traded corporations are particularly under pressure to see their profit margins grow over time. A variety of different profit margins may be calculated from the figures on a company's income statement. Three important profit margin indicators are gross margin, operating margin and net margin.

Gross Margin

Gross margin is simply an organization's net revenues minus its COGS (Bloomenthal, 2020; Piper, 2013; Skonieczny, 2012; Taparia, 2004). Gross margin is typically shown as the gross profit as a percent of net sales.

The gross margin represents the portion of each dollar of revenue that the organization retains as gross profit after paying the *direct* labor and production costs that go into producing the product or service. The expected gross margins of industries and the companies within them can vary widely depending upon the fixed and variable cost structure mix of an industry. Industries such as software, digital services and professional services generally have relatively high gross margins (Damodaran, 2020).

This ratio is gross profit divided by net revenues. So for fiscal 2019, the gross margin for Alphabet on a percentage basis was 55.6% ($90 billion/$161.9 billion). This gross margin shows modest contraction from the prior two years, which was 56.4% in fiscal 2018 ($77.2 billion/$136.8 billion) and 58.9% in fiscal 2017 ($65.3 billion/$110.9 billion). In essence, Alphabet retains almost $0.56 of each dollar of revenue generated after paying COGS. These remaining funds are then used to cover other costs, such as G&A expenses.

Operating Margin

Operating margin, also known as return on sales, is an important measure of operational efficiency (Kenton, 2019b; Piper, 2013; Skonieczny, 2012; Taparia, 2004). This measure shows how much money an organization makes (or loses) on each dollar of net revenue it generates (before taking into account interest, taxes and dividends). The operating profit margin represents the portion of each dollar of revenue that the organization retains as operating profits after paying *all operating expenses* (i.e., COGS and the typical selling, general and administrative costs of running the organization, but before paying any interest or taxes).

This ratio is operating income (or operating profit) divided by net revenue. So for fiscal 2019, Alphabet's operating margin on a percentage basis was 21.1% ($34.2 billion/$161.9 billion). This represents margin expansion compared to the 20.1% figure for fiscal 2018 ($27.5 billion/$136.8 billion), but margin contraction when compared to two years earlier when the operating margin reached 23.6% for fiscal 2017 ($26.2 billion/$110.9 billion).

Net Margin

Net margin, also known as net profit margin, is a commonly used measure of the bottom-line profitability of an organization (Piper, 2013; Segal, 2020; Skonieczny, 2012; Taparia, 2004). This measure shows how much money an organization makes (or loses) on each dollar of net revenue it generates after every expense, including taxes, interest and any one-time or special expenses, has been deducted from revenue. Unlike with calculating operating margin, which only takes into account *operating* expenses, net margin also takes into account any *non-operating* expenses, such as taxes and interest, and any non-operating income, such as investment gains, dividend income or the sale of an asset or assets.

This ratio is net income (or net profit) divided by net revenues. So for fiscal 2019, Alphabet's net margin on a percentage basis was 21.2% ($34.3 billion/$161.9 billion), meaning that $0.21 of every dollar of revenue essentially flowed down into Alphabet's coffers. This marks a small decline from a net margin of 22.4% for fiscal 2018 ($30.7 billion/$136.8 billion), but a significant improvement from a net margin of just 11.4% for fiscal 2017 ($12.7 billion/$110.9 billion). Note that, as shown in Table 8.2, in 2017, Alphabet incurred a larger than typical provision for income taxes, as well as generated less other income than usual, which had the effect of substantially pulling down its net margin. As this example shows, operating margin may at times provide a cleaner picture year-to-year of a company's financial performance.

CALCULATING EARNINGS PER SHARE

All public companies not only report their net income or earnings on its income statement, but also convert this figure to an EPS basis and report the EPS figure. This critical calculation essentially shows a shareholder how much of a company's profits (or losses) is associated with *each individual share of stock* they own. In essence, each share of stock represents a tiny slice of ownership in that company and its earnings. EPS is calculated by dividing the company's reported net income (i.e., net earnings or profits) by the total number of shares of stock outstanding for the company. Investors often pay more attention to a company's EPS number than to the net income figure, particularly how the reported EPS for a period compares to the EPS projections of the company and/or investment analysts (Chen, 2018).

The share count for calculating EPS is usually included near the bottom of the income statement in a section below the net income line. The conservative approach to calculating EPS is to use the *diluted* average shares outstanding total rather than the *basic* average shares outstanding total.

The diluted total includes all possible additional shares that may be issued in the future from the execution of stock options, warrants, preferred shares or related securities.

For example, Alphabet posted diluted earnings per common share of $49.16 for fiscal 2019. This figure was calculated by dividing Alphabet's reported net income of $34.3 billion for 2019 by the company's diluted average shares outstanding count of nearly 698.6 million shares. This represents a 12.5% improvement from the $43.70 in EPS that Alphabet posted in the prior year. The EPS figure forms the basis for widely used financial valuation metrics, such as the price-to-earnings (*P/E*) ratio, which are used to assess the value of a company and its stock price relative to its EPS. The *P/E* ratio is discussed in more detail later in this chapter.

READING A BALANCE SHEET

While an income statement shows an organization's revenues, expenses and the resulting profit or loss generated for the period under review, a balance sheet shows an organization's assets (i.e., what it *owns* that is a source of value) and liabilities (i.e., what it *owes*) for a certain point in time. The balance sheet also shows shareholders' equity or net worth for the enterprise, which roughly indicates how much money would be left over for shareholders if the organization sold off all of its assets and paid off all of its liabilities. The name balance sheet comes from the fact that an organization's total assets must equal or "balance" relative to the organization's total liabilities plus shareholders' equity (Piper, 2013; Skonieczny, 2012; Taparia, 2004). Balance sheets provide an important snapshot view of an organization's financial staying power and ability (or inability) to endure significant disruptions to operations (Winkler, 2020a, 2020b).

For example, at year-end fiscal 2019, as shown in Table 8.3, Alphabet reported total assets of nearly $276 billion, a staggeringly large sum. There were corresponding liabilities and shareholders' equity of the same amount (with total liabilities of nearly $74.5 billion and total stockholders' equity of $201.4 billion). Stockholders' equity less any preferred stock divided by the company's total number of shares outstanding equals a company's so-called "book value" per share (Kenton, 2020a). Alphabet's book value at year end was around $288.37 per share. Assuming the stated accounting values carried

Table 8.3:   Alphabet, Inc. Balance Sheet (2017–2019).

Alphabet, Inc.

BALANCE SHEET (2017–2019)

(Amounts in millions, except share amounts)	2017	2018	2019
ASSETS			
Current assets			
Cash and cash equivalents	$10,715	$16,701	$18,498
Marketable securities	91,156	92,439	101,177
Total cash, cash equivalents, and marketable securities	101,871	109,140	119,675
Accounts receivable	18,336	20,838	25,326
Income taxes receivable, net	369	355	2,166
Inventory	749	1,107	999
Other current assets	2,983	4,236	4,412
Total current assets	124,308	135,676	152,578
Non-marketable investments	7,813	13,859	13,078
Deferred income taxes	680	737	721
Property and equipment, net	42,383	59,719	73,646
Operating lease assets	0	0	10,941
Intangible assets, net	2,692	2,220	1,979
Goodwill	16,747	17,888	20,624
Other non-current assets	2,672	2,693	2,342
Total assets	$197,295	$232,792	$275,909
LIABILITIES AND STOCKHOLDERS' EQUITY			
Current liabilities			
Accounts payable	$3,137	$4,378	$5,561
Accrued compensation and benefits	4,581	6,839	8,495
Accrued expenses and other current liabilities	10,177	16,958	23,067
Accrued revenue share	3,975	4,592	5,916
Deferred revenue	1,432	1,784	1,908
Income taxes payable, net	881	69	274
Total current liabilities	24,183	34,620	45,221

(Continued)

(Amounts in millions, except share amounts)	2017	2018	2019
Long-term debt	3,969	4,012	4,554
Deferred revenue, non-current	340	396	358
Income taxes payable, non-current	12,812	11,327	9,885
Deferred income taxes	430	1,264	1,701
Operating lease liabilities	0	0	10,214
Other long-term liabilities	3,059	3,545	2,534
Total liabilities	44,793	55,164	74,467
Stockholders' equity			
Convertible preferred stock, $0.001 par value per share	0	0	0
Class A and Class B common stock, Class C capital stock and additional paid-in capital, $0.001 par value per share	40,247	45,049	50,552
Accumulated other comprehensive loss	(992)	(2,306)	(1,232)
Retained earnings	113,247	134,885	152,122
Total stockholders' equity – Alphabet, Inc.	152,502	177,628	201,442
Total liabilities and stockholders' equity	$197,295	$232,792	$275,909

on a firm's books are accurate, book value (also known as net book value or net asset value) theoretically represents the total value of a company's assets that shareholders would receive if the company were to be liquidated.

Assets

An asset is something an organization owns that has value with the potential to generate revenues and contribute to profits. Examples of assets include cash, cash equivalents and marketable securities; accounts receivable (i.e., money owed to the organization); inventory; property, plant and equipment; operating leases; deferred income tax credits; intangible assets, such as copyrights, trademarks and patents; and goodwill, an intangible asset that accounts for the excess purchase price of another company's assets. Current assets are assets the organization may convert to cash typically in a year or less, while non-current assets are longer-term assets. As shown in Table 8.3, at year-end 2019, Alphabet reported total current assets of nearly $152.6 billion and non-current assets of approximately $123.3 billion.

The current assets section of the balance sheet, specifically the cash, cash equivalents and marketable securities lines, is also used to calculate an organization's "burn rate" (also called its "cash burn") and to assess the general health of its balance sheet. The burn rate is the rate at which a money-losing organization spends its cash on hand and other readily available assets over a certain period of time (such as on a monthly or even a weekly basis) to cover its operating expenses. During the coronavirus outbreak and economic slow-down, there was a heightened interest by stakeholders in the cash balances and burn rates of every type of enterprise, from small startup companies to multinational corporations (Francis & Gryta, 2020; Winkler, 2020a, 2020b). In the case of Alphabet, as of year-end 2019, it had a fortress-like balance sheet with a staggering $119.7 billion in cash, cash equivalents and marketable securities on hand.

Liabilities

A liability is, as the name implies, some sort of monetary obligation that the organization owes to someone else and for which it is liable. Examples of liabilities include accounts payable (i.e., money the organization owes to suppliers and vendors); income taxes payable or deferred; accrued and deferred revenues; long-term debt; operating lease liabilities; and other long-term liabilities. Long-term debt may include debts owed to banks, bondholders or other parties. Current liabilities are liabilities that the organization expects to pay within a year, while non-current liabilities have an expected payback duration of beyond a year. Typical non-current liabilities include long-term debt and long-term lease obligations (Taparia, 2004).

As shown in Table 8.3, at year-end 2019, Alphabet reported total current liabilities of approximately $45.2 billion and non-current liabilities of approximately $29.2 billion.

Shareholders' Equity

Shareholders' equity, also called stockholders' equity, is the remaining amount of assets available to an organization's shareholders after all liabilities have been paid (Chen, 2020a). Shareholders' equity comes from two main sources: the amount of money originally and subsequently invested in the company, and through retained earnings, which the firm accumulates over time as it generates profits. A company with negative shareholders' equity (i.e., liabilities exceed assets) may indicate it is at risk of bankruptcy (Clark, 2020). Company boards and management teams generally seek to increase the value of shareholders' equity over time.

Alphabet's shareholders' equity consistently grew from 2017 to 2019. As shown in Table 8.3, Alphabet reported shareholders' equity of approximately $201.4 billion at year-end fiscal 2019. This compares with shareholders' equity of around $177.6 billion and $152.5 billion in fiscal 2018 and 2017, respectively.

FINANCIAL VALUATION ESSENTIALS

There are many different financial valuation metrics and models that businesspeople, investors and other financially oriented stakeholders pull from financial statements to assess the current and future potential value of a business. A valuation is an estimation of the economic worth of a business asset, unit or the entire enterprise (Hayes, 2019). For publicly traded companies, the company's stock price changes each trading day, thereby providing a near real-time view of the company's ascribed total market value. For private companies, share ownership is more difficult to value due to the absence of a public market for the company's shares. Private companies may hire an outside independent party, such as investment bank, to conduct a valuation analysis (Nguyen, 2019). Public companies also hire bankers to conduct such analyses.

Many financial valuation metrics and concepts are beyond the scope of this book. A more detailed knowledge of valuation metrics and concepts are probably only needed for those communication professionals working in investor relations, financial communication or another finance-intensive specialty area (Feldman, 2016; Laskin, 2018; Penning & Bain, 2018; Ragas, 2019a, 2019b). However, any strategic communication professional, particularly those working in and with corporate communication and corporate affairs teams and/or with public company clients, would meaningfully benefit from understanding at least these three financial valuation concepts: market capitalization, enterprise value (EV) and the *P/E* ratio.

Market Capitalization

Market capitalization, also known as simply "market cap," is a measure that determines the total market value of a company. Market cap is calculated by multiplying a company's stock price at a certain date in time by its total number of issued shared outstanding. As you may recall, the shares outstanding figure is typically provided at the bottom of the income statement. For public companies, a firm's stock price is often published on the investor relations section of the corporate site, as well as on many financial news and information websites, such as Bloomberg, CNBC.com, MarketWatch, WSJ.com or Yahoo! Finance. Stock charts use the stock price to provide a graphical representation of a company's stock price performance over time. It is important to note that a stock chart *does not* directly display a company's revenues or earnings performance – only its stock price.

As of year-end 2019, Alphabet had a market capitalization of nearly $934 billion, making it one of the world's most highly valued companies by market cap (PwC, 2019b). This is based on Alphabet having approximately 698.6 million shares outstanding as of year-end 2019, multiplied by Alphabet's closing stock price on December 31, 2019 of $1,337.02 per share.

Enterprise Value

While market cap is a widely used valuation metric, it also has its limitations. Market cap is only based on a company's equity value; it does not take into account a firm's cash position, debt outstanding and any preferred stock issuance (Murphy, 2020). EV, a more comprehensive measure of company value, takes these variables into account and represents the minimum price someone would have to pay if they wanted to acquire the entire company. For example, there are firms that carry significant amounts of outstanding debt so valuing such companies based on just market cap (i.e., equity value) would paint a misleading picture.

Alphabet ended 2019 with an EV of nearly $806 billion. This is based on the company's market cap of almost $934 billion plus total debt of just around $4.6 billion subtracted from cash, cash equivalents and marketable securities of around $132.8 billion.

P/E Ratio

The *P/E* ratio is perhaps the most widely used financial metric for valuing a company. The *P/E* ratio is sometimes called "the earnings multiple." This ratio is the company's stock price divided by its EPS. The *P/E* ratio tells an investor, a businessperson or anyone else interested in a company's finances, how much value the stock market is assigning to a company's current or projected future earnings *on a per share basis*. Valuation metrics such as the *P/E* ratio allow for apples-to-apples comparisons of companies' stock.

For example, a stock priced at $5.00 per share isn't necessarily "cheap" from an investment perspective, just as a stock priced at $500 per share isn't necessarily "expensive." To make an accurate comparison, an investor must know much (or how little) earnings are associated with each company's share of stock. *P/E* ratios allow for this important valuation comparison between companies across industries or even the overall stock market. This is the same idea behind not just looking at the price of two items of different sizes on a grocery store shelf, but rather looking at the price per ounce of both items to get a direct comparison of value.

Alphabet's stock price for year-end 2019 was $1,337.02, which, when divided by its 2019 diluted EPS of $49.16, gives the parent company of Google a trailing *P/E* multiple of 27× earnings. For fiscal 2021, Wall Street analysts expect Alphabet to post EPS of around $56.00. Using the same stock price and this EPS estimate gives Alphabet a forward *P/E* of 24× earnings. For comparison, the historical average *P/E* ratio of the information technology sector and the communication services sector is around 20× and 16×, respectively (Butters, 2020). By these comparisons, Alphabet shares could be viewed as "overvalued." On the flipside, investors generally are willing to pay more for market leaders, particularly those that generate fairly consistent earnings growth over time, such as the market-dominant Alphabet.

Besides the *P/E* ratio, there are a range of other ratios that use a company's stock price along with another financial metric to calculate a valuation measure. This includes the price-to-sales ratio and the price-to-earnings growth ratio. Companies are also valued on multiples of EV using ratios such as enterprise value-to-revenue and enterprise value-to-earnings before interest, taxes, depreciation, and amortization.

BENEFITS OF BECOMING FLUENT IN THIS SECOND (OR THIRD) LANGUAGE

As a field, PR and strategic communication has long argued that it needs a seat at the leadership table (or to at least serve as a trusted advisor to those at the table) to do its job most ethically and effectively (Bowen, 2008; Neill & Barnes, 2018; Nothhaft, Werder, Vercic, & Zerfass, 2020; Ragas & Culp, 2018a). The CFO almost always has a seat at the table. Those at this leadership table are also likely to consider an organization's financial statements and financial performance when developing, implementing and tracking organizational strategies, programs, goals and objectives. While arguably *too much emphasis* may get placed at times on the shorter-term dollars and cents impact of organizational decisions and policies, communicators would be unwise to cast aside finance and accounting concepts. This remains a lingua franca of business and often of those sitting around the leadership table.

By building a proficiency in at least the basics of accounting and finance concepts, communication professionals are better prepared to contribute more meaningfully and persuasively to leadership discussions (Beiser, 2018; Hine, 2018; Spangler, 2014). Organizations today must create much more than simply economic value for a sub-set of their stakeholders, such as investors, or simply create quality products and services for their customers. The creation of broader societal value grounded in organizational purpose and values has become a strategic imperative for every enterprise (Bolton, Stacks, & Mizrachi, 2018; McCorkindale, Hynes, & Kotcher, 2018).

At the same time, all organizations, whether major corporations or mom-and-pop corner businesses, also owe it to their stakeholders to make decisions that, over the long haul, position the enterprise to become and remain financially self-sustaining and fiscally healthy. The strategic communication professional, whether working in-house or as an agency partner, who can bring this holistic, multi-sided perspective to the leadership table will be invaluable.

KEY TERMS

Balance sheet	Burn rate
Book value	Cash flow statement
Bottom line	Chief financial officer (CFO)

Chief operating officer (COO)

Earnings per share (EPS)

Enterprise value (EV)

Financial statements

Form 990

Generally Accepted Accounting
Principles (GAAP)

Income statement

International Financial Reporting
Standards (IFRS)

Market capitalization

Price-to-earnings ratio (*P/E* ratio)

Profit margin

Quarter-over-Quarter

Stock chart

Top line

Valuation

Year-over-year (YoY)

DISCUSSION QUESTIONS

(1) Do you think accounting and finance will become less important "languages of business" and those in the C-suite and in the boardroom in the future? Why or why not? Explain.

(2) Select a publicly traded company that you admire and respect. Now without looking this up, guess the company's *annual* "top line" revenues and "bottom line" profits.

(3) Go to the Web and look up the company's most recent annual earnings report, specifically its annual income statement (aka "the P&L"). How did you do? What was the firm's actual reported annual revenues and profits?

(4) Using this same company and its annual income statement, calculate the company's operating profit margin. Did its profit margin expand or contract YoY?

(5) Sticking with this same company, what was its reported EPS? Look up its stock price. Now calculate its *P/E* ratio. What does this say about its valuation?

By Valerie Barker Waller, Chief Marketing and Communications Officer, YMCA of the USA

As the child of two professors, I understand the firsthand benefits of being passionate about academic pursuit, which has helped me to develop a lifelong love of learning.

In college, I was fortunate to study what I was curious about and good at – Finance and Business Economics. I enjoyed learning theory. But, as it turns out, what I truly enjoyed about theory was no fun in practice. So, after spending time doing internal audits and business unit financial planning, which both really do help you learn a business from the inside, I decided to do something completely different – make TV commercials.

While on the surface, understanding financial controls has nothing, literally, to do with making ads, it has everything to do with it. Whether it is from within the organization or as a trusted partner agency, it is critical for communicators – who are helping to craft and share a company's story – to understand all aspects of a business to truly add value at every level and every table where important discussions happen.

Throughout my career, I have had the opportunity to help position brands and organizations in multiple sectors, from consumer packaged goods to telecommunications to airlines to the brand that is the Olympic Games. In all cases, understanding the financials and the other key performance indicators for the product, division, company and sector has been beneficial, and has ensured I can participate in important conversations that have helped me deliver the best possible communications output.

Key to this pursuit has been understanding how a specific business works and how it makes money. Here are questions that I find helpful to get answers about any business:

- What are its sources of revenue and what are its expenses?

- How does the economy impact the sector and the company or organization?

- For the publicly traded companies, what was shared on the most recent quarterly earnings calls; for the non-profits, what was included in the organization's most recent 990's (filed each year with the Internal Revenue Service and usually is available on the organization's website)?

Here are a few ways to become a more financially savvy communicator:

- *The daily news:* Read and follow journalists that focus on your industry or category and be sure you are regularly looking at the stock price for your company or your client's company.

- *Tricks of the trade:* Subscribe to trade publications. While not written for communicators, there is always invaluable insight about the sector, key competitors and business threats.

- *Buddy up:* Connect with a colleague in Finance or Accounting to understand the basics and learn the lingo. As part of your professional development plan, ask for the opportunity to partner with someone at your company. Whether you are just starting out or further along in your career, you will benefit from a partnership like this.

- *Night school:* Take a Finance for Non-financial Managers online class; many universities offer them, including Harvard Business School. Be sure to see if your company will sponsor you and/or cover the cost. If you have some prior coursework or academic background, you can also pick up a book that covers the same type of content.

- *Profit from non-profit:* If volunteer board service is something you already do or would consider, ask to be on the Finance and/or Audit Committee. While not likely to be directly applicable to your sector or specific business, this is a great way to get exposure to and learn more about key financial information.

I had both the benefit and good fortune of studying what was interesting – money and numbers – and being able to use it to do what I love – communications. Understanding financial statements and key financial information has allowed me to be an informed and knowledgeable voice. For strategic communicators to be a true partner, whether internally or with clients, solid grounding in and understanding of "the money and the numbers" is key.

9

CORPORATE DISCLOSURE: LAWS, RULES AND REGULATIONS

Transparency is the name of the game today for strategic communication. But so is learning and following "the rules of the game" when it comes to corporate disclosure of mandatory and voluntary information related to financial and business matters. Most organizations, particularly publicly traded companies, cannot simply say *what they want, when they want, whenever they want* to *whomever they want* through *whatever channel* they so please.

Business leaders, spokespeople and other communicators must navigate the myriad laws, rules, regulations and ethics that guide corporate disclosures, and the broad communication of timely, fully accurate and truthful statements and claims to investors, other stakeholders and the public at large. Companies that violate these rules of the game face a variety of negative consequences ranging from regulatory fines, penalties and restrictions to reputational loss and a trust deficit among stakeholders and the public. Companies also must guard against potential shareholder lawsuits and related litigation as a result of what they do – and do not – say publicly.

Billionaire inventor and entrepreneur Elon Musk learned about these potential negative consequences the hard way. In August 2018, Elon Musk, the founder and chief executive officer (CEO) of electric vehicle and clean energy company Tesla, feeling frustrated with how Wall Street was valuing his public company, fired off a quick tweet to his millions of followers. In the tweet, Musk (2018) claimed that he had "funding secured" for a buyout to take Tesla private at $420 a share. The tweet sparked a jump in Tesla's stock price and forced the NASDAQ stock exchange to halt trading in Tesla shares until the firm gave an official response (Goldstein, 2018). Following the tweet, the US Securities and Exchange Commission (SEC) moved quickly to investigate the claim. Musk tried to clarify the market-moving statement, which not only seemed pre-mature at best and inaccurate at worst (i.e., there did not in fact appear to be an actual buyout offer in place), but had not been approved by Tesla's board of directors (Gelles, Stewart, Silver-Greenberg, & Kelly, 2018).

The notorious Musk $420 tweet ultimately set off an almost year-long battle between the SEC and Musk with Tesla stuck in the middle. Following an initial settlement in September 2018 between the two sides, the SEC asked a federal court in February 2019 to hold Musk in contempt for allegedly violating the agreement. Musk appeared to have not learned his lesson by tweeting an updated Tesla production outlook *without* first seeking approval from the company's lawyers, as required under the settlement. In another tweet, Musk had seemingly mocked the SEC. In April 2019, following pressure from a federal judge to reach a revised and clearer agreement, Musk agreed to a laundry list of stock price sensitive Tesla subjects he would not tweet about without first obtaining the pre-approval of an experienced securities lawyer (Goldstein, 2019). These additional restrictions came on top of Musk having previously agreed to step aside as chair of the board of Tesla for three years and to pay a $20 million fine. Tesla also agreed to add two new independent directors to its board and to create a permanent committee to monitor disclosures and potential conflicts of interest (Goldstein, 2018).

All in all, this was a quite expensive series of tweets for Musk and Tesla stakeholders. In spite of these transparency issues, Tesla has defied critics of its business model, and in late 2020 it was added as a company to the prestigious S&P 500, the most widely tracked stock market benchmark (Santilli, 2020).

Strategic communication professionals are often on the frontlines of helping organizations become more transparent when it comes to the quantity and quality of information they disclose to stakeholders and the public. Such transparency increasingly extends beyond advising the C-suite on the crafting of messages, but to the actual company actions that help make these words matter more (Arthur W. Page Society, 2016a, 2019b; Hynes, 2017, 2018). Publicly held companies are particularly in the spotlight when it comes to corporate and financial communication, but the disclosures of privately held companies are also scrutinized, particularly those operating in more regulated industries (Laskin, 2018; Ragas, 2019b). As such, while strategic communication professionals don't necessarily need to be corporate legal, regulatory, policy, compliance and ethics experts, they should gain at least a working knowledge of key corporate disclosure-related laws, rules, regulations and concepts, particularly within the industries and sectors in which they work (Remund & Kuttis, 2018).

THE ALPHABET SOUP OF REGULATORS AND RULES

There is "an alphabet soup" of regulatory agencies at the federal, state and municipal levels that keep an eye on corporate policies and behaviors with an eye on protecting consumers and the general public (Wilcox, Cameron, & Reber, 2015). See Table 9.1 for a list of federal regulatory agencies that are particularly relevant to communicators. All told, according to the Federal Register (2020), there are more than 450 government agencies just at the federal level in the United States.

Within the United States, federal regulatory agencies go by acronyms like the EEOC (Equal Employment Opportunity Commission), FDA (Food and Drug Administration), FTC (Federal Trade Commission), SEC and the USDA (US Department of Agriculture). The Federal Reserve Board does not go by a pithy acronym, but is simply known as "the Fed." The Fed is responsible for providing the country with a safe, flexible and stable monetary and financial system. Embedded in the mission of these regulators is making sure that organizations, whether multinational corporations or startup companies, make timely, accurate and truthful statements and claims. There is an equivalent alphabet soup of regulators internationally. For example, the Canadian equivalent to the SEC and its Electronic Data Gathering, Analysis, and Retrieval (EDGAR) system for filing securities information is the Canadian Securities Administrators and System for Electronic Document Analysis and Retrieval system.

Some regulators have oversight that cut across industries and sectors, such as the FTC and the SEC, while some regulators are specific to particular industries and sectors, such as the Consumer Financial Protection Bureau for the banking and financial services sector and the Federal Energy Regulatory Commission for the energy sector. Certain industries are particularly heavily regulated, such as banks and financial services, energy and utilities, pharmaceuticals and transportation, which can lead to companies in these industries generally being more cautious and requiring more approvals around marketing and strategic communication plans. Every company and industry has its

Table 9.1:   The Alphabet Soup of US Federal Government Agencies.

US Federal Agency	Agency Role and Responsibility
Commodity Futures Trading Commission (CFTC)	Regulates the US derivatives markets, including financial instruments like futures, swaps and certain kind of options
Consumer Product Safety Commission (CPSC)	Promotes the safety of consumer products by addressing unreasonable injury risks and developing uniform standards
Consumer Financial Protection Bureau (CFPB)	Responsible for consumer protection in the financial sector and created by the 2010 Dodd–Frank Wall Street Reform Act
Environmental Protection Agency (EPA)	Enforces rules and standards that protect the environment and human health, including controlling pollution
Equal Employment Opportunity Commission (EEOC)	Administers and enforces civil rights laws against workplace discrimination against job applicants and employees
Federal Aviation Administration (FAA)	Regulates all aspects of civil aviation within the United States as well as over its surrounding international waters
Federal Communications Commission (FCC)	Regulates interstate and international communications by radio, television, wire, satellite and cable
Federal Energy Regulatory Commission (FERC)	Regulates the interstate transmission and wholesale sale of electricity, natural gas and oil, including pipelines
Federal Reserve System (The Fed)	The central banking system of the United States with an expanded mandate that includes supervising and regulating banks
Federal Trade Commission (FTC)	Responsible for the enforcement of civil (non-criminal) US antitrust law and the promotion of consumer protection
Food and Drug Administration (FDA)	Responsible for monitoring the safe consumption of medical products (drug approvals), some foods and tobacco items
National Labor Relations Board (NLRB)	Assure fair labor practices and workplace democracy nationwide. Investigates and remedy unfair labor practices
Occupational Safety and Health Administration (OSHA)	Responsible for ensuring safety in the workplace, including limiting work-related injuries, illnesses and deaths
Securities and Exchange Commission (SEC)	Responsible for enforcing federal securities laws, proposing securities rules and regulating the securities industry
Small Business Administration (SBA)	Bolsters and promotes the economy by providing assistance to small businesses, including capital, contracts and counseling

Note: This is a very abbreviated list of US federal government agencies relevant to communicators. The Federal Register shows a complete list of more than 450 federal government agencies: *federalregister.gov/agencies*.

own unique regulatory landscape and expectations; this makes it imperative for communication professionals, whether working in-house or as an agency partner, to learn this landscape and then make realistic recommendations.

Within most corporations, the general counsel and/or the chief legal officer almost always has a seat at the leadership table and is a senior member of the C-suite (CristKolder Associates, 2019; Neatby, 2016; Neill, 2015). Depending on the size and complexity of the organization, the general counsel may not only oversee the internal legal function (and any outside law firm and consultant relationships), but may also have oversight for related areas, such as government affairs, regulatory and policy, risk, compliance and ethics matters. The general counsel's team is typically responsible for overseeing organization-wide compliance with the web of federal, state and local laws, rules, regulations and standards. This includes providing legal advice on how the organization can manage compliance and risk, while advancing its business strategy, goals and objectives (Tabuena, 2006). Legal reviews and approvals are a fact of life for communicators and marketers working inside of or with larger organizations. As such, it is critical for corporate communication professionals to develop and maintain strong working relationships with their colleagues in the legal, government affairs and regulatory departments (Bain, 2018).

"The relationship between communications professionals with their allies in regulatory affairs, legal, government affairs, and ethics & compliance is critical, yet often underappreciated by new communications professionals," says Moyra Knight, VP of corporate communications, Astellas US LLC, and president, Astellas Global Health Foundation (personal communication, April 3, 2020). "Collectively, these groups of highly-trained individuals help communicators compliantly navigate the turbulent seas of highly-regulated industries." Knight credits these professionals with using their specialized expertise to help communicators create strong programming, bring research and insights into a communicator's overall program and for being willing to collaborate to get to a solution.

THE SECURITIES LAWS AND REGULATION FAIR DISCLOSURE

Timely, accurate and truthful information is the lifeblood of markets, whether buying or selling securities, such as stocks or bonds, or purchasing any kind of product or service (Morrill, 1995; Rickard, 2019). Regulators try to ensure a "balanced playing field" in marketplaces and protect the public from unscrupulous behavior. Directly before the stock market crash of 1929 and the ensuing Great Depression, unbeknownst to regular investors and the public, some corporate insiders saw the performance of their businesses deteriorating and secretly dumped their stock holdings ahead of the stock market crash (Taparia, 2004).

In the wake of this nefarious conduct, two pieces of landmark federal legislation were passed to reform the US capital markets, The Securities Act of 1933, also known as the Truth in Securities Act, and the Securities Exchange Act of 1934. This latter act established the formation of the SEC. Decades later, many modern corporate securities regulations and disclosure requirements for public companies still have their roots in the 1933 and 1934 Acts (Remund & Kuttis, 2018). More recent legislation relevant to corporate disclosure is the Sarbanes–Oxley Act of 2002 (also known as SarbOx or SOX), which established sweeping auditing regulations for public companies, and the Dodd–Frank Wall Street Reform and Consumer Protection Act of 2010 (often called simply Dodd–Frank), which overhauled financial sector regulation in the aftermath of the Great Recession, which officially started in December 2007 and ran through June 2009.

As previously discussed, by the nature of being a public company, the SEC and the stock exchanges mandate that publicly traded companies must report their business performance, including releasing detailed financial statements, on a so-called periodic basis (i.e., quarterly for the US markets). US public companies must disclose their quarterly business performance in a document called a Form 10-Q that is filed with the SEC's EDGAR system. On a yearly basis, US public companies must disclose their annual business performance in an even more detailed document called a Form 10-K, which is essentially a company's formal annual report.

10-Qs are filed three times a year (for Q1, Q2 and Q3) and the 10-K is filed once a year (for Q4). The financial statements found in 10-Q reports are *unaudited*, whereas the financials found in a 10-K are required to have been audited by an accounting firm (Taparia, 2004). Most US companies, whether public or private firms, tend to operate on the rhythm of quarterly reporting and planning, which can lead to a focus on short-term results (Dimon & Buffett, 2018). Many companies follow a fiscal year (12-month accounting period) that matches the calendar year (i.e., January 1– December 31), while firms in certain industries, such as retail, have a fiscal year that may close on an alternate date, such as the end of January, due to the busy holiday season.

In between these mandatory periodic reports, US public companies are required to keep investors current as to any developments that are "material" in nature (U.S. Securities and Exchange Commission, n.d.-a, 2012a). The US Supreme Court has defined "materiality" as being when there is a substantial likelihood that a reasonable investor would consider the information important in making an investment decision (U.S. Securities and Exchange Commission, 2012a). Whenever a significant corporate event triggers a disclosure, companies must promptly file a current report, known as an 8-K filing, with the SEC's EDGAR system (U.S. Securities and Exchange Commission, n.d.-a). Examples of unscheduled material events that would warrant an 8-K disclosure include a merger or acquisition, a bankruptcy, a change in auditor, a resignation of a company director or other major corporate governance changes. The vast majority of public firms go beyond these required disclosures and also choose to make voluntary disclosures that provide additional details about their business operations and expected future performance (National Investor Relations Institute, 2014; Ragas, 2019b).

The passage in August 2000 of Regulation Fair Disclosure, commonly known as Reg FD, marks perhaps the most significant change in corporate disclosure and the practice of investor relations (IR) since the formation of the SEC (LaBranche, 2019). During the dot com boom of the 1990s, there were instances in which Wall Street analysts and large professional investors received market-moving, non-public material information from company executives ahead of smaller investors. During this time period, the rise of low-cost online stock brokerages and investment websites helped make smaller investors aware of key information sources for which they lacked access, such as joining quarterly earnings conference calls and investment conference presentations to hear directly from company CEOs, chief financial officers (CFOs) and other executives.

Reg FD seeks to eliminate the practice of so-called "selective disclosure" in which a public company discloses material information to a particular investor or a small group of investors, as opposed to broadly disclosing the information to *all investors at once* (National Investor Relations Institute, 2014; U.S. Securities and Exchange Commission, 2004). Reg FD helps to bring greater transparency to IR and further democratizes the flow of key corporate information (Ragas, 2019b; Ragas & Culp, 2014a; Remund &

Kuttis, 2018). In the case of an unauthorized or inadvertent selective disclosure, the company must promptly take corrective action by broadly disclosing this material information via an 8-K filing and/or issuing a news release. "Promptly" typically means as soon as reasonably practical, but in no event after the later of 24 hours or the start of the next day's trading (National Investor Relations Institute, 2014).

"The National Investor Relations Institute was an early proponent of Reg FD and was consulted on its drafting by the SEC," says Gary A. LaBranche, president and CEO of National Investor Relations Institute (NIRI), the largest professional IR association in the world, with more than 3,000 members (personal communication, April 3, 2020). "Reg FD helps to ensure the fairness of the capital markets and encourages broader participation by individual investors." According to LaBranche, "given the interconnected world that companies and stakeholders operate in today," communication professionals should also "become versed in Reg FD" as messages and information flow across audiences and platforms.

HANDLE WITH CARE: MATERIAL, NON-PUBLIC INFORMATION

Company executives, employees and consultants may come into possession of material, non-public information through the nature of their work. For IR and corporate communication professionals, this can include working on drafts of quarterly earnings news releases, as well as on major corporate announcements, such as a merger or acquisition or a change in the C-suite or on the board of directors. There are significant negative consequences, including reputational loss, fines, being barred from serving as an officer or director of a public company and even jail time, for those who misuse material, non-public information for the benefit of themselves and/or others. During the stock market turbulence around the COVID-19 global pandemic, the SEC even issued an advisory reminding company executives, directors, employees and consultants to carefully handle confidential corporate information (Merle, 2020).

To guard against inadvertent violations of the securities laws, many public companies implement a formal or informal "quiet period" prior to the release of a quarterly earnings report (National Investor Relations Institute, 2016). A quiet period is a specific period of time during which the officers and representatives of a company will not talk about the company's financial results (National Investor Relations Institute, 2016; U.S. Securities and Exchange Commission, 2017). To reduce the risk and even the possible appearance of insider trading, many public companies also have "blackout periods" around quarterly earnings reports. During these blackout periods, company insiders, such as officers, directors and employees with access to sensitive corporate information, cannot buy or sell the company's stock (Sandler, 2012).

As per SEC regulations, even when company policies allow corporate insiders to buy and sell their stock, they must disclose these activities on a timely basis to the public. These regulations are designed to help bring transparency into the process of stock ownership for investors and the public. Whenever a public company officer or director buys or sells their stock (or executes stock options), they must disclose this activity through a Form 4 filing with the SEC's EDGAR system. Similarly, whenever an investor acquires a beneficial ownership stake of more than 5% in a public company, they must disclose this position with the SEC through a Schedule 13D filing, which is also called a beneficial ownership report (Kenton, 2019a). The 13D not only identifies the shareholder, but the investor is also required to state why they have taken a significant ownership stake. An alternative to the 13D under some circumstances is a 13G filing. The business news media often report on the contents of these SEC filings.

There have been a variety of high profile insider trading cases in recent years that have made the news (Merle, 2020). For example, in 2018, former NFL linebacker Mychal Kendricks was indicted by federal authorities on insider trading charges (Abelson & Gillette, 2018; Schad, 2018). Kendricks received non-public information about pending corporate mergers from a friend, Damilare Sonoiki, who worked at Goldman Sachs. The two individuals used the information to buy stock in firms that were about to be acquired. In 2019, former US Congressman Chris Collins (R-NY) pled guilty to insider trading and lying to federal authorities (Breuninger, Mangan, & Higgins, 2020). Collins was sentenced to more than two years in prison. Collins tipped off his son about a failed clinical drug trial at Innate Immunotherapeutics, a small biotech company for which he served on the board. Collins' son and others quickly dumped their stock in Innate before the failed test results were made public and the stock had plummeted in value.

Looking beyond insider trading to selective disclosure violations, in 2019, the SEC brought an enforcement action against TherapeuticsMD for alleged

Reg FD violations (Posner, 2019). The SEC says that the firm selectively communicated the prospects of gaining FDA approval for one of its drugs to stock analysts, while failing to simultaneously or promptly disclose this information to the broader market and all investors as required by Reg FD.

YOU RANG? QUARTERLY EARNINGS CALLS

For the vast majority of public companies, the quarterly earnings conference call is the centerpiece for financial communication and corporate disclosure to the financial community (National Investor Relations Institute, 2013, 2014, 2016). Earnings conference calls are not only closely followed by investors, but often are covered by the news media (Roush, 2016) and also attract interest from internal stakeholders, such as employees and contractors (DiStaso, 2012). Often, a public company will release its quarterly earnings news release with its financials via a paid wire service and post the release to the IR section of its corporate website (DiStaso, 2012). As part of the earnings release (and sometimes in an earlier advisory that announces the date and time of the quarterly report), the dial-in and log-in details for joining the conference call will be provided. Some companies provide a slide deck and supplemental information that goes along with the conference call (National Investor Relations Institute, 2016). As a best practice, an archived copy of the earnings call and/or transcript of the call and any associated materials should be posted to the IR website.

The earnings call is almost always hosted by the company's CEO and CFO within a month or so of completing the quarter. At some companies, other members of the C-suite, such as business unit leaders, may also participate on the call and provide updates (and/or answer investor questions). The investor relations officer often helps manage the call. The typical format of the call features prepared remarks by the CEO and/or CFO commenting on the company's previous and current performance, followed by an operator-assisted question and answer session (National Investor Relations Institute, 2013, 2016). At large companies, typically only Wall Street analysts and institutional investors are allowed to ask questions. The contents of these calls often represent weeks of collaboration among various corporate teams and departments, including finance, accounting, legal, IR and communication (Lev, 2012; Lev & Gu, 2016). In addition to holding quarterly conference calls for earnings, a company may also schedule a special call to discuss a major corporate event, such as a merger or acquisition. Since these calls must be open to meet disclosure requirements, they typically provide an important source of competitive intelligence, including for communication professionals working for competitors in associated industries or sectors (Ragas & Culp, 2014a).

In addition to quarterly earnings conference calls, the CEO, CFO and other senior executives typically use a variety of other channels for corporate disclosure and relationship building with the financial community. In addition to holding annual shareholder meetings, many public companies hold an analyst/investor day on an annual basis (or sometimes less frequently) at a company facility, such as headquarters, or a major money center city. Often these analyst/investor days are webcast as well, which open them up to a larger audience. In addition to analyst/investor days, public companies generally make the rounds and present throughout the year at investment conference hosted by investment banks. These presentations may be webcast and the presentation materials, such as slide decks, may be made available online.

In addition to analyst/investor days and investment conference presentations, company management teams may also go on what is called a "non-deal road show" or NDR. A road show consists of a series of meetings between company management and current or prospective shareholders from investment firms in major money center cities. Companies must be careful to follow Reg FD and not engage in selective disclosure in such meetings. The COVID-19 pandemic resulted in public companies having to hold virtual meetings for investor outreach (Posner, 2020). Following this experience, there is an expectation that videoconferencing will become more prevalent for IR in the years ahead (Human, 2020).

In recent years, the SEC has become more accepting of the use of social media for corporate disclosure – assuming public companies properly notify the public that a social media channel may be used for disclosure purposes. Netflix CEO and co-founder Reed Hastings caused a stir in 2013 when he used his personal Facebook page to share a key Netflix viewership milestone that had *not* been previously reported through Netflix corporate communication channels (Vigna, 2013). After opening an inquiry, the SEC declined to bring an enforcement action against Hastings and Netflix. Instead, the SEC used this case to provide clarification on Reg FD (U.S. Securities and Exchange Commission, 2013).

In essence, US public companies may use social media channels like Facebook and Twitter to announce material information as long as investors have been previously alerted about which social media may be used to disseminate such information (National Investor Relations Institute, 2014). For example, Twitter, Inc. (2020) includes the following language in its quarterly SEC filings:

> We have used, and intend to continue to use, our investor relations website, as well as certain Twitter accounts (@jack, @nedsegal, @twitter and @twitterIR), as means of disclosing material non-public information and for complying with our disclosure obligations under Regulation FD. (p. 10)

The growing range of communication channels available for corporate disclosure and relationship building adds to the complexity. Effective corporate and investor communication "is not as easy as many people assume," according to Ruth Venning, executive director, IR for Horizon Therapeutics plc (personal communication, April 29, 2020). "I liken it to a game of chess – the rules may not seem that complicated and it may even sound simple, but once in the game, you often realize it is multi-faceted, highly nuanced and the stakes can be high," says Venning, also the 2021 national chair of the NIRI. "The quality and credibility of your communications – which often become that of your company or senior management – are your currency" (personal communication, April 29, 2020).

EARNINGS GUIDANCE AND FORWARD-LOOKING STATEMENTS

No discussion of corporate disclosure would be complete without discussing what is called earnings guidance – the practice of public companies broadly disclosing expectations about future financial and business performance to investors and other stakeholders (Alpha IR Group, 2020; Leder, 2003; Lev, 2012). Within the US markets, a survey of IR professionals finds that more than 9 out of 10 (94%) US public companies provide some form of guidance (National Investor Relations Institute, 2016). US public companies tend to provide guidance that spans an annual basis with the most common metrics shared being expectations on revenue, tax rate, capital expenditures, earnings/earnings per share (EPS) and operating expenses margins (National Investor Relations Institute, 2016). Large capitalization US public companies are more likely to provide some form of guidance than small capitalization public companies. On a global basis, around three out of four (73.4%) IR professionals report that their public companies provide guidance on a quarterly or annual basis (BNY Mellon, 2020). Private companies will rarely choose to provide any sort of external earnings guidance and typically keep any business forecasting or projections internal.

At its best, *annual* earnings guidance helps manage the expectations of the financial community in terms of future company business performance and may help reduce stock price volatility and the cost of capital (Babcock & Williamson, 2018; P. Hodgson, 2017; National Investor Relations Institute, 2018). Wall Street analysts generate financial models and financial estimates about a public company whether the firm comments or not on how it will perform in the future. These analyst estimates are then aggregated by financial data providers into consensus estimates for company earnings, revenue and other metrics. When a company reports its quarterly earnings results, Wall Street reacts in part to whether the company's reported results "beat," "met" or "missed" these consensus projections (Leder, 2003; Lev, 2012; National Investor Relations Institute, 2018). Providing annual guidance in some ways is like when a sports team's head coach or general manager comments on what goals they have for the season ahead (e.g., number of wins and making the playoffs). These comments can help manage the expectations of the team's fans and sports reporters' and commentators' projections.

The counterargument to providing earnings guidance, especially regarding companies that do so on a *quarterly* basis, is that these projections can promote short-term thinking and behaviors among company management, employees and potentially other stakeholders. Well-regarded business leaders Warren Buffett and Jamie Dimon penned an influential op-ed in *The Wall Street Journal* in 2018 titled, "Short-Termism is Harming the Economy." In this article, Dimon and Buffett (2018) argued that, in their experience, "quarterly earnings guidance often leads to an unhealthy focus on short-term profits at the expense of long-term strategy, growth and sustainability" (para. 2). Buffett and Dimon are not opposed, though, to company reporting of detailed quarterly financial and non-financial operating performance. The Buffett and Dimon stance is supported by the Business Roundtable (2018), an influential non-profit association made up of several hundred large company CEOs, which argues that public firms should be managed for long-term prosperity and *not* to try to meet and exceed the latest quarterly forecast.

There is litigation risk that comes with companies providing guidance and then falling short of such guidance or worse. The Private Securities Litigation Reform Act of 1995 helps stem the filing of frivolous or unwarranted securities lawsuits, including suits involving a public company missing a previously released forecast (Chen, 2020b). Whenever a public company makes a "forward-looking statement," such as providing guidance, it should include along with such information what is called "safe harbor language" (Alpha IR Group, 2020; National Investor Relations Institute, 2014). This safe harbor language outlines company-specific risk factors that could materially impact the firm's future financial performance. This language is typically read before the start of earnings conference calls and investor presentations; it is also included at the front of slide decks and at the bottom of earnings releases. The communicator who understands the rules of the game around making forward-looking statements can help educate colleagues about these rules, and ensure the proper use of such language in company or client communication beyond IR.

NAVIGATING THE WEB OF LAWS, RULES AND REGULATIONS

Stakeholders and the public are hungry for greater transparency from organizations and organizational leaders (Bolton, Stacks, & Mizrachi, 2018; DiStaso & Bortree, 2012; Nothhaft, Werder, Vercic, & Zerfass, 2020; Rawlins, 2008, 2009). In turn, communicators generally favor more and better corporate disclosures for their organizations and clients. But there is a web of applicable laws, rules, regulations and ethical obligations to learn and navigate when it comes to such communication. Unfortunately, this is not a subject that is often studied much within college and university communication, public relations and marketing programs, but such knowledge is critical to the success and effectiveness of corporate communication teams and the counsel they provide (Ragas, 2019b). Strong relationships with corporate legal, compliance, regulatory and government relations professionals are essential for communication professionals, whether they are working in-house or as agency professionals (Penning & Bain, 2018; Ragas & Culp, 2014a, 2018b).

Mark Bain (2018), a former corporate chief communications officer and head of communications for a global law firm, has joked that, "'I'm so excited about my meeting with legal today,' said no communicator, ever." (p. 115). Bain (2018) notes that the relationship between lawyers and communicators can be rocky at times with the two occasionally wrangling over "what the company should – or should not – do and say" (p. 121). The overlapping skills and responsibilities of communicators and lawyers, as well as professionals in affiliated areas like regulatory, risk, policy, compliance and ethics, make them essential partners on business issues and reputational matters – even if they may not always see eye to eye.

Strategic communication professionals do not need to become experts in each of these aforementioned disciplines, but if they want to gain respect and build trust with their colleagues in these areas, then they do need to demonstrate a working understanding and fluency in the relevant laws, rules, regulations and concepts. As Bain (2018) has quipped, with this important shared foundational knowledge in place, "some communicator, somewhere, will get excited about their upcoming meeting with legal" (p. 121).

KEY TERMS

Analyst/investor day	General Counsel
Blackout period	Material information
Chief legal officer	Non-deal road show
Consensus analyst estimate	Regulation Fair Disclosure (Reg FD)
Corporate disclosure	Quarterly earnings call
The Dodd–Frank Act	Quiet period
Earnings guidance	Safe harbor language
Form 4	The Sarbanes–Oxley Act
Form 8-K	Schedule 13-D
Form 10-K	The Securities Act
Form 10-Q	The Securities Exchange Act
Forward-looking statement	Selective disclosure

DISCUSSION QUESTIONS

(1) What are up to three large organizations that you think practice transparent communication and business practices? Explain how you made your decisions.

(2) Think specifically of one of the organizations that you feel does a good job at transparency. Which regulatory agencies does this organization likely work with?

(3) Visit the corporate website of this organization and look up the leadership team. Do they have a general counsel and/or a chief legal officer? If so, what are their responsibilities?

(4) Select a public company you are interested in learning more about. Go to the IR section of its corporate website. Did you find any archived materials for quarterly earnings conference calls? What did you find?

(5) In your opinion, should public companies issue earnings guidance and provide forward-looking statements? If yes, what types of business metrics do you recommend providing as part of guidance?

By Rodrigo A. Sierra, Chief Communications Officer, SVP, American Medical Association

Imagine a natural gas main rupturing and sending a 200-foot column of flames crawling up the side of a public housing senior citizen high-rise. Now imagine working for the utility company, being new on the job, and having full responsibility for managing the communication stream and helping mitigate a potential public relations (PR) disaster.

That was the situation I found myself in as the new manager of PR for Chicago-based Peoples Gas. I had only been in the role about six months, following eight years as a news reporter. Jumping into the fray, I went directly to the site and began managing this fast-moving event that was capturing the city's attention. My journalism experience made me very comfortable and well prepared for getting peppered with questions by a swarm of print, radio and TV reporters pressing for information ... Who was at fault? When would the gas be securely shut off? How long would it take to restore service to the neighborhood?

But here's something else to consider. Gas mains break, construction accidents happen and heating bills go up. These are typical issues someone in a communications role at a public utility might reasonably expect to encounter – and could generally prepare to manage carefully and proactively. What I didn't know, but would soon learn, was that my role required much more than keen crisis communications skills and confidence in front of the camera.

Communicators at highly regulated entities like public utilities must also understand the financial side of the business, as well as the abundance of fiduciary and disclosure requirements that go with it. This necessitates working hand-in-hand with the office of general counsel, investor relations and regulatory affairs. The same applies for communicators in banking, transportation, automotive manufacturing, pharmaceutical companies and health care, among others.

Shifting business environments is another important consideration for communicators to track and understand. For example, during my tenure at Peoples Gas, the utility annually faced the scrutiny of the Illinois Commerce Commission, which approves and denies changes to utility rates. Following the Enron scandal and the 2002 passage of the Sarbanes–Oxley Act that established sweeping auditing and financial regulations for public companies, Peoples Gas ended up on the wrong side of a $100-million settlement with the Illinois Attorney General. This was another delicate corporate communication challenge to navigate. Later, Peoples would enter into a merger with another energy company. Such M&A activity requires filings with an array of city, state and federal agencies, as well as shaping communications that persuade those agencies – and the public – that synergies and advantages gained from increased scale would lead to lower operating costs and present opportunities to pass savings on to customers.

As if all of these experiences and reasons were not enough to get me thinking about how to better equip myself to do my job, a dinner conversation with my chief executive officer regarding my ability to continue taking on more responsibilities confirmed my need to seek an MBA. Soon after I applied to the executive MBA program at the Kellogg School of Management at Northwestern.

While my MBA program solidified what I'd already learned on-the-job, it also greatly enhanced my knowledge and gave me new tools and frameworks to tackle business issues with confidence. The program also taught me the importance of building a network *across* industries and disciplines that I could tap into for thinking through tough business challenges. This network and education prepared me well for my next role as chief marketing officer of a storied but struggling publishing company and my current role as chief communications officer for the American Medical Association.

PART V

BUSINESS MODELS

10

STRATEGIC COMMUNICATION AGENCIES AND CONSULTANCIES

It was the cold call that started a relationship which helped build one of the world's most valuable consumer brands and one of the largest US-based public relations (PR) agencies.

In 1957, a then 28-year-old Al Golin cold called Ray Kroc. Kroc, a milk-shake mixer salesman turned entrepreneur, had only several years earlier bought the franchising rights to a promising, but still fledgling quick ser-vice restaurant concept called McDonald's. Golin pitched Kroc on PR being an economical way for him to help rapidly grow McDonald's locations around the country. After inviting Golin to pitch him in person, Kroc was so impressed with Golin's ideas that he hired the small agency, agreeing to pay a $500-a-month retainer, which in today's dollars would be worth around $4,500 (GOLIN, 2017; Roberts, 2017).

Kroc praised Golin and his now eponymously named firm, GOLIN, for being key to the growth and success of McDonald's (Golin, 2006; Roberts, 2017). In Kroc's (1992) memoir, he says that Golin and his agency "deserve a lot of the credit for making McDonald's a household word" (p. 100). For example, Golin is credited with helping develop many of the community-focused initiatives for which McDonald's is still known, including expanding Ronald McDonald House nationally and creating the McDonald's All-American High School Basketball Game and the All-American High School Marching Band (GOLIN, 2017).

The agency–client relationship between GOLIN and McDonald's has endured for more than six decades and has been critical to the agency's own sustained growth and success (Golin, 2006). At the time of Golin's passing in 2017, GOLIN, a unit of Interpublic Group (IPG), had become one of the world's 10 largest PR and communication agencies, employing more than 1,200 people in more than 50 offices around the world (GOLIN, 2017; Roberts, 2017).

At its core, agencies and consultancies are all about relationships: building, sustaining and growing relationships with clients and helping clients to build stronger relationships with their stakeholders and society. Underneath these relationships are the reality that almost all agencies and consultancies are structured as *for-profit* entities that must create enough value for clients to generate the revenues needed to cover the agency or consultancy's expenses and produce a healthy level of profits. However, not enough time is spent in many college and university programs helping young professionals to learn "the business of the business." Much about agency and consultancy business models is often learned over time on the job.

"When you work at an agency or consultancy, you get to help run a business – you get to sell your ideas, work with dynamic clients, manage projects and help build a business," says Kathy Cripps, senior counselor at Prosper Group, a consultancy that advises owners of agencies. Cripps, a former president of the PR Council, is an agency veteran, having founded, built and sold a mid-sized healthcare PR firm (personal communication, June 3, 2020). "The agency business marries creativity, management and strategy. Aspiring and new agency pros who roll up their sleeves and really learn 'the business of the business' make themselves invaluable."

This chapter provides an overview of the media, marketing and communication ecosystem; the strategic communication agency and consultancy landscape in particular; the nuts and bolts of agency business models; the process of pitching and winning business; and this chapter reviews some of the disruptive forces to agency and consultancy business models. The chapter concludes with a look at the future of agency–client relationships in light of these disruptive forces.

THE MEDIA, MARKETING AND COMMUWNICATION ECOSYSTEM

Media, marketing and communication is a big business. On a global basis, annual spending within the media, marketing and communication ecosystem is estimated to total more than $1 trillion dollars (PQ Media, 2020).

Many hundreds of thousands of people work within this industry, in jobs at content providers like newspapers, magazines and online publishers; in cable, satellite, broadcast, mobile and streaming networks; at in-house marketing and communication departments at all different types of organizations; and in marketing, media, advertising and PR agencies and consultancies. For over a century, organizations have relied upon the outside expertise of agencies and consultancies for everything from the development and launch of marketing and communication campaigns and programs to counsel and guidance on specific issues affecting organizational reputations (Cutlip, 1994, 1995).

Total US revenue for more than 400 agencies and agency networks tracked by *AdAge* topped $55 billion in 2019 (B. Johnson, 2020b). Digital work accounted for a little more than a majority (54%) of total US agency revenue in 2019, compared with just around a quarter (25.8%) of total revenue a decade earlier. On an annual basis, the organic growth rate for the US agency business in 2019 was almost flat (+1.2% revenue growth) compared to the prior year, which is the slowest growth rate since the Great Recession of 2008–2009 (B. Johnson, 2020a). Given the weakened economic backdrop following the impact of the COVID-19 global pandemic, the expectation is for a decline in agency revenue and staffing levels in 2020 and that a full recovery in spending may take up to several years (B. Johnson, 2020a). Besides digital work, a bright spot for growth in recent years for agencies and consultancies has been in healthcare spending, which posted a healthy growth rate (+7.3%) in 2019 and reached $5.7 billion in revenue. For comparison, advertising and PR spending was approximately $10.1 billion (+1.4% growth) and $4.1 billion (+1.5% growth), respectively (B. Johnson, 2020b).

There are many different types of marketing, advertising, media and PR agencies. Very broadly speaking, they may be divided into two categories: *full-service* agencies and *specialty* agencies. As the name implies, a full-service agency generally offers a wide range of services, whereas a specialty agency may concentrate on serving a particular industry or sector and/or discipline within communications. For example, specialty agencies may have expertise specifically within aspects of digital communication and social media, health communication, sports and entertainment, crisis communications, customer experience, direct marketing, financial communication and investor relations, business-to-business marketing or analytics, measurement and evaluation. The national and international agency networks are often full-service and will generally offer practice groups covering a variety of disciplines, industries and sectors. This said, even the large agencies may be known for having a strength in a particular area, such as leaning more toward serving consumer accounts or doing more corporate work.

THE AGENCY AND CONSULTANCY LANDSCAPE

While there are exceptions, many of the larger agency brands are owned by one of the major agency holding companies. These holding companies include Omnicom Group, Inc., IPG of Cos., Publicis Groupe, WPP plc, Dentsu Aegis Network and Havas Group. A 2013 planned merger between Omnicom and Publicis was eventually called off due to personality clashes and disagreements between the leadership of the two firms (Gelles, 2014).

Other major investors and/or owners of agency assets include MDC Partners, S4 Capital and Stagwell Group. MDC and Stagwell have agreed to a merger, which will vault the combined company into a top 10 global marketing services firm (Washkuch, 2020). Many of the holding companies are publicly traded so they have shareholders to answer to, as well as quarterly reporting requirements and financial targets to meet. The holding companies generally direct the agencies they own to share knowledge and resources, collaborate on integrated solutions for clients and achieve economies of scale through common back office systems and consolidating their real estate footprints in major markets.

With annual revenue of approximately $15 billion, the largest US-based agency holding company is New York City-headquartered Omnicom Group, Inc. (2020a). Omnicom is illustrative of the impressive breadth and depth of the agency networks owned and managed by the largest holding companies. Omnicom employs 70,000 professionals operating in 1,500+ agencies serving 5,000+ clients in 100+ countries around the world (Omnicom Group, Inc., 2020a). While a US-based firm, almost half (46%) of Omnicom's 2019 total revenue came from work outside of North America. See Fig. 10.1 for a revenue breakdown by geography. Looking at total revenue on an industry basis, the largest sector is pharma and health (14%), followed by food and beverage (13%) and automotive (10%). See Fig. 10.2 for a more complete revenue breakdown by industry.

Omnicom's portfolio includes three of the world's top global advertising agency networks (BBDO, DDB and TBWA); three of the world's top media agencies (OMD, PHD, Hearst & Science); and a global diversified agency services group (DAS) of award-winning agencies across 30+ different marketing

Fig. 10.1:   Omnicom Group Total Revenue by Geography.

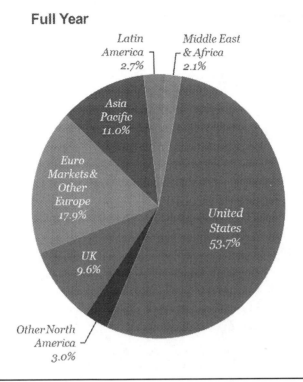

Full Year

Latin America 2.7%
Middle East & Africa 2.1%
Asia Pacific 11.0%
Euro Markets & Other Europe 17.9%
United States 53.7%
UK 9.6%
Other North America 3.0%

Source: Omnicom Group, Inc.

and communications disciplines (Omnicom Group, Inc., 2020a). Some of the world's largest PR agency networks are housed under the DAS group of companies at Omnicom, including FleishmanHillard, Ketchum and Porter Novelli. Advertising work (56.5%) represents the largest slice of the total revenue pie at Omnicom, followed by CRM consumer experience work (17.5%), PR services (9.2%), CRM execution and support (9.1%) and healthcare work (7.7%) (Omnicom Group, Inc., 2020a).

Over the past decade, some of the world's largest management consulting and information technology services firms have become major new players in the agency world (Schultz, 2017). These consultants have bulked up on their marketing services and creative services capabilities through a combination of agency acquisitions and internal investments in these units. These new competitors to the agency holding companies and their networks include

Fig. 10.2:   Omnicom Group Total Revenue by Industry.

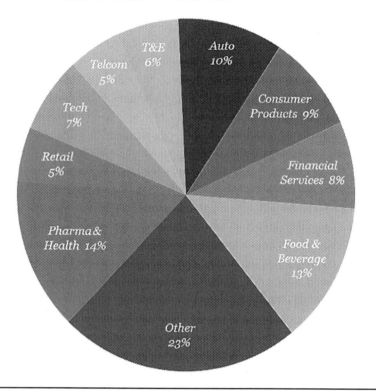

Source: Omnicom Group, Inc.

Accenture Interactive, Cognizant Interactive, Deloitte Digital, IBM iX and PwC Digital (Pollack, 2019). In addition, mid-sized management consulting firms with strategic communication groups include FTI Consulting, Inc., the parent of FTI Strategic Communications and ICF International, Inc., the parent of ICF Next. Accenture Interactive turned heads in 2019 when it acquired Droga5, among the best known independent agencies in the United States, in one of the largest acquisitions to date made by one of the giant consulting firms (Maheshwari, 2019). Accenture, the parent company of Accenture Interactive, is a Fortune Global 500 company with annual revenue of approximately $41 billion and nearly 460,000 employees with offices dotting the world (*Fortune*, 2019).

Even with waves of consolidation in recent decades, many local and regional (and even some national and international) agencies and consultancies remain independently owned and operated. For example, with nearly 6,000 employees in more than 60 offices around the world, Edelman is not only the world's largest global PR agency network, but the only top five global PR agency *not owned* by one of the major holding companies (see Table 10.1 for PR agency rankings based on global annual revenue). Founded in 1952 by former journalist Dan Edelman with one office in Chicago, Edelman has always been an independent, family-owned firm (Daniel J. Edelman Holdings, Inc., 2020). An advantage for privately held and independently owned agencies and consultancies is that agency owners may take a longer-term orientation and not need to please outside investors who may wish to maximize short-term profits. A disadvantage may include having more limited access to capital for growth and expansion.

Edelman has used its independent, family-owned status and longer-term orientation as sources of strategic advantage over its approximately 70-year history. This includes the agency's leadership being prepared to take the business down to temporary "zero profit" levels during economic recessions before engaging in any employee layoffs and furloughs (Marszalek, 2020). "The best decision by my father and me was to remain independent," says Richard Edelman, president and chief executive officer (CEO) of Edelman, who took over the top spot from his father, Dan, in 1996 (personal communication, July 11, 2020). "It has enabled us to diversify, so that we are now truly a communications firm with a core PR business but one third of our talent in creative, planning, digital, influencer, experiential and research."

THE NUTS AND BOLTS OF AGENCY BUSINESS MODELS

Billable brainpower is still at the core of most agency and consultancy business models (Luttrell & Capizzo, 2019a, 2019b). While there are exceptions, many agencies and consultancies are largely fee-income based, charging clients for the amount of time and number of agency employees working on the account, as well as the scope of the business that the agency handles (Monllos, 2019; Smith, 2017). This labor and expertise-based fee model is used across the professional services landscape, including by law firms, accounting

Table 10.1:   PR and Communication Agency Rankings Table.

Agency Name	2019 Global Revenue	Annual Revenue Change (%)	2019 Global Staff	Revenue Per Staff	Headquarters
Edelman	$892.0 million	0%	5,703	$156,416	Chicago, IL
Weber Shandwick	$869.0 million	+3%	4,865	$178,623	New York, NY
Burson Cohn & Wolfe	$720.0 million	+1%	4,160	$173,077	New York, NY
FleishmanHillard	$606.9 million	0%	2,850	$212,947	St. Louis, MO
Ketchum	$502.0 million	−2%	2,550	$196,863	New York, NY
MSL	$444.5 million	−3%	2,045	$217,359	Paris
Hill+Knowlton Strategies	$366.0 million	−9%	2,250	$162,667	New York, NY
BlueFocus (Citizen Relations)	$320.0 million	−9%	2,535	$126,233	Beijing
Brunswick Group	$307.0 million	+12%	1,006	$305,169	London
Ogilvy	$300.0 million	−23%	2,000	$150,000	New York, NY
MC Group	$274.6 million	+17%	1,238	$221,824	Berlin
ICF Next	$266.6 million	+7%	1,497	$178,061	Fairfax, VA
FTI Consulting	$243.1 million	+9%	728	$333,915	Washington, DC
Havas PR Global Collective	$225.0 million	+2%	1,340	$167,910	New York, NY
Golin	$223.5 million	+3%	1,700	$131,471	Chicago, IL
W2O Group	$222.0 million	+25%	926	$239,741	San Francisco, CA
Vector	$219.5 million	+17%	984	$223,069	Tokyo
Porter Novelli	$145.0 million	−4%	700	$207,143	New York, NY
WE	$143.5 million	+13%	1,177	$121,920	Bellevue, WA
APCO Worldwide	$142.3 million	+6%	784	$181,457	Washington, DC

Source: Adapted from 2020 PRWeek Agency Business Report.

firms and management consultants. Human capital is arguably the most precious asset in the professional services world.

Key to the fee model is the billing rate, which is the hourly rate the agency charges clients for each level of staff that work on the account (Gould+Partners, 2019b; Wilcox, Cameron, & Reber, 2015). Research by

Gould+Partners (2019b), a provider of valuation and benchmarking services to PR and communication agencies, suggests that the average billing rate for the junior most staff (account coordinator) is around $130 an hour, while the average billing rate for the most senior agency leader (president/CEO) is around $410 an hour. The blended rate, which is the rate charged regardless of level of staff working on the account, is approximately $224 an hour. The hourly rate charged will vary not just by staff title and experience level, but by the type of work performed, the sector/industry, geography/region and other factors. Those new to agency life learn quickly about carefully tracking billable hours through time sheets and associated systems.

Fee-based relationships between agencies and clients may be retainer based and/or project based. A retainer is a fixed monthly base charge paid in advance by the client for a pre-determined minimum amount of agency support and services (Smith, 2017). Retainers help provide a predictable revenue stream for agencies and consultancies. In recent years, as corporate clients have sought to cut costs, project-based agency–client relationships have become more common (Monllos, 2019). Clients may also request fixed or flat-fee-based pricing for a project, which places more risk onto the agency and consultancy to appropriately price out and deliver the project. An alternative arrangement is an incentivized or performance-based model, which is fee based with the potential for the agency to earn incentive payments, based upon agreed upon performance metrics being achieved (Pathak, 2019; Stein, 2017). Finally, in select cases, some agencies will agree to work for reduced fees in exchange for also receiving an equity ownership stake in the actual client, which has been the case with direct-to-consumer brands like Allbirds, Birchbox, Casper, Keeps and Warby Parker (Battan, 2018; Beer, 2019; Pathak, 2019).

As clients put more pressure on agencies and consultancies to reduce fees, agencies and consultancies are generally seeing their profit margins come under pressure (RFP Associates, LLC, 2019). Agency leaders use a variety of different metrics and indicators to measure the productivity and profitability of agency professionals and accounts. This includes tracking average annual revenue generated per agency account professional and the utilization rate per billable professional.

Based on one benchmarking analysis, annual revenue generated per professional for "best in class" model PR agencies was approximately $253,000 (Gould+Partners, 2019a). The utilization rate is the total *actual* billable hours divided by the baseline hours (i.e., total *available* billable hours) expressed as a percentage for a certain period of time (e.g., month, quarter and year). This same benchmarking analysis indicates that utilization rate for account executives at these model PR agencies was a little over 85% (Gould+Partners, 2019b). The operating profit margin at the model agencies was approximately 16% (Gould+Partners, 2019a). This means that for every $100 in revenue generated by clients, $16 flowed through to the agency's pre-tax bottom-line after paying employee salaries, benefits and bonuses, as well as overhead expenses like office space and utilities, and before any debt service. An ideal operating profit margin for a professional services firm like a PR, advertising or marketing agency is 20% or higher.

PITCHING AND WINNING NEW BUSINESS

Winning new pieces of business and growing accounts are key to the sustained success and vibrancy of an agency or consultancy, whether it is a boutique agency with just one or a handle of employees or a practice group with many employees inside of a larger firm (Luttrell & Capizzo, 2019b). As agency professionals progress in their careers, they generally take on more responsibility for not just managing and servicing accounts, but also helping to "make it rain" by growing existing accounts and consistently winning new business (Burson, 2017; Wisner, 2012).

The types of relationships between clients and agency partners vary. An agency may serve as a primary agency and be responsible for a broad scope of client work on an ongoing basis or the scope of work may be more focused and project based. More large companies seem loathe in recent years to officially name an agency as its agency of record. Instead, the trend seems to be for large companies to have a primary agency and then a streamlined roster of specialized agencies that bring subject matter expertise to the table for particular projects, programs, issues and/or geographies (Daniels, 2019a; RFP Associates, LLC, 2019).

Even long-time client–agency relationships are being closely scrutinized and, in some cases, ended (Pasquarelli, 2019; Rittenhouse & Pasquarelli, 2020). Both agencies and clients are well aware of the disruption to agency business models and relationships. A survey by *PRWeek* found that more than 7 out of 10 agency respondents (72%) believe that this is a period of agency disruption and more than 6 out of 10 clients (62%) agree with this statement (Daniels, 2019a).

Research suggests that, among surveyed chief communications officers (CCOs) and senior executives at Fortune 1000 companies and large non-profit organizations, almost half (49.5%) report having worked with three or more agencies within the past year (RFP Associates, LLC, 2019). Nearly 95% of respondents report having worked with *at least one* agency in the past year. Respondents to this same survey report that nearly 6 out of 10 (57%) of them spend between $100,000 and $999,999 dollars annually on the PR agency for which they have the most significant relationship (RFP Associates, LLC, 2019). Another quarter (25%) of respondents say they spend $1 million dollars or more each year with their most significant agency partner.

A client will customarily conduct an annual review with the agency to review the agency's work and performance. A client may choose to put an account "up for review." Due to any number of factors, from changes in leadership at the client or team on the account to the client seeking new perspectives or needing additional outside expertise on a subject, a company may decide to seek out new agency partners. An incumbent agency may or may not participate.

Depending on the organization, the prospective client may choose to run a formal agency search process and may engage with an external search consultant to help run the process. In an era of increasing scrutiny on corporate budgets, often the communication and/or marketing department will need to formally work with the company's procurement and sourcing function on the agency search and selection process (PR Council, 2019). Procurement and sourcing focus on supply chain partner selection, spending and management. Many senior communication and marketing executives say they rely upon their experience and industry knowledge, and "word of mouth" among colleagues, to identify potential new agency partners (RFP Associates, LLC, 2019).

Often a formal agency search process will make use of a request for proposal (RFP) (PR Council, 2019). The RFP may be sent to a small number of agencies that the client has identified as serious candidates for the work. Prior to the RFP, a client may choose to issue a request for information (RFI) to collect information about the capabilities of various agencies. The information resulting from the RFI may help the client narrow the pool to then invite to participate in the RFP. A strong, clear RFP for an agency search usually includes the following components: statement of purpose, situation, company information, business objective, audience, scope of work, goals of project, what success looks like, project timeline, opportunities, bidder qualifications, budget and proposal guidelines/requirements (PR Council, 2019).

The client will then typically use the agency proposals submitted in response to the RFP to select up to several finalists. The agency finalists will then be invited to pitch to the prospective client in what might be termed a "shoot out" or a "bake off." Considerable staff time and agency money goes into the entire new business process, including developing the presentation and rehearsing the pitch, therefore it is important that an agency participates in searches they are confident they have a good chance of winning. Whether the pitch is done on-site at the client or remotely, the end goal is the same: *win the business* (Rittenhouse, 2020a).

"New business is a high stakes game and agencies must win more than their fair share to grow. Albeit stressful at times, pitching can be one of the most exhilarating opportunities in agency life," says Kim Sample, president of the PR Council, which is comprised of 110+ global, mid-size, regional and specialty firms across every discipline and practice area (personal communication, May 15, 2020). Sample was previously an agency executive and founder. "For young talent who want opportunities to be seen and heard, raising your hand for new business is a career-enhancing and fun move."

DISRUPTIVE FORCES TO AGENCY AND CONSULTANCY BUSINESS MODELS

Embracing change and adaptation – or maintaining the status quo and experiencing a possible decline or worse – is the new normal for business and society. Due to a confluence of disruptive forces, many signs point to the velocity and magnitude of change within the business world accelerating in the years ahead (Anthony, Viguerie, Schwartz, & Van Landeghem, 2018; Rossman, 2019; Schultz, 2019; Stone, 2017).

"Agencies need to be agile, creative and adaptable in order to survive in the post-COVID era. Client and consumer expectations are changing at warp speed; progressive agencies will adapt to using technology-enabled creative, lean heavily into technology and streamline their operations in order to support their clients moving forward," says Chris Foster, president, North America for Burson Cohn & Wolfe, a WPP Group agency network (personal communication, September 15, 2020). "As information moves faster and consumers expect more at a moment's notice, agencies will need to adapt and flex at speeds we've never seen."

There are many forces at work that are transforming the strategic communication profession as a whole (Daniels, 2019a, 2019b, 2020; USC Annenberg Center for Public Relations, 2019, 2020a, 2020b) and challenging the value propositions (Osterwalder, Pigneur, Bernarda, & Smith, 2014) of communication agencies and consultancies in particular (Barrett, 2020; Davis & Gilbert LLP, 2019; B. Johnson, 2020a, 2020b; RFP Associates, LLC, 2019).

Here are four disruptive forces of note influencing the agency and consultancy world:

(1) *Technological innovations:* Perhaps the leading force of disruptive change for agencies and their clients are the vast array of new digital technologies that are gaining adoption and transforming business and society (Arthur W. Page Society, 2019a). Technological innovations, such as artificial intelligence-based big data applications, have the potential for savvy agencies to create value for themselves and their clients through enabling more effective marketing and communication. On the flipside, agencies and consultancies that *cannot* successfully harness these technologies for their clients are at risk of being marginalized. Human capital will always be at the core of the agency business model, but, increasingly, so will technology. For example, a survey of PR students finds that 7 out of 10 young people believe that technology will be *more important* or *of equal importance* as human capital to the communication industry in the future (USC Annenberg Center for Public Relations, 2019).

(2) *Changing competitive landscape:* The competitive landscape has changed significantly for advertising, PR and communication agencies in recent years (Schultz, 2017). Some of the world's largest consulting firms (e.g., Accenture, Deloitte, IBM and PwC) have emerged as major players in providing marketing and creative services to clients (Maheshwari, 2019; Pollack, 2019). The size, scale and capabilities of the consultants can no longer be ignored. For example, 2020 saw Accenture Interactive displace IPG as the world's fourth largest agency company (D. Johnson, 2020). Agencies and consultancies must also walk a delicate tightrope in which they sometimes partner with

and other times they compete with the giants of Silicon Valley, such as Google and Facebook, for clients and work. Finally, best of breed specialized agencies and consultancies are taking market share in some cases from traditional full-service agencies.

(3) *Rise of the in-house agency:* Recent years have seen corporations invest in beefing up and building out agency-like capabilities within their marketing and corporate communication departments (Pasquarelli, 2019; Wohl, 2017). This includes the rise of more in-house agencies handling everything from creative services to data and analytics. The growth of in-house agencies and bringing more work in-house has put greater scrutiny on spending with external agency partners. In some cases, the investment in building out and operating in-house agencies has even contributed to some companies ending long-time agency relationships that have produced award-winning work. For example, in 2020, Allstate ended its six-decade relationship with Leo Burnett after moving more creative work in-house (Rittenhouse & Pasquarelli, 2020).

(4) *Attracting, retaining and developing agency talent:* As agency business models attempt to adapt to the above disruptive factors, it is critically important that they do a strong job of attracting, retaining and developing agency talent. Satisfaction levels with agency careers appear mixed (Daniels, 2020). This leads to some professionals moving in-house and others leaving the industry entirely. One study suggests that agency staff turnover rates can top 20–25% per year (Gould+Partners, 2020). To better retain and develop talent, agencies and consultancies should invest more in professional development and training programs (Jain & Bain, 2017; Penning & Bain, 2018). A pressing strategic priority for agencies is to foster more diverse, equitable and inclusive agency cultures (Mundy, 2019). More clients are challenging their agencies to meet diversity, equity and inclusion metrics in order to win and/or keep their business (Ford, 2019; Neptune, 2020).

"Diversity, equity, and inclusion is without a doubt, more than ever before, a business imperative," says Kim L. Hunter, CEO of LAGRANT COMMUNICATIONS and chairman and CEO of The LAGRANT Foundation (TLF), a nonprofit organization dedicated to increasing the number of ethnic minorities in the fields of advertising, marketing and PR (personal communication, May 20, 2020). "Those agencies who hire, develop, and retain ethnically diverse talent among their workforce, will be the true beneficiaries to their clients and organizational cultures." Since its formation, TLF has awarded more than 725 scholarships and more than $2.7 million to ethnic minority students entering the field (The LAGRANT Foundation, 2020).

SOME THINGS JUST GO BETTER TOGETHER

Some things just go better together, whether it is peanut butter and jelly or wine and cheese. Each can be enjoyed on their own, but they really do great in pairs. The same can be said for organizations and agencies when it comes to effective strategic communications management (Argenti, 2017; Nothhaft, Werder, Vercic, & Zerfass, 2020; Zerfass & Volk, 2018).

Organizations with the talent, time and treasure can indeed do their own advertising, PR and communication in-house. But organizations that also choose to work with the right outside agency and consultancy partners are typically better positioned to succeed (Goodman, 2019). There is much that can be gained from the independent and outside knowledge, expertise and judgment that agencies and consultants bring to the table and provide to their clients (Luttrell & Capizzo, 2019a, 2019b). Therefore, it is hard to imagine a future in which agencies and consultancies won't continue to be critical to the communication and marketing functions, from providing high-level counsel, idea generation and problem solving to tactical program implementation and "arms and legs" day-to-day support.

This is not to say that agency business models are not in flux, as they try to address a range of disruptive factors that produce both challenges and opportunities for agency leaders. The value propositions offered by agencies and consultancies must continue to evolve to the wants and needs of clients (their customers) and to the marketplace as a whole (Osterwalder & Pigneur, 2010; Osterwalder et al., 2014; Osterwalder, Pigneur, Smith, & Etiemble, 2020).

The reality that agencies and consultancies are businesses that must find ways to generate enduring profits and get paid appropriately for their work is likely to be made starker in the years ahead. As such, both young professionals that are new to the agency world, as well as seasoned professionals that are going to the agency side for the first time, would benefit more than ever from learning about "the business of the business." An argument may be made that those working in-house would also benefit from understanding the essentials of agency business models; this may even help make for better and more enduring agency–client partnerships.

KEY TERMS

Agency holding company   Performance-based model
Agency of record   Project-based work
Agency search   Primary agency
Billable hours   Procurement and sourcing
Billing rate   Request for information (RFI)
Business model   Request for proposal (RFP)
Equity ownership model   Retainer
Fee-based work   Specialty agency
Full-service agency   Utilization rate
In-house agency   Value proposition

DISCUSSION QUESTIONS

(1) Look up the website of one of the major agency and consultancy holding companies. What seems to be the value proposition offered by them? Do you find it compelling?

(2) What do you think the future holds for strategic communication agencies and consultancies? How will they address the disruptive factors highlighted in this chapter?

(3) Imagine you were planning to launch your own agency and consultancy. What area(s) of the strategic communications world would you focus upon? Explain your thinking.

(4) Pretend you are a CCO of a Fortune 500 company on an agency search. What would be the most important requirements in the agencies you hire?

(5) If you were an agency leader, what are specific steps you would take to make a career at your agency more attractive, and would improve talent acquisition, growth and retention?

By Karen van Bergen,
Dean, Omnicom University

As trusted advisors for our clients, we must always be looking ahead, anticipating and activating change. Here are three ways agencies are evolving their business to anticipate client needs in today's environment:

(1) Measuring business impact:
Demonstrating business impact of communications strategies must be at the core of any agency/client partnership. We exist today in a data-driven world where we can link our value through key performance indicators (KPIs) and measurement focused on business impact. There is less and less tolerance for squishy, inaccurate measurement metrics like ad equivalent value, media impressions and share of voice. Being able to demonstrate business impact is intimately tied to your value as an agency partner to a client. If you cannot measure impact, you lose relevance.

That's why you must start every agency/client engagement with a discussion on measurement. How will communications drive business goals through a campaign? What are the tangible KPIs we must achieve? By starting with measurement, we can then build campaigns that can clearly be tied to business impact – whether that means driving sales or eliciting behavior change.

(2) Building a diverse and inclusive workforce:
In this business, talent is all we have. Getting in front of diversity in its many forms, such as increasing the number of women and other minorities in leadership roles will soon be table stakes. If we do not reflect the diversity of the target audiences we are trying to influence, why should clients trust us as their strategic advisors?

Right now the PR industry is a bit of an echo chamber. For the most part, we're the same types of people thinking in the same types of ways. We need to expand our definition of diversity to include a diversity of perspectives and backgrounds. When I was the chief executive officer at Porter Novelli, I developed the mantra "Think like a startup," and started actively pursuing new hires from industries that don't typically feed PR firms. We even hired real entrepreneurs, who had started their own firms! This was by no means an easy thing to do. But we made a couple of very successful hires that brought in an entrepreneurial mindset that was a great asset to our growth and development.

(3) *Increasing collaboration across agencies:*
As clients increasingly want more integrated communications strategies to drive sales and brand reputation, they are interested in working with cross-agency teams within or across marketing disciplines to support the business.

In 2009, Philips Royal Electronics had a single global goal to change their reputation and be known as a global healthcare solutions leader. It was of the utmost importance to have consistency and control of *all* messaging across markets and business units, which is why they hired Omnicom's OneVoice Team, a united cross-agency Ketchum and FleishmanHillard team, to execute all the communications work globally.

Today, these cross-agency teams – like Disney's OMG23 and P&G's Woven – are commonplace and include agencies from across marketing disciplines and even across holding companies. These teams need to be led by a single leader to be accountable for everyone's performance across agencies. This individual must ensure that the work is fully integrated, clients get the best talent for the job, agreed-upon processes are adhered to and that agencies work together – not compete – for business.

While there are multiple ways to run an agency, demonstrating business impact, building a diverse workforce and creating a culture of inclusivity and collaboration are required to succeed and exceed the needs of clients today.

11

IN-HOUSE COMMUNICATION DEPARTMENTS AND TEAMS

Stature of the communication function in an organization often rises following a crisis and distress (J. E. Grunig, 1992; L. A. Grunig, Grunig, & Dozier, 2002; Toth, 2006). During periods of volatility, disruption and/or transformation, the communication function often has the opportunity to prove its mettle to organizational leaders and demonstrate why it should regularly contribute to strategic decision-making (Berger, 2019; Berger & Meng, 2014; Meng, 2014).

The last two decades have witnessed no shortage of business and society defining events and time periods, such as the aftermath of the September 11, 2001 terrorist attacks and the 2008–2009 Great Recession, to recent social movements on the climate crisis, sexual harassment and gender equality in the workplace, gun violence and mass shootings and police brutality and racial injustice.

The COVID-19 global pandemic thrust communicators around the world into the organizational spotlight and working side-by-side in many cases with company leaders. In general, communicators seem to have risen to the challenge and shined under trying and stressful circumstances (McCorkindale & Cody, 2020). Surveys indicate that at least eight out of 10 communication executives felt that the communication function was very important and very involved in its company's external and internal COVID-19 response (Peppercomm & Institute for Public Relations, 2020a, 2020b). Only 10% of communicators indicated their department and team were *not* part of the cross-functional response team (Peppercomm & Institute for Public Relations, 2020a).

Human resources (HR) and operations, along with communication, were the functions most mentioned as being part of the response (Peppercomm & Institute for Public Relations, 2020b). Even assuming communication executives may be overstating their role and importance at least a bit during COVID-19, there is little debating that the chief communications officer (CCO) and the communication team inside many organizations has risen in stature, responsibility and relevance to the C-suite, stakeholders and the public in recent years.

There is very much a business model, so to speak, that underpins the functioning of in-house communication departments and teams, whether the team is housed inside of a corporation, a start-up company, a non-profit organization or a government agency. Whether planning to work in-house or already in-house, or working on the agency or consulting side, *all* communication professionals would benefit from better understanding the evolving business of communication departments and teams. As such, this chapter traces the rise of the CCO and the communication function within organizations; reviews the roles and responsibilities of in-house departments and teams; examines the careers and characteristics of in-house communication professionals; and assesses trends in budgets for in-house departments and teams. The chapter concludes with a look at the future of CCOs, communication departments and teams.

THE RISE OF THE CCO

As summarized in the first chapter, public relations (PR) pioneer Harold Burson argued that the communication function inside of organizations has evolved through at least three stages over the past half century (Burson, 2017; Christian, 1997). In the first stage, the C-suite asked communicators "how do I say it?" In the second stage, the C-suite started asking communicators "what do I say?" In both of these stages, the C-suite often came to the senior most communicator in the organization *after* a decision had already been made. The communicator's focus was on leading the messaging rather than also contributing to organizational policy-making. In the third stage, the C-suite asks communicators "what do I do?" – recognizing that the most effective organizational communication is about not just "talking the talk" but "walking the walk." Words must be grounded in tangible and consistent actions and behaviors.

Chief executive officers (CEOs) and other members of the C-suite increasingly recognize the value of intangible assets, such as organizational reputation, trust, brand, culture and purpose, in contributing to organizational success (Arthur W. Page Society, 2017, 2019a). Research generally shows that, in a growing number of organizations, the senior most communication professional often has access to the C-suite and may even be a member of the C-suite (e.g., APCO Worldwide, 2016; Daniels, 2019a; Korn Ferry, 2020a, 2020b; Neill, 2015, 2018, 2019; Spencer Stuart & Weber Shandwick, 2016; Swerling et al., 2014). For example, an industry survey of in-house PR and communication professionals found that close to half (45%) of respondents indicate that the communication department reports to the organization's CEO/president (USC Annenberg Center for Public Relations, 2019). More than a quarter (28%) of communication departments report to marketing. The remainder (27%) of departments report to various other functions, such as strategic planning, human resources, operations and legal (USC Annenberg Center for Public Relations, 2019).

The rise of the CCO and the communication function within the enterprise generally traces to the formation and growth of the Arthur W. Page Society, a professional association for senior PR and corporate communications executives and educators, which was founded in 1983 (Arthur W. Page Society, 2020). The Page Society, now often known simply as Page, is named after Arthur W. Page, who served as the senior most communication professional at AT&T from 1927 to 1946. Page was one of the first communication executives to serve as an officer and member of the board of directors of a major public company (Jones & Kostyak, 2011). The mission of Page is to strengthen the enterprise leadership role of the CCO and its purpose is to unite the world's best communicators to transform business for the better (Arthur W. Page Society, 2020). Since 2007, Page has released an ongoing stream of influential thought leadership research focused on the evolution of the roles, responsibilities and competencies of the CCO and the communication function in the enterprise and to society.

Some in-house communication executives officially have CCO as part of their job titles, while others more informally hold this title. In an advertising context, CCO can stand for chief client officer or chief creative officer. In a communication and PR context, CCO stands for chief communications officer. The formal job title held by the senior most communicator within an organization can vary significantly. For some organizations, this professional holds the formal title of a vice president (VP), while for other organizations, this position may be at the senior vice president (SVP) level or, in more limited cases, even at the executive vice president (EVP) level. Some CCOs are members of the executive committee of the organization and an executive officer (aka formally part of the C-suite), while others are not. Current and former CCOs are also starting to pop up more on corporate boards of directors, as more corporations recognize the unique multi-stakeholder perspectives provided by communicators, particularly by those that also have business acumen (Spencer Stuart, 2018b).

Each year *PRWeek*, an industry trade publication, publishes US and UK editions of The Power List, which is a list of the 50 most influential communication leaders in the field as determined by the publication. The range of formal job titles held by CCOs are evidenced by the top five in-house names on the 2020 US edition of The Power List (*PRWeek*, 2020):

- Damon Jones, CCO, Procter & Gamble (P&G)

- Jay Carney, SVP, global corporate affairs, Amazon.com, Inc.

- Dan Bartlett, EVP, corporate affairs, Walmart, Inc.

- Zenia Mucha, SVP and CCO, The Walt Disney Company

- Nigel Powell, EVP and CCO, NIKE, Inc.

While the number of women and people of color holding the CCO and chief marketing officer (CMO) titles is rising, these senior-most communication and marketing positions are still most often held by white men. For example, as of 2019, a little more than 4 out of 10 (43%) CMOs from 100 of the most-advertised US brands were women (Korn Ferry, 2019). A few years earlier, in 2017, closer to one out of four (28%) of these CMOs for these top brands were women.

The level of racial and ethnic diversity is considerably lower among this same group of CMOs. In 2019, just 14% of these CMOs came from racially or ethnically diverse backgrounds, compared to 10% in the prior year (Korn Ferry, 2019). In a positive sign of change, of those CMOs who began their tenure in 2019, nearly half (48%) were women, and almost one out of five

(19%) of them were from racially and/or ethnically diverse backgrounds (Korn Ferry, 2019).

By comparison, women hold an estimated one quarter (25%) of the top positions in the C-suite (i.e., CEO; chief financial officer, CFO; chief human resources officer, CHRO; CMO; and chief information officer/chief technology officer, CIO/CTO) among the 1,000 largest US companies based on annual revenue (Korn Ferry, 2019). Among these C-suite positions, women hold the majority of these spots for only one of these C-level positions, the CHRO. An estimated 55% of all CHRO positions at these firms are headed by women (Korn Ferry, 2019). The data indicate that women hold a little over a third (36%) of CMO positions among this larger sample of companies. In comparison, the percentage of women holding the title of CEO (6%), CFO (12%) or CIO/CTO (18%) are all considerably lower (Korn Ferry, 2019).

ROLES AND RESPONSIBILITIES OF IN-HOUSE DEPARTMENTS AND TEAMS

In-house strategic communication teams within organizations may be organized under a variety of names, such as strategic communication, corporate communication, corporate affairs, corporate relations or often simply: communications (Argenti, 2017; Arthur W. Page Society, 2019a). In some cases, in-house positions may have PR or advertising in the job title. Within some organizations, the communication team has its own department and function headed by a CCO, who may report to the president or CEO. In other organizations, the communication team may be part of a larger department or function, such as marketing, or the combined department and function may have an integrated title such as: marketing and communications. In such cases, the senior most communication professional may report to the CMO or another C-level executive (e.g., human resources, strategic planning, operations and legal) (USC Annenberg Center for Public Relations, 2019).

Regardless of the formal structure, there is a notable trend in recent years toward closer cross-functional collaboration and integration between the communication and marketing functions within organizations, particularly within larger corporations (Burton, 2019; Daniels, 2019a; *PRovoke*, 2019, 2020; Spencer Stuart & Weber Shandwick, 2016; Swerling et al., 2014;

USC Annenberg Center for Public Relations, 2019). For example, a survey of communication professionals finds that nearly 90% of them believe that PR and marketing will become somewhat more integrated to a lot more integrated within the next five years (USC Annenberg Center for Public Relations, 2019). On the contrary, the investor relations (IR) function typically collaborates with the communication and marketing teams, but IR is almost always separate from these two departments, or part of the larger finance and treasury team (Laskin, 2018; National Investor Relations Institute, 2019; Ragas, Laskin, & Brusch, 2014).

The communication function and department are typically responsible for managing an organization's external and internal communications. While external communication areas, such as media relations, remain important, the rise of organizational purpose, culture and values has seen internal communication, including employee communication/engagement and change communication, rise in prominence inside of many communication functions and departments in recent years (Men, 2019; Men & Bowen, 2017).

The core roles and responsibilities that typically fall at least partially under CCOs and their communication teams include media relations; crisis management or reputation management; employee communication; social media or digital communication; corporate social responsibility or corporate responsibility; foundation or charitable giving; marketing, branding or advertising; and government relations or public affairs (Spencer Stuart & Weber Shandwick, 2016). CCOs expect the communication function to place a greater focus on digital communication, reputation management, employee advocacy engagement and branding or corporate identity in the future. Research from the Arthur W. Page Society (2019a) indicates that that communicators are gaining a greater responsibility within companies for defining and stewarding the corporate brand on behalf of *all* stakeholders.

Departments that the majority of global CCOs report working closely with inside of organizations include the office of the CEO, digital/social media, marketing, human resources, legal, government affairs/public affairs, IR, finance and information technology (Spencer Stuart & Weber Shandwick, 2016). Global CCOs particularly expect to work more closely in the coming years with their colleagues in digital/social media, marketing, human resources, the office of the CEO, government affairs/public affairs and customer experience. Not surprisingly, the communication function and team often plays the role of cross-functional integrator and collaborator across the enterprise in helping advance organizational goals, strategies and priorities with a focus on decision-making grounded in organizational purpose and character (Arthur W. Page Society, 2012, 2013, 2016b, 2017, 2019a).

The size and structure of in-house communication departments and teams can vary widely due to a range of factors, including often in relation to the size and scale of the organization and its operations. For example, a start-up company or community non-profit organization might employ just one or up to several communication and/or marketing professionals, whereas a large company, such as a Fortune 500 company, or a large non-profit organization, such as a major professional association, are more likely to employ a larger communication team. This team is typically based at headquarters but may even have some team members based at other office locations around the country and/or the world. During the COVID-19 pandemic, many teams successfully worked virtually, which likely will alter traditional staffing models in the future.

Very generally speaking, business-to-consumer (B2C) brands tend to have larger in-house communication teams than their business-to-business (B2B) brand counterparts. A *PRovoke* (2020) survey of top CCOs and CMOs found that a little less than a quarter of respondents (22%) report managing small teams of 1–20 team members, while a little less than a third (29%) manage mid-sized teams of 21–100 people. The largest number of respondents, at nearly half of CCOs and CMOs (49%), report managing large teams of 100+ people.

With a heritage stretching back more than 200 years, New York-based Colgate-Palmolive Company is the home to iconic consumer brands, including Colgate, Palmolive, Softsoap, Tom's of Maine and Hill's Science Diet, that are sold in more than 200 countries and territories. A Fortune 500 firm, the B2C leader has more than 34,000 employees and worldwide annual net sales of nearly $16 billion (Colgate-Palmolive Company, 2020). Colgate's corporate communication team collaborates with the marketing teams across the company's various divisions to "look for great stories and tell them" (P. Davis, personal communication, July 27, 2020). Agility is key for the corporate communication team so, for example, the function chooses to not divide itself by internal communication and external communication.

"We are organized like an agency with internal clients (our divisions and functions) and we develop comprehensive communications strategies to inform, inspire and engage," says Paula S. Davis, VP and CCO for Colgate (personal communication, July 27, 2020). "We then leverage our communications colleagues with specialized skills in digital, social, graphic design, and editorial to package and distribute the content in different and unique ways for different audiences."

On the contrary, B2B brand Cummins Inc. has adopted a fully integrated communication and marketing team model. Founded in 1919, Columbus, Indiana-based Cummins designs, manufactures and distributes a broad portfolio of power solutions, such as backup power generation for sports stadiums and arenas like Wrigley Field, home of the Chicago Cubs. A Fortune 500 company, Cummins has more than 60,000 employees with annual revenue of nearly $24 billion (Cummins Inc., 2020). The integration of corporate communication and marketing communication responsibilities under one team mirrors Cummins's structure of five operating segments and supporting corporate functions across its global business.

"With an integrated approach, we are best positioned to provide consistent levels of support and messaging across our wide range of expertise for internal and external audiences," says Carole Casto, VP of marketing and communications at Cummins. "As a combined communications function, we are better positioned to support the long-term success of our team through increased leadership development and skill-enhancing opportunities."

See Fig. 11.1 for an overview of the integrated structure of the Cummins corporate communication and marketing communication team.

CAREERS AND CHARACTERISTICS OF IN-HOUSE COMMUNICATION PROFESSIONALS

PR, advertising and communication agencies and consultancies are training grounds for young talent. Many in-house communication professionals started their careers working in agencies and consultancies. Some stay on the agency side as they progress, while others then move to the client side. For example, the group of top CCOs and CMOs selected by *PRovoke* (2019), formerly *The Holmes Report*, to make up "The Influence 100" self-report that the majority (58%) of them have worked at an agency at some point in their careers (*PRovoke*, 2019). For in-house communication and marketing leaders that started their career in a field other than strategic communication, their first career was most likely to be in journalism.

Fig. 11.1:   Integrated Corporate Communication and Marketing Team at Cummins.

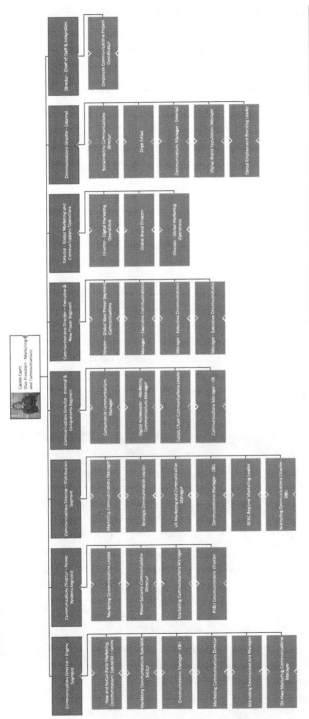

Virtually all (98%) of the C-level communication and marketing executives that make up the 2020 edition of "The Influence 100" say they hold a bachelor's degree and nearly half of them (48%) hold an advanced degree as well (*PRovoke*, 2020). There are signs that, as communication as a field has been elevated into more of a strategic management function at many large organizations, more communicators are seeking out advanced degrees, particularly with an emphasis on management and business administration, such as an MBA (Daniels, 2020).

"Agencies are such a unique ecosystem, and even after working in-house for years, the lessons I experienced then serve as the foundation for how I approach communications to this day," says Bjorn Trowery, consumer communications manager for Facebook, Inc. Bjorn, a LAGRANT Foundation scholarship recipient, started his career on the agency side with Edelman. "Agency life puts you through the ringer, and gives you such a full range of experiences that make even younger professionals feel like seasoned veterans, who can take on anything without skipping a beat" (B. Trowery, personal communication, July 19, 2020).

With in-house communication professionals increasingly expected to work in cross-functional teams across enterprises, there is a growing need and expectation for communicators to have a broader skill set and knowledge base than the specialist and technician roles of years past (Dozier, 1992; Dozier & Broom, 2006; Dozier & Grunig, 1992). Research by Korn Ferry (2020a, 2020c), an executive search firm, indicates that chief communications and public affairs officers believe that the skills required of successful in-house team members are changing as the roles and responsibilities of the communication function evolve. Specifically, chief corporate affairs officers (CCAOs) indicate that the skills they value the most in adding to their talent bench are data analytics; change management communications; and content, in-house editorial and storytelling skills (Korn Ferry, 2020a). This represents a shift from three years earlier when these leaders emphasized skills such as speechwriting, media relations and social media. CCAOs believe that the following three skills make for a great senior communication leader: the ability to influence without authority; having business acumen and decision quality; and courage of conviction (i.e., the ability to speak truth to power regardless of the consequences) (Korn Ferry, 2020a).

In-house corporate communication professionals as a group are generally more highly compensated than agency professionals. This is in part because there tends to be fewer junior positions on in-house communication teams compared with entry-level positions being common at many agencies and consultancies. For example, salary survey data from *PRWeek* indicates that the median annual salary for a communication professional is $100,000 with a median annual salary of $145,500 for in-house corporate PR professionals and $90,000 for PR agency professionals (Daniels, 2020). The median annual salary for an in-house non-profit PR professional is $85,000. Broadly speaking, the data in recent years reveal stronger satisfaction with base salaries among in-house practitioners compared to their agency counterparts (Daniels, 2018, 2019a, 2020). There remains a gender pay gap in the field with men overall paid a median salary of $107,000, while women overall are paid a salary of $95,000 (Daniels, 2020).

The communication field says the right things about diversity, equity and inclusion, but its workforce, within agencies, in-house departments and academia, does not fully reflect these commitments (Landis, 2019; Tindall, 2018; Tindall & McWilliams, 2011). For example, the PR field in the United States is predominantly white and female (Brown, Waymer, & Zhou, 2019; Wallington, 2020). Data released in 2020 by Omnicom Group, the largest US-based agency holding company, reveal that 7 out of 10 (70%) of its agency employees are white (Rittenhouse, 2020b). This percentage rises to more than 8 out of 10 (84%) employees being white at the executive management level. For comparison, as of 2019, black, indigenous and people of color collectively make up approximately 40% of the US population (United States Census Bureau, 2020). While women comprise as much as 70% of the PR workforce, by some estimates, they hold only around 30% of agency executive positions (Chitkara, 2018). In the past few years, more agencies and firms are naming women and people of color to top strategic communication jobs, but there remains much work to be done on diversity, equity and inclusion *across all levels of the profession* (Mundy, 2016, 2019; S. Spector & Spector, 2018).

The cultural demographic shift of the United States makes diversity, equity and inclusion "a business imperative" for any organization, according to Andy Checo, an associate VP at Havas FORMULATIN, an award-winning agency for clients seeking to connect with the US Latinx community (personal communication, June 22, 2020). "Currently, diversity and inclusion lacks within communications departments," says Checo, who is also the president of the Hispanic Public Relations Association (HPRA). "Given we are tasked with making meaningful connections with our stakeholders, it is vital that our communication strategies are anchored on the insights that reflect the point of views and understanding of diverse audiences."

BUDGETS FOR IN-HOUSE DEPARTMENTS AND TEAMS

As with staff size, the size of a communication department's budget can vary significantly, in part due to the size and scale of the organization and the amount of resources the C-suite dedicates to the communication function (Daniels, 2019a). Surveys of communication leaders generally indicate that in-house communication budgets in recent years have risen or at least stayed flat through year-end 2019 (Swerling et al., 2014; USC Annenberg Center for Public Relations, 2019). However, the recession sparked by the COVID-19 global crisis in spring 2020 has resulted in significant cost cutting activities across the board by corporations and other organizations, including staff furloughs, layoffs and reduced departmental budgets, particularly on discretionary spending. Corporate budgets and staffing levels may take up to several years to fully recover with communication and marketing spending often cut noticeably during recessions. Such spending has historically been slower to completely recover than the overall economy (B. Johnson, 2020).

A survey of top CCOs and CMOs found that about a quarter (24%) of them report managing in-house communication and marketing budgets of more than $100 million per year (*PRovoke*, 2020). The majority (53%) of these communication and marketing leaders report being responsible for an annual budget of more than $25 million. Of course, some have significantly less resources to work with, as nearly one out of five (19%) CCOs and CMOs in this group report managing a departmental budget of $10 million or less (*PRovoke*, 2020). The top 10 areas in which these senior leaders anticipate spending the most in the future are corporate reputation, PR, social media – organic, content development, employee engagement and change management, data and analytics, measurement and evaluation, social media – paid, crisis management and influencer marketing (*PRovoke*, 2020).

As is the case with agencies, staff salaries and associated expenses (aka human capital) are typically the largest budget line on in-house communications and marketing budgets. An extensive global study of communication and PR industry practices found that almost half (49%) of communications and PR department and/or function budgets are dedicated to staff salaries and related costs (Swerling et al., 2014). The next largest budget line is often PR/communication program execution (31% of total budget allocation), followed by outside agency/consultancy fees (14% of budget allocation) and spending on PR/communication measurement and evaluation (6% of budget allocation) (Swerling et al., 2014). Some communication teams and functions may spend more or less of their total budget on a percentage basis on outside agency and consultancy fees than others, depending in part on the breadth and depth of the in-house skills and capabilities of the team and the function (RFP Associates, LLC, 2019). In addition, measurement and evaluation is generally growing in importance.

Corporate department and function budget cycles are typically set on an annual basis (Kenton, 2020b). Some budgets are based on a calendar year (i.e., a year-end of December 31), while others are based on a fiscal year with a different year-end date (e.g., January 31, June 30 and September 30). The budgeting process usually begins several months prior to the new fiscal year when managers are required to submit estimates for anticipated communication projects and staffing. Proposed budgets often are reviewed by the CFO prior to approval by senior management or the CEO. Corporate annual communication budget planning includes assessing fixed costs such as personnel and support services required for the coming year. This is sometimes an anxious time for the in-house team, as well as its agencies, who are eager to confirm anticipated budgets so they can do their own planning for the coming year.

The concept of zero-based budgeting (ZBB) has gained traction within some large companies over the past decade as they look for cost savings (Geller & Naidu, 2019). Under ZBB, the department or team leader must start from a "zero base" each year in justifying all aspects of the proposed budget's expense lines and items, rather than simply building off the prior year's budget. ZBB is a budgeting process that ostensibly allocates funding based on program and department-level efficiency and necessity rather than budget history in an effort to make an organization leaner and more streamlined (Deloitte Development LLC, 2015; Mahler, 2016).

Many communicators did not study finance or accounting in school. Budget management is often not a favorite activity of communication professionals. But the days of when a marketer or communicator might say, "I know half of my marketing or communication budget didn't work; I just don't know what half!" are long over. Strategic communication practitioners, particularly those in manager and above roles, are increasingly expected to be effective budget managers able to track spending, stay within budgets and demonstrate tangible results from communication programs and initiatives (Goodman, 2019; Men, Robinson, & Thelen, 2019).

"The most effective communicators leverage both the art and science of their roles in order to achieve the greatest impact," says Leslie Sutton, VP of corporate communications for Discover Financial Services, a Fortune 500 financial services company best known for the Discover card. Sutton serves on the board of advisors for The Plank Center for Leadership in Public Relations and on the board of trustees for the Institute for Public Relations. "The ability to measure the ROI of communications programs enables teams to demonstrate value in a way that's consistent with business discipline and it is critical to the prioritization of activities and future planning" (L. Sutton, personal communication, June 30, 2020).

THE FUTURE OF COMMUNICATION DEPARTMENTS AND TEAMS

Strategic communicators have long argued they need *access* to "the room where it happens" and that they also deserve a seat at the leadership table (Berger, 2019; Ragas & Culp, 2018a, 2018b). The former has become a reality at many organizations and the latter is also the case at some places. The strategic communication function is increasingly getting a voice in organizational decision-making and opportunities to serve as trusted advisors and counselors to leadership on a growing range of meaningful business and societal matters (Argenti, 2017; Arthur W. Page Society, 2019a; Bolton, Stacks, & Mizrachi, 2018). This is a far cry from the days when the communication function was far from the halls of power and largely relegated to generating publicity, handling media requests and planning and managing announcements and events.

While the future for in-house communication departments and teams is bright, it is also not a future without challenges. The coming years will almost certainly bring closer collaboration and integration – if not outright combining of departments – between communication and marketing teams in larger organizations (Bronn, Romenti, & Zerfass, 2016; Nothhaft, Werder, Vercic, & Zerfass, 2020). Such integration may have the effect of amplifying or reducing the influence and unique viewpoints of PR and communication professionals within organizations (Ragas & Culp, 2018a, 2018b).

Such integration may also accelerate the need for greater business literacy among in-house communication professionals (Ragas, 2016b). Many marketing professionals went to business school and are fluent in the language and thinking of business. Communicators will also likely benefit from greater training in areas at the nexus of management, marketing, communication and society, such as data analytics and measurement, data visualization, project management, change management, compliance and ethics and social responsibility and social justice (Neill, 2018; Neill & Barnes, 2018; van Ruler, 2014, 2015).

As stated by the so-called Peter Parker principle (of Spider Man fame), "with great power, comes great responsibility." With living out an organization's stated purpose, principles, and values in the spotlight, many CCOs and their in-house communication colleagues arguably hold more soft power and organizational influence than perhaps at any time in the profession's history. Given this greater opportunity to lead at an organizational level and to do a better job of developing talent at all levels of the profession (Jain & Bain, 2017; Penning & Bain, 2018), CCOs, their teams and agency partners can choose to be forces for positive change in business and society in the years ahead. Or they can default to supporting "business as usual." The choice is theirs.

KEY TERMS

Agency side

Business model

Business-to-business (B2B)

Business-to-consumer (B2C)

Calendar year

Chief communications officer
  (CCO)

Chief corporate affairs officer
  (CCAO)

Chief financial officer (CFO)

Chief human resources officer
  (CHRO)

Chief information officer (CIO)

Chief marketing officer (CMO)

C-suite

Fiscal year

In-house side

Zero-based budgeting (ZBB)

DISCUSSION QUESTIONS

(1) Go to the corporate website of a brand you respect. Look up the management team. Is there a CCO and/or a CMO?

(2) Sticking with this same brand, if there is a CCO and/or a CMO listed as part of the management team, what is this leader's stated role, responsibilities and experiences?

(3) In your opinion, what are some of the potential *advantages* of the full integration of the communication and marketing functions within the same organization?

(4) In your opinion, what are some of the potential *disadvantages* of the full integration of the communication and marketing functions within the same organization?

(5) Look into your crystal ball. What do you think the future holds for the in-house communication function inside of organizations? What future trends do you foresee?

By John Onoda,
Onoda Consulting

The team of communicators inside corporations own a continually changing set of high-stakes roles and responsibilities. More than any other function within large organizations, the communications group must be nimble and adept at quickly mastering new skills and becoming experts on new topics.

Why is this?

Unlike professionals in other corporate functions – legal, HR, finance, etc. – communicators are not constrained by laws and dense regulations. Unlike people in operations, they require no special equipment, factories, special technology, expensive software, fleets of vehicles or anything else that takes time and money to acquire.

So, communicators only need to change what's inside their heads and they are ready to tackle new challenges. The best ones can drop what they're doing and jump into a new assignment in a moment's notice, if need be.

Having led communications departments at four major corporations (Levi Strauss, General Motors, Visa USA and Charles Schwab) and consulted with dozens more, I have observed the career paths of hundreds of professionals. I am confident asserting that the most successful communicators share certain traits. These traits are:

- A knack for learning quickly.

- A talent for mastering new skills rapidly.

- Unusually high productivity.

- An appetite for risk.

- Great energy.

- An endless hunger to grow professionally.

- A comfort with continual change.

- The ability to let go.

- A gift for building new working relations with all kinds of people.

There is a body of professional literature and many academic studies about the structure of in-house communications departments. Much money and time is often spent redesigning org charts and tinkering with workflows before jobs are redesigned and regrouped, which happens every few years. A lot of this effort is wasted. The truth is that *the people* in a communications department determine its effectiveness, not its structure. Because they work in such a dynamic environment, how communicators organize themselves and work naturally is more important than what some consultant puts on a slide; and, if the communicators lack the necessary skills and attitude, even a perfectly designed department will fall short of expectations.

Another key aspect of the way in-house communications departments function is that they reflect the political power structure of the organization. Because the value of communications is hard to prove, especially to senior management, the department tends to focus manpower and budgets on the voices that most determine the perception of its success or failure. In short, the squeaking wheel gets the grease.

So how do communicators thrive in such a subjective environment?

They must acquire skills and knowledge necessary to be champions of corporate gamesmanship. Such skills and knowledge are:

- Strategic thinking.

- Business acumen.

- Alliance building.

- Leadership.

- High emotional intelligence.

- The ability to accept failure.

- Resilience and the knack of learning from failure.

- Authenticity.

Most of these traits are not taught in schools. They are best learned from mentors or coaches. If career help from more seasoned professionals is unavailable, they can be acquired through observation and experimentation. Also, there are many fine books on how to become a leader in large organizations. I suggest you read them.

PART VI

PRACTICE MAKES PERFECT

12

BUSINESS ACUMEN AND
PROFESSIONAL DEVELOPMENT

The classic phrase "practice makes perfect" may not be perfect but it has some truth to it. The more one practices, generally the better they get at something.

This idea was encapsulated in "The 10,000 Hour Rule" introduced by Malcolm Gladwell (2011) in his bestselling book *Outliers: The Story of Success*. Gladwell argues that it generally takes at least 10,000 hours of practice to acquire expertise in complex domains such as sports, arts or the sciences. Closer scrutiny of this rule-of-thumb indicates that it is not just the *amount* of practice, but the *quality* of practice, known as deliberate or purposeful practice, that is particularly important (Ericsson, Krampe, & Tesch-Römer, 1993). Further, while prolonged deliberate practice seems to improve performance at something, the innate talent, skills and abilities of the individual, as well as myriad other factors, come into play (Macnamara & Maitra, 2019).

In short, Gladwell's (2011) "rule" is far too simple but should not be fully dismissed either. For example, a meta-analysis of scientific studies on this subject finds that, while practice alone may not turn you into an *elite-level* performer, practice will very likely improve your performance and boost your level of expertise (Macnamara, Moreau, & Hambrick, 2016).

Developing one's business acumen is not all that different than becoming good at many other things in life, including learning a second or even a third language. Few people take two years of high school classes in a second language like Spanish or French and then simply become fluent. Those that choose to keep immersing themselves beyond high school or college in the language, the culture and its people and who regularly practice reading, writing and speaking this second or third language are more likely to become reasonably fluent. As you may have guessed by now, developing and elevating one's business IQ takes a sustained commitment to learning – and pursuing opportunities for deliberate practice – that should go on beyond completing this book.

Many in communication are attracted to the profession because much of the work is "in the creative sphere" according to Ray Kotcher, former chief executive officer (CEO) and chair of Ketchum, one of the world's largest public relations (PR) agencies (personal communication, August 10, 2020). Kotcher finds that fewer communicators are comfortable with the analytical work at the intersection of communication and business strategy, "yet those who can develop an essential understanding of the vocabulary of business and apply it, will provide greater value and have a clear competitive advantage." He gives the following example: "Imagine being out there in the world of work and being asked into a meeting with clients or colleagues from finance – or any of the other C-suite functions – and not being able to grasp adequately what is being discussed at the table, and then being asked what you see as the related strategic communication opportunities and challenges."

In the experience of Kotcher, now a professor of the practice at Boston University's College of Communication teaching, among other classes, business fundamentals to graduate communication students, learning about business "doesn't need to be scary" and "even can be fun" (personal communication, August 10, 2020). "Think of developing your business acumen in the same way you would make a personal commitment to go regularly to the gym to build new muscle," says Kotcher, a recipient of lifetime achievement awards from the Public Relations Society of America (PRSA), the Institute for Public Relations (IPR), and the Page Society. "You know what happens when you begin to miss workouts! It's continuous training. Adapt and keep learning."

BUSINESS ACUMEN MOVES TO CENTER STAGE

Business acumen has moved from out of the shadows and onto center stage. Over the past decade, there has been growing recognition from educators and practitioners of the importance and value of greater business and financial literacy to the success of mass communication professionals (e.g., Claussen, 2008; Roush, 2006). More specifically, there is greater acknowledgment that – for strategic communication to better live up to the "strategic" part of its name and contribute to *strategic decision making* – communication professionals need a heightened business IQ (Berger, 2019; Duhé, 2013; Krishna, Wright, & Kotcher, 2020; Ragas, Uysal, & Culp, 2015).

Perhaps now more than at any time in the field's history, senior communication professionals are being invited into "the room where it happens" (in which decisions get made and policies are set by organizational leadership). In a growing number of cases, communicators are helping drive storytelling grounded in policies that they have helped not just communicate but shape before they have been announced (Hynes, 2017, 2018; Ragas, 2019a; Ragas & Culp, 2018b).

"CEOs are increasingly looking for communications leaders with a deep understanding of the business who can serve as trusted advisors that aid their decision-making," says Mike McGrew, executive vice president and chief communications and CSR officer for Constellation Brands, a top international producer and marketer of beer, wine and spirits with a brand portfolio that includes Corona, Modelo, Pacifico, Robert Mondavi and Kim Crawford. "This requires spending a significant amount of time in the business, getting in tune with the day-to-day realities that commercial and operations leaders face, understanding the decisions they make and why, getting acclimated to their distinct languages, and engaging in meaningful business conversations" (M. McGrew, personal communication, August 18, 2020).

"Exhibiting a deep understanding of the business is critical to gaining the trust of senior executives," says McGrew, who reports to Constellation's president and CEO and is a member of the executive management committee for this Fortune 500 company. "Enhanced business acumen and trust earned among senior leaders, combined with the unique perspective communicators bring to the table, allows for greater influence in shaping and driving an organization's strategic priorities."

In 2013, one of the co-authors of this book wrote an article for the *Chronicle of Higher Education* titled, "Require Business 101 for Every Student," arguing that students in the social sciences and the liberal arts (and not just in business schools) would benefit from completing some coursework in business (Ragas, 2013). The generally positive reactions to this article, coupled with interest from PR and advertising students at DePaul University in business basics and leadership, sparked the co-authors to write their first book, *Business Essentials for Strategic Communicators* (Ragas & Culp, 2014a). The co-edited book, *Mastering Business for Strategic Communicators* (Ragas & Culp, 2018b), with essays contributed by current or former chief communications officers (CCOs), followed. Today, there is a growing number of strategic communication, PR, advertising and communication management programs that are incorporating coursework in business and financial literacy into the curriculum. The 2018 recommendation by the Commission on Public Relations Education, a group comprised of top educators and practitioners, that business literacy should be a new recommended area of study for an undergraduate PR education marked an important point for future classroom education.

Outside of the classroom, more communication agencies and consultancies in recent years have incorporated elements of business and financial training into agency talent development and leadership programs (Ragas & Culp, 2014b). We have also seen more in-house communication departments offering business acumen workshops and programs to their teams (Ragas & Culp, 2015). While this is positive progress, the pace of change continues to accelerate and with it the knowledge, skills and abilities expected of practitioners. We think that more resources need to be devoted as a field to the training and development of talent on critical competencies in the years ahead (Jain & Bain, 2017). Younger professionals, in particular, cite the importance of professional development opportunities when it comes to employee recruitment, engagement and retention (Daniels, 2017, 2018, 2019b, 2020). We wonder if a greater commitment to talent development and mentoring programs might even help accelerate the rise and growth of more diverse voices across the profession (S. Spector & Spector, 2018).

"Young professionals and their supervisors should seek out training and development opportunities that allow them to gain a solid command of business terms and bottom-line expectations," says Victor Arias, managing director and partner, DiversifiedSearch, one of the top search firms in the United States (personal communication, July 26, 2020). "This knowledge will allow them to elevate their credibility and future performance with clients and peers. Combined with mastering 'unwritten rules' of expected behaviors in the workplace creates a winning combination for future business leaders."

CAREER STAGES: FROM STUDENT TO SENIOR LEADER

While good habits are good habits, the opportunities and ways to develop one's business literacy through purposeful practice will vary over the course of one's career. As such, we have provided some professional development recommendations for readers based on career stage:

Strategic communication students: For communication majors, we implore you to expand your media diet and to start following business news. Staying on top of popular culture news is important for communicators but following business news – and learning what is on the minds of business leaders and getting familiar with the language of business – is important too. Think about doing a double major or a minor in a business subject, such as marketing, management or entrepreneurship. At a minimum, take electives that include business coursework. Start networking as a student, including developing relationships with your professors, fellow students and class guest speakers. Get involved in campus co-curricular organizations like the Public Relations Student Society of America (PRSSA) and the American Advertising Federation (AAF) college chapters. Even better, pursue leadership opportunities in such student organizations. Join competition teams for student competitions, such as the PRSSA Bateman case study competition, the AAF National Student Advertising Competition and the Page and IPR case study competition in corporate communication.

New graduates and young professionals: For recent graduates, staying on top of business news and immersing yourself in business materials related to your employer and/or clients will prove beneficial. Raise your hand for any professional development opportunities with your employer. Join and become an active member of at least one professional association and think about volunteering with a local non-profit organization you are passionate about. Consider joining a committee of one of these organizations to build more leadership experience. You may want to consider pursuing a graduate degree, such as a master's in strategic communication with a business emphasis or an MBA that incorporates strategic communication coursework (Rennie, Byrum, Tidwell, & Chitkara, 2018). Look for opportunities to help students at your alma mater. Ramp up your professional networking, both with those in your field and with those outside of it.

Mid-career professionals and rising leaders: Double down on professional development efforts, both with your employer and on your own, related to strengthening your business acumen. This might include completing work-shops, certificate programs and/or pursuing that graduate degree that you had thought about but have not yet done. Seek out opportunities to gain more managerial and budgetary responsibility and experience. Look for opportunities to get on and chair committees and groups with your employer and/or where you volunteer. For some rising leaders, if you have advanced to one of the top positions on your in-house team or/at your agency, look into being nominated by an Arthur W. Page Society member for the Page Future Leaders Experience and/or membership in Page Up, its sister organization for rising leaders.

Senior leaders: Just because you have climbed to near the top of the professional mountain does not mean that the learning stops, and "giving back" may even accelerate. Seek out new leadership opportunities outside of your comfort zone that further hone your business acumen and related skills. Aspire to get on to the leadership committee(s) of your employer and become a bonafide member of the C-suite. Serve on the boards of organizations and look for more opportunities to give back and help advance the profession. Create and support professional development opportunities that help advance the careers of your teams and other professionals. Aim for being nominated for membership into organizations for senior strategic communication leaders like the Arthur W. Page Society, the PRSA College of Fellows and The Seminar.

TEN WAYS TO BUILD BUSINESS ACUMEN

Through our writing, research, speaking and consulting on business acumen, we have learned that professionals are hungry for tangible steps they and their teams may take to improve their business literacy and develop their business acumen. We have personally seen time and again how recent graduates and younger professionals, who work on developing their business fluency, use this competency to differentiate themselves and rise faster in their careers. While the communication profession seems to be getting more serious about talent development and mentorship programs (Brown, Waymer, & Zhou, 2019; Jain & Bain, 2017; Wallington, 2020), professionals still need to proactively *take ownership* of their own professional development and career paths whenever possible.

Former CCO and strategic communication counselor Charlene Wheeless says it is important to "do what you love and love what you do" (personal communication, July 12, 2020). "If you are in a work situation that you don't like, quit whining and change your circumstances," says Wheeless, chair of the Arthur W. Page Society for 2020 and 2021. Wheeless has held senior positions at Bechtel, Raytheon, American Management Systems and DynCorp. "No one is coming to rescue you – rescue yourself."

In this vein, we have compiled a list of 10 recommendations for building business acumen, the majority of which are recommendations professionals can initiate *on their own* without relying on their current or future employers for support. Further, many of these recommendations are purposely low cost. Such recommendations primarily require "sweat equity": rolling up one's sleeves and spending the ongoing time and effort needed to turn some of these recommendations into healthy *habits*. Of course, we would note that there are many more ways to build your business IQ beyond the recommendations listed in the following pages. But we have found through trial and error that the recommendations on this list generally work well together.

Without further ado, here are 10 of our favorite ways to develop business acumen as a communication professional and, more generally, to power up your career prospects:

(1) *Expand your news diet to more business news:* Perhaps the best habit to get into when it comes to learning the language, terminology and thinking of business and business leaders is to regularly follow business news. For national business and finance news, we particularly recommend *The Wall Street Journal*, the business section of *The New York Times*, and business cable news channel CNBC and its CNBC.com website. At a local level, follow the business section of your local newspaper and, if you are based in a large city, follow the local business news journal. For gaining international perspective, we recommend the English language international publications the *Financial Times*, *The Economist* and *South China Morning Post*. For younger communication professionals, business news providers *Business Insider* and *Cheddar* may particularly resonate. We also remain fans of business news magazines like *Bloomberg Businessweek* and *Fortune*, as well as the radio programs and podcasts of the non-profit news organization *Marketplace*, which is distributed by American Public Media.

(2) *Read more business books – not just this one:* Get into the habit of reading more business books. Every year the *Financial Times* and McKinsey & Co. select a best business book of the year and publish a short list of the best new business books. Reading books on such lists will help keep you on top of the latest thinking of business leaders and will also provide you with good conversation fodder. While not specifically written for strategic communicators, there are several books focused on building business acumen (e.g., Charan, 2017; Cope, 2012). We particularly recommend books by bestselling author Michael Lewis. Not only do fellow business journalists rate Lewis as one of the most influential business journalists around (Ragas & Tran, 2015; Tran & Ragas, 2018), but the writing style and storytelling approach of Lewis is accessible and compelling. Several Lewis books have been made into movies (*The Blind Slide, The Big Short*).

(3) *Read the writings and interviews of top business leaders:* Another great way to become versed in the language and thinking of business is to read the writings and interviews of closely followed business leaders, such as top CEOs and senior executives. We recommend following the writings and interviews of leaders such as Mary Barra (General Motors), Jamie Dimon (JPMorgan Chase), Larry Fink (BlackRock), Mellody Hobson (Ariel Capital Management), Jack Ma (Alibaba Group and Ant Group) and Robert F. Smith (Vista Equity Partners). The annual letters authored by many of these leaders are good starting points. It is important to go beyond the perspectives of just white male business leaders. Check out the annual "Most Powerful Women in Business" list published by *Fortune* and the annual "The World's Hundred Most Powerful Women" list published by *Forbes*.

(4) *Add business edutainment shows to your viewing queue:* Over the past decade, there has been an explosion in television programming focused on business subjects, particularly the camera-ready drama of the start-up life, entrepreneurship and/or running small businesses. For example, the Emmy-winning ABC television show *Shark Tank* has almost single-handedly sparked greater interest by the public in innovation, start-ups and pitch competitions. While shows like *Shark Tank* are indeed entertainment, they also do have some educational value (i.e., edutainment) in introducing business and finance concepts and terminology.

There are also movies that help explain the world of Wall Street, such as the Oscar-winning film *The Big Short* about the global financial crisis of 2007–2008 and its aftermath. The Oscar-winning documentary *Inside Job* provides a sobering look at Wall Street and government's interconnected roles in this crisis.

(5) *Seek out formal training and development programs:* In addition to self-directed study, seek out internal and/or external opportunities to participate in training and development programs focused on building business acumen and related subjects. Some organizations and agencies have developed and offer virtual and/or in-person internal workshops on business acumen (or you may be able to push for the development of such a program). Another option is to explore participating in external programs, such as workshops, classes and certificates offered by industry associations, publishers, colleges and/or universities. For example, the National Investor Relations Institute offers finance essentials courses geared to non-finance professionals. More of these programs are being offered in online formats. Participating in such training programs will not only help sharpen your business IQ but may also provide good networking opportunities.

(6) *Consider going back to school:* For those who have already gotten their feet wet with a training and development program, they may want to consider going back to school and enrolling in a graduate program or a certificate program. Popular options include the Master in Business Administration (MBA) or a Master's program in strategic or integrated communication that emphasizes business management and strategy in coursework. When evaluating graduate programs, look carefully at the reputations of the faculty and the alumni network of the program, including the positions held by alumni. One way to assess whether an MBA program may take strategic communication and PR seriously is to see whether the program is part of the PRSA MBA/Business School Program initiative (Public Relations Society of America, Inc., 2020; Rennie et al., 2018). By some indications, less than a third of PR professionals hold a graduate degree (Daniels, 2017). For comparison, more than half of investor relations (IR) professionals have earned an advanced degree, with an MBA being the most popular choice (National Investor Relations Institute, 2017).

(7) *Pick a public company and track its investor communications:* A great way
to learn about a business from the perspective of the C-suite and investors
is to track the investor communications of a publicly traded company.
This company might be your employer, your client or perhaps a company
headquartered where you live. Visit the IR section of the company's website. Here you will find a wealth of IR materials, such as the CEO letter
to shareholders, the annual report, quarterly earnings news releases and
potentially an archive of quarterly earnings presentations and transcripts.
A good free source of earnings call transcripts is SeekingAlpha.com. To dig
deeper, you might gain access to Wall Street analyst notes about the firm.
You might also track the business media coverage of the company in relation to company news releases. Finally, follow your favorite companies on
LinkedIn and other social media platforms.

(8) *Get some "skin in the game" and invest in the stock market:* While the stock
market is one of the best ways to create generational wealth, only a little over
half of American households directly or indirectly (such as through retirement accounts) invest in the stock market (Parker & Fry, 2020). Whether
through buying individual stocks or investing in an exchange traded fund
or a mutual fund, by investing in the market (and we suggest starting small),
you will almost certainly become more attuned to business and economic
news and will likely boost your business IQ over time. There are many different financial technology (aka "fintech") companies focused on serving
the needs of millennials and Generation Z. For example, companies such as
Acorns specialize in micro-investing, allowing individuals to automatically
invest their "spare change" from everyday purchases.

(9) *Develop a network of pros across business functions:* Work on developing,
growing and cultivating a network of professionals *across business functions* throughout your career. Within some organizations, it is easy to limit
your networks primarily to those working within your function or department. Proactively inviting colleagues in other departments and functions
to coffee/tea or lunch is not only smart relationship building but builds
a network of subject matter experts to call upon when you have questions. Bonus points go to finding experts that have the "heart of a teacher"
and enjoy explaining complex business topics in accessible ways. Getting
actively involved in professional and civic organizations, including serving
on committees and boards, is a great way to expand a network beyond the
direct networks of current and former employers and/or clients.

(10) *Develop your own personal board of directors:* Every established company has a board of directors. The board provides oversight, accountability and strategic guidance to the management team. Whether a new graduate or a senior leader, communicators at all career stages benefit from having mentors they can turn to for guidance, insights and as sounding boards. Mentors need not be limited exclusively to professionals from within the world of communication or even business. Perspectives from those in other industries, backgrounds and/or from lived experiences different from your own can be invaluable. Develop your own personal board of directors filled with those you consider mentors. You might think of the chair of your personal board of directors as a *sponsor* – someone who is more than a mentor and will actively advocate for your career growth and success.

See Fig. 12.1 for a visual representation of the concept of a personal board of directors that you commit to building and helping mentor you, while still ultimately taking responsibility for your own career choices. Just like a professional board, the members of your board may be "refreshed" over your career by you or them as mentor–mentee relationships evolve and change.

Fig. 12.1: Personal Board of Directors.

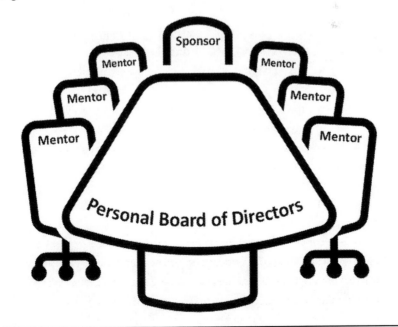

LIFELONG LEARNING AND THE MINDSET
OF CHAMPIONS

As proud Chicagoans, we have a fondness for all Chicago professional sports teams (we only disagree over rooting for the Chicago White Sox or the Chicago Cubs). So we watched with great anticipation the ESPN documentary series *The Last Dance* about the Chicago Bulls and their successful quest to win six NBA championships over an eight-year stretch during the nineties (ESPN, 2020). This documentary reminded us that Michael Jordan, widely viewed as one of the greatest basketball players of all time, *did not* even make his high school varsity team as a sophomore. Jordan credits this setback as motivating him to become an absolute "gym rat" – always practicing and striving to get better at his game (D. Johnson, 2020). Even long after Jordan had become a perennial All-Star player, he was known for pushing himself and his teammates through arduous practices and training regimes. This work ethic and drive for continual learning and growth was a hallmark of Jordan's Hall of Fame career and success.

In our experience, many of the top strategic communication professionals "in the game" also never stop honing their craft and trying to elevate the profession. [Read the thinking and insights of some of these communication leaders in Bolton, Stacks, and Mizrachi (2018), Ragas and Culp (2018b) and S. Spector and Spector (2018).] We have observed that the top leaders often show a dedication to continual learning and competency development throughout their careers. They generally do not stop learning when they get to the top – be it as a CCO, a senior agency leader or an esteemed senior scholar-practitioner – and they often commit to helping others on their teams and those around them, such as mentees and junior colleagues, to getting better too. In our estimation, if this attitude is adopted more broadly across the profession in the years ahead, there will be many more "championship seasons" to come for strategic communication as a field.

KEY TERMS

Board of directors

Business acumen

Business literacy

Chief communications officer (CCO)

C-suite

Exchange Traded Fund

Executive committee   Stock market
Investor Relations (IR)   Strategic communication
Mutual fund   Talent development

DISCUSSION QUESTIONS

(1) Looking at the list of 10 ways to develop greater business acumen, which of these recommendations do you plan to do in the future? Which one(s) might you already do?

(2) This list of recommendations should be viewed as a starting point and is *not* all encompassing. What are three recommended additions that you would make to this list?

(3) Development of diverse talent is key to the vitality and future relevance of the profession. What are ways the profession can attract, retain and develop more diverse talent?

(4) The strategic communication field in recent years has placed a greater emphasis on mentorship programs. What do you feel are the keys to success with such programs?

(5) Looking beyond business acumen, what other competencies would you focus upon as part of training and development programs for strategic communication professionals?

**By Katie Boylan,
SVP and Chief
Communications Officer,
Target Corp.**

When I think about what I learned in college or in the early part of my career, the single most important thing is that I *learned how to learn.*

Being curious and eager to learn something new is what allows you to turn a vulnerability – not knowing an answer – into an opportunity to stand out. And that mindset is what turns professional development from something you do at specific times, like at a conference or a team training event, into something you do every day.

I started my career in consumer marketing, where I had to think about public relations from the standpoint of the customer. Every day I confronted different challenges and questions from a wide variety of clients. Some were big ... "how do we maximize an Olympic sponsorship?" ... and others were small ... "how do we get people to our spring fashion event?"

I was in my 20s. Nothing I had done professionally or lived personally prepared me for these tasks. But the willingness to dive in and do research, to ask a lot of questions, and to look at things from the perspective of the customer helped me succeed in this work – and, honestly, really enjoy it.

So when I got to Target in 2011, I had a great base of experience that had grown from consumer-driven challenges to crisis management and corporate affairs.

But in some ways joining the Target enterprise, with its scale and complexity, put me right back where I had started at the beginning of my career. It was at once exciting, overwhelming and, at times, frustrating. But I knew that if I let all I *didn't know* become the dominant narrative in my head, I'd never be able to do the work necessary to grow and advance in my career here.

So I took comfort in the fact that, while I had no experience with things like Generally Accepted Accounting Principles (GAAP), earnings per share (EPS), supply chains or commercial real estate development, *I knew how to learn about these things.*

For me, that meant doing a few basic things – many times a day:

- When I came across acronyms I didn't know or business initiatives I didn't understand, I made time to figure them out.

- When going through strategy slide decks, I didn't gloss over sentences. I'd force myself to go through them line-by-line and figure out how the pieces came together.

- And I studied other leaders and brands carefully, and expanded what I was reading and watching.

Almost a decade later, my commitment to learning is still a source of credibility. I can't deliver the high-quality counsel that Target's leaders need if I don't also have a solid grasp on their areas of the business – from merchandizing and marketing to public policy and investor relations.

I am still learning and I enjoy it. Whether you go from company to company, or stay in the same place for a while, there's no such thing as mastery in business. There is always some unknown event on the horizon, which will present a new challenge and an opportunity to learn and deliver for the people who count on you.

My career at Target alone is a great example of this. Every couple of years, Target has needed to adapt to major events – ranging from a data breach over the 2013 holiday season, to a total overhaul of our business strategy in 2017, to the COVID-19 crisis in 2020.

So while I'm not asking the same questions today as I did when I first started, I'm still asking a lot of questions and challenging myself to learn. Every day.

GLOSSARY

Accelerator — In an innovation context, an accelerator is typically an application-based, fixed-length program in which startup teams receive support to help develop and scale their business.

Accounting — The process of summarizing, analyzing, recording, and reporting business and financial transactions. The field of accounting is guided by detailed principles and procedures.

Accounts Payable — A line on the balance sheet that is a liability, this figure is money the company owes to a supplier for a good or service purchased, but for which has not yet been paid.

Accounts Receivable — A line on the balance sheet that is an asset, this figure is money owed to the company such as from the sale of a good or service for which funds have yet to be collected.

Accretive — In corporate finance, this refers to a business transaction, such as an acquisition, that leads to an increase in earnings for the acquiring company. The opposite of *dilutive*.

Acquisition-driven Growth — Business growth generated via *external* acquisition. This form of growth is distinct from organic business growth, driven through *internal* growth initiatives.

Actuary — A professional who uses analytical skills and business knowledge to find ways to manage risks. Actuaries largely work in insurance, financial organizations and multinational corporations.

Advertising Value Equivalence — AVE is a controversial media metric that attempts to place a financial value on earned media coverage based on the cost to buy ad space in that publication.

Agency Problem — Also known as "agency costs," this problem arises when the interests of an organization's board of directors and/or management diverge from that of its stakeholders.

Agency Holding Company — Many of the larger agencies and consultancies are owned by an agency holding company, which provides shared infrastructure and support services for its portfolio of agencies and consultancy brands.

Agency of Record (AOR) — The AOR refers to the communications agency selected by the client and responsible for taking the lead on providing a full range of ongoing services to the client.

Agency Search — The process of a client running a search to hire an agency or consultancy for a piece of work. Such a search may use a request for information and/or a request for proposal.

Agency Side — In a communication context, this term refers to professionals that work externally for an agency or consultancy rather than for the in-house department or team of a client.

Agency Theory — Theory that conceptualizes shareholders as the "principals" of an organization and the board of directors as the "agents" that act on behalf of shareholders in creating value.

Agenda Building Theory — A theory that explores the role of organizational information subsidies in influencing how information is used and interpreted by influencers and stakeholders.

Agenda Setting Theory — A theory that examines how the media's presentation of topics in the news over time focuses and shapes the public's perceptions of the world around them.

Agile — A term used to describe a mindset of values and principles set forth in the Agile Manifesto. Agile methods and approaches are widely used in information technology.

Agile Management — A management approach that incorporates the Agile mindset, values and principles. Agile management is associated with disruptive change, adaptation and innovation.

Agile Manifesto — A broad document created at an influential meeting of software developers and project managers in 2001 that outlined the original definitions of Agile values and principles.

Amortization — In corporate accounting, the deduction of capital expenses over the useful life of an intangible asset, such as a copyright, trademark, patent or other intellectual property.

Analyst/Investor Day — A half- or full-day event held at a company facility and/or virtually in which management provides the financial community with a detailed look at its business.

Analytics — A collection of numeric metrics or indicators that help track the performance of a communication campaign or program in meeting a stated objective or objectives.

Annual Meeting — A meeting held by a company typically after the end of its fiscal year. Many of these meetings are largely procedural with low in-person attendance, but there are exceptions.

Annual Report — Document published annually that reviews the company's performance in the prior year. This document typically includes a letter from the chief executive officer. May just be a 10-K wrap.

Applied Research — Research that is conducted by or on behalf of an organization to solve a business challenge or address an opportunity. This research may be proprietary and non-public.

Arthur W. Page — Served as the vice president of public relations for AT&T. The first public relations executive to serve as an officer and member of the board of a major public company.

Arthur W. Page Center for Integrity in Public Communications — A research center at Penn State University dedicated to the study of ethics and responsibility in public communication.

Arthur W. Page Society — Now often known simply as Page, this professional association for senior communicators has a mission of strengthening the enterprise leadership role of the chief communications officer.

Asset — A source of value for an organization. In a financial context, an asset is something that the organization owns or controls which is expected to contribute to the creation of future profits.

Association for Education in Journalism and Mass Communication (AEJMC) — Founded in 1912, AEJMC is the largest association of journalism and mass communication educators and students.

Balanced Scorecard — Strategic management approach popularized by Robert Kaplan and David Norton that gauges organizational performance using both financial and non-financial metrics.

Balance Sheet — This statement tracks a company's assets, liabilities and net worth on an accounting basis. It summarizes what a company owns and owes at the stated period in time.

Bankruptcy — A legal process in which an organization restructures its financial obligations to creditors (known as a Chapter 11) or liquidates its assets and shuts down (known as a Chapter 7).

The Barcelona Principles — A set of seven measurement principles agreed to at a meeting of communication measurement and evaluation experts held in Barcelona, Spain in summer 2010. The principles were updated in 2015 and 2020.

Baseline — Used in measurement and evaluation, a baseline is an initial measure of a campaign or program indicator that is used to assess future change in the performance of that indicator.

Basic Research — Research that is conducted with the primary purpose of developing theory and contributing to the general body of knowledge. Academicians often conduct basic research.

Basis Point — Also known as BPS, a basis point represents one $1/100^{th}$ (0.01%) of 1.0%. A unit used to track percentage changes in interest rates and bond yields. A 100 BPS equals 1.0%.

B Corp Certification — A certification awarded to for-profit firms by B Lab, a global non-profit organization, based on a review of the social and environmental performance of the business.

Bear Market — A market that is declining or expected to decline in value is said to be a "bear market." This phrase refers to the symbolism of a bear's claws pulling downward.

Bearish — An expression used to convey negativity about the overall stock market or a particular security. May also be used in a broader business context to convey negativity about something.

Behavioral Economics — Sub-field of economics which studies the effect of emotional factors and the seemingly "irrational" economic decisions made by individuals and organizations.

Behavioral Finance — Sub-field of finance which uses human and behavioral psychology to explain market behavior. Research in this field runs counter to the efficient market hypothesis.

Benefit Corporation — A type of for-profit corporate entity which explicitly states it has a broader purpose beyond privileging profits for investors, but rather making a material positive impact on society and the environment. Also known as a public benefit corporation.

Best Practice — In a communication measurement context, a method or technique that has consistently demonstrated superior results compared to using other approaches.

Billable Hours — The "bread and butter" still of many agency revenue models, the amount of billable time charged to the client for work performed based upon the agreed upon hourly rates.

Billing Rate — The hourly rate, also known as the billable rate, upon which a professional services firm such an agency charges the client for each level of staff that work on the account.

Blackout Period — The period around quarterly earnings reports in which company insiders cannot buy or sell shares of company stock. This limits the risk of insider trading charges.

Bloomberg News — A subsidiary of Bloomberg, L.P., Bloomberg News is one of the world's largest news agencies with news bureaus around the world and a focus on business news.

Bloomberg Terminal — This computer system is a high-end, real-time subscription-based data, news and information service focused on financial professionals. Competing products include Eikon, FactSet, and Capital IQ.

Blue Chip Company — A company with a high credit rating that has generated strong and predictable financial performance for years, if not decades, is said to be a "blue chip" company.

Board of Advisors — A group that provides informal, non-binding advice to an organization's management. A board of advisors does not have the fiduciary obligations of a board of directors.

Board of Directors — In a public company, the board of directors is elected by the company's shareholders to provide oversight and guidance to the company's senior management.

Boardroom — Besides being the physical room in which a board of directors meet, this term refers to the directors of a company or organization when considered collectively.

Bond — Generally considered safer than stocks, a bond is a form of debt that pays interest to the holder. Unless a convertible bond, a bond does *not* represent an ownership interest in a firm.

Bonus — In the context of compensation, an additional payment added to wages, above and beyond the normal payment expectations, as a reward for achieving good performance.

Book Value — The stated net asset value of a company as carried on a company's accounting balance sheet (aka "the books"). Many intangible assets are not accounted for in this figure.

Bottom Line — Refers to an organization's net income. The name "bottom line" comes from the fact that net income is generally a line near the bottom of an organization's income statement.

Breakup Fee — This is a fee that an acquiring company agrees to pay the to-be-acquired company if the transaction is not approved or the acquirer decides to back out of the agreement.

Warren Buffett — Known as "the Oracle of Omaha," Buffett, the chief executive officer of Berkshire-Hathaway, is regarded as one of the greatest investors of the century; also co-created "The Giving Pledge."

Bull Market — A market that is rising or expected to rise in value is said to be a "bull market." This phrase refers to the symbolism of a bull thrusting its horns upward (i.e., a rising market).

Bullish — An expression used to convey optimism about the overall stock market or a particular security. May also be used in a broader business context to convey optimism about something.

Burn Rate — Also called the "cash burn," this is the rate at which a money-losing organization spends its cash on hand and other readily available assets over a certain time period (e.g., monthly or quarterly) to cover its operating expenses.

Harold Burson — Called the most influential public relations (PR) leader of the twentieth century, the late Burson was the founder of Burson-Marsteller, now known as BCW, one of the world's largest PR agencies.

Business Acumen — In a strategic communication context, business acumen means becoming knowledgeable about business functions, stakeholders and markets that are critical to organizational success; using this understanding to assess business matters through a communications lens; and providing informed strategic recommendations and actions.

Business Literacy — The ability to understand the vocabulary and language of business. May also be referred to as business fluency or business IQ. Foundational to developing business acumen.

Business Marketing Association (BMA) — Founded in 1922, BMA is a national association of business-to-business marketing and communications professionals.

Business Model — A brief explanation of how an organization provides a solution to a customer problem, thereby creating value for the organization's stakeholders, including generating sustainable profits, and the factors that influence this value creation process.

Business-to-Business — B-to-B, also written as B2B, refers to a business that primarily markets and sells its products or services to other businesses as its customers rather than to consumers.

Business-to-Consumer — B-to-C, also written as B2C, refers to a business that primarily markets and sells its products or services to consumers rather than to other businesses.

Buyout — A term used in mergers and acquisitions which occurs when one firm acquires a controlling interest or completes a full takeover (i.e., purchase) of another company.

Calendar Year — The 12 month period running from the beginning of January until the end of December. Many companies choose to set their fiscal year schedule to the calendar year.

Capital — Money, property and other assets of value that serve as the lifeblood of any organization. Investors provide capital to organizations with the goal of generating a profit.

Capital Expenditure — Also known as "CapEx," funds spent on buying or improving fixed, physical, long-term assets such as property, plants, and equipment to generate future value.

Capital Markets — Includes the stock market and the bond market. This is where organizations go to raise capital and where buyers and sellers trade securities like stocks and bonds.

Capitalism — An economic system based on the private ownership by businesses and individuals of the means of production. A criticism of capitalism is that it privileges owners and investors.

Capitalized — Under accounting rules, an expenditure is capitalized if the item's useful life is believed to be longer than a year. Capitalized costs are amortized or depreciated over time.

Carbon Footprint — The amount of greenhouse gases, often specifically carbon dioxide (CO_2) emissions, associated with an individual, group, or company during a given period of time. More companies and organizations are setting long-term "net zero" carbon emission goals.

Andrew Carnegie — Late nineteenth century industrialist and philanthropist who wrote the "Gospel of Wealth" in which he urged the wealthy to devote their resources to bettering society.

Case Study — A research approach that relies upon multiple sources of data to study a topic. This may include both quantitative and qualitative data sources as well as primary and secondary data.

Cash Flow Statement — This statement literally "follows the money" and shows the amount of cash generated or spent by an organization in its course of business over the stated time period.

Cause Marketing — A form of marketing in which a company partners with a non-profit organization and agrees to donate a portion of sales to the cause supported by the non-profit.

C Corporation — A C Corp, the default or standard corporation type under Internal Revenue Service (IRS) rules, is a legal structure for a firm in which the profits of the business are taxed at both the corporate and personal levels. Many large corporations are structured as C Corps.

CEO Activism — Public engagement by a chief executive officer (CEO) in political or social issues that do not necessarily directly relate to the company's business. The CEO may use public forums such as social media.

Chair — Also known as the chairperson, chairwoman, or chairman, the chair of the board serves as the leader of the organization's board of directors. The chair serves as a key conduit between the board and senior management.

Change Management Communication — Strategic communication focused on change management: the process, tools, and techniques to manage the people side of change initiatives.

Chief Communications Officer (CCO) — The senior most communication executive in an organization, the CCO is tasked with leading the organization's communication function and advising leaders.

Chief Corporate Affairs Officer (CCAO) — The CCAO is a senior executive responsible for leading the corporate affairs of an organization. This title may be instead of chief communications officer.

Chief Digital Officer (CDO) — A relatively new C-level title only appearing in some organizations, the CDO is often responsible for driving organizational transformations around digital technologies.

Chief Diversity Officer (CDO) — A relatively new C-level title, the CDO is the executive responsible for leading an organization's diversity, equity and inclusion (DE&I) efforts.

Chief Executive Officer (CEO) — The CEO is the top executive in an organization's C-suite, tasked with setting and implementing firm strategy. The CEO often sits on the company's board of directors.

Chief Financial Officer (CFO) — A member of the C-suite, the CFO is increasingly tasked with not just overseeing an organization's finances, but other executive level functions like firm strategy.

Chief Human Resources Officer (CHRO) — A member of the C-suite, the CHRO is a senior executive responsible for leading the human resources function and matters of the organization.

Chief Information Officer (CIO) — A member of the C-suite, the CIO is a senior executive often responsible for leading the *internal* information technology efforts of the organization.

Chief Legal Officer (CLO) — A member of the C-suite, the CLO, also known as the General Counsel, is responsible for leading the legal affairs of the organization and provides counsel to leadership.

Chief Marketing Officer (CMO) — The senior most marketing executive in an organization, the CMO is tasked with leading the organization's marketing function and advising leaders in the C-suite.

Chief Operating Officer (COO) — A member of the C-suite, the COO is tasked with the day-to-day management of an organization's operations. This person may also carry the title of president.

Chief Technology Officer (CTO) — A member of the C-suite, the CTO is a senior executive often responsible for leading the organization's *external-facing* information technology efforts.

Classified Board — For companies that have a classified or "staggered" board of directors, all directors do not come up for shareholder vote annually, but rather over a multi-year period.

Clawback Provision — A provision included in an employment contract which allows the company to "clawback" previously paid compensation upon certain circumstances occurring.

Closely Held — A closely held company refers to the fact that a company only has a small number of shareholders and is likely privately owned. The opposite would be a public company.

Commission on Public Relations Education — With representatives from across industry and academia, the commission provides research-based recommendations for public relations education.

Common Stock — Security that represents an ownership interest in a firm and holds voting rights. In the event of a liquidation, creditors and preferred holders get paid before common holders.

Communist Party of China (CPC) — The CPC, also referred to as the Chinese Community Party, is the founding and governing political party of the People's Republic of China and controls many of the state-owned companies in China.

Company Insider — As defined by US federal securities laws, company insiders are executive officers, members of the board of directors, large shareholders, and potentially outside advisors.

Consensus Analyst Estimate — This figure is based on the combined estimates of investment analysts covering a public company. Such estimates are made on a quarterly and annual basis.

Consent Solicitation — Some public companies allow corporate actions to be taken outside of the annual meeting format if a written consent solicitation receives majority shareholder support.

Consumer Confidence — Survey-based measures of how the public feels about current and future economic performance. Consumer confidence can be predictive of future economic behavior.

Consumer Price Index (CPI) — A popular gauge of the rate of inflation. The US CPI measures changes in the average value of a basket of goods and services purchased by urban households.

Content analysis — A research method that may be quantitative or qualitative depending upon the approach. The analysis of the frequency and contents of textual and image-based messages.

Corner office — An office located in the corner of a building, which typically has two windows, and are often given to senior executives. This term is used to refer collectively to the C-suite.

Corporate character — The unique, differentiating identity of the enterprise. The major elements of corporate character: brand stewardship, corporate culture, and societal value.

Corporate conscience — The role of strategic communication professionals, such as the chief communications officer, as the ethics counsel to organizations, helping to guide ethical decisions and behaviors.

Corporate disclosure — The communication of timely information, particularly involving any material changes, about a company that may influence an investor's decision-making about the firm's securities. The Securities and Exchange Commission enforces disclosure requirements for US public companies.

Corporate finance — Concerned with the raising and managing of funds (i.e., capital) with the goal of maximizing value for stakeholders, particularly shareholder and investor interests.

Corporate gadfly — Individual investor that attempts to affect change at public companies. Pioneering gadflies have included the Gilbert brothers and Evelyn Davis among others.

Corporate governance — The system of "checks and balances" that attempts to make boards of directors and management more accountable and better aligned with stakeholder interests.

Corporate officer — A member of the C-suite, this is one of the senior most executives in a corporation who is responsible for the day-to-day leadership and management of the company.

Corporate philanthropy — The charitable donations of profits and resources by corporations to non-profit organizations. Such donations may be made through a corporate foundation.

Corporate purpose — The fundamental reason for which a corporation exists and what it does to create value for its stakeholders, beyond simply generating profits for the corporation's investors.

Corporate reputation — An overall assessment of a company by its stakeholders using a company's various dimensions as the evaluative criteria. The attitude held toward a firm.

Corporate Social Advocacy (CSA) — CSA is the act of a firm intentionally or even unintentionally aligning with a controversial social–political issue outside its normal sphere or corporate social responsibility interest.

Corporate Social Responsibility (CSR) — CSR is voluntary actions taken by a firm to fulfill perceived obligations that go beyond maximizing profits, and following laws, rules, and regulations.

Cost of Capital — A concept in corporate finance, cost of capital is the cost of obtaining funds to grow a business. Generally speaking, a lower cost of capital helps improve profitability.

Cost of Goods Sold — Also known as "COGS" or "COS" (for cost of sales), these are the *direct* costs that go into producing a good or service. Indirect costs are excluded from this figure.

Council of Institutional Investors (CII) — Founded in 1985, CII is a non-profit association of investment funds with combined assets of $4 trillion dollars that is a driving force in corporate governance.

Council of Public Relations Firms — With more than 100 public relations agencies as members, the Council advocates for and advances the business of public relations firms.

Co-working Space — An open office space and shared infrastructure that encourages the collaboration of ideas and expertise among a community of people, such as entrepreneurs.

Credit — Entered on the right-hand side of an accounting ledger, a credit entry is made to record changes in value due to a business transaction. A debit is the opposite of a credit.

Crowdfunding — The process of raising small amounts of money through a large number of people (i.e., a crowd). Popular crowdfunding platforms include Kickstarter and GoFundMe.

C-suite — The group of C-level executives (e.g., chief financial officer, president, and chief financial officer) that comprise the senior leadership team within an organization. These are the leaders in "the room where it happens."

Cumulative voting — At some public companies, shareholders have the right to pool their votes all for one director nominee, thereby amplifying the voice of minority shareholders in elections.

Currency exchange rate — The rate at which one currency will be exchanged for another. Exchange rates fluctuate based on shifts in the economic conditions of the various countries.

Dun & Bradstreet (D&B) Hoover's — A subsidiary of D&B, Hoover's is the world's largest commercial database of 120 million business records and industry specific information.

Debit — Entered on the left-hand side of an accounting ledger, a debit entry is made to record changes in value due to a business transaction. A debit is the opposite of a credit.

Debt — A bond, loan note, mortgage, or other obligation, which states repayment terms on borrowed money and, if applicable, the interest owed as a condition of the borrowed money.

Declassified Board — A board of directors in which all board of director seats come up for vote annually rather than a classified board where there is a staggering of terms for directors' seats.

Delphi Panel Method — A research method developed by the Rand Corporation originally for forecasting, which seeks to build consensus on a subject among a panel of subject matter experts.

Deflation — The opposite of inflation. Deflation is when prices for goods and services decline. Deflation leads to consumers delaying purchases and the value of assets declining.

Depreciation — In corporate accounting, the deduction of capital expenses over the useful life of a tangible asset, such as fixtures, equipment, vehicles, buildings, and improvements.

Depreciation and Amortization — Also known as D&A, these related "non-cash" expenses on the income statement take into account the wear and tear of assets over the life of the asset.

Depression — A severe, long-term downturn in the economy. A depression is a deeper downtown than a recession. The most well-known US depression is the Great Depression of the 1930s.

Depth Interview — A qualitative research technique in which a researcher conducts a detailed interview with a subject one participant at a time. Also known as a one-on-one interview.

Diffusion of Innovation Theory — Theory that seeks to explain how, why, and at what rate innovations are communicated through certain channels over time through a social system.

Dilutive — In corporate finance, this refers to a business transaction, such as an acquisition, that leads to a decrease in earnings for the acquiring company. The opposite of *accretive*.

Direct Listing — Also known as a direct public offering, a direct listing is a lower-cost way to become a public company without going through the traditional initial public offering process.

Dividend — The distribution of some of a company's earnings to its shareholders, as determined by the board of directors. Dividends may be paid out as cash or the issuance of additional stock.

Disclosures — In an organizational and communication context, the release of organizational information that aids stakeholders in decision-making and reduces information asymmetry.

Disruption — In the context of disruptive innovation, a disruption is a major innovation that creates a new market and value network, displacing market-leading firms, products, and alliances.

Diversity, Equity, and Inclusion — Known as DE&I or DEI, this is a term used to describe programs, policies, and initiatives that encourage greater diversity, equity, and inclusion.

DocuSign® — A cloud-based electronic signature technology platform that allows you to legally sign documents, such as contracts, tax documents, and legal materials, virtually.

The Dodd–Frank Wall Street Reform and Consumer Protection — Passed in 2010 in the wake of taxpayer-funded bailouts of Wall Street, this landmark legislation tightened and placed new regulations over corporations, particularly those operating in the financial services sector.

Dow Jones Industrial Average (DJIA) — Often known as simply "the Dow," the DJIA is a widely followed stock market index comprised of 30 very large, well-known US public companies.

Dual Class Stock — A type of ownership structure in place at some companies in which there are two or more classes of stock with one class having greater voting rights than the others.

Earnings — Terminology usually used with public companies, refers to the amount of money a company made or lost over a set time period. Earnings are the same at net income or net profits.

Earnings Before Interest, Taxes, Depreciation, and Amortization (EBITDA) — EBITDA is a measure of an organization's *operating* profitability. This measure excludes the impact of financing decisions, accounting decisions, or tax environment. An alternative to EBITDA is EBIT.

Earnings Call — Generally held quarterly, a conference call at which company management discusses the company's latest financial performance and takes questions from investors.

Earnings Guidance — Informational disclosures specifically focused on conveying expectations about future company earnings performance to investors. The contents and level of specificity of these forward-looking statements may vary widely.

Earnings Per Share (EPS) — EPS is a measure of earnings or profits. EPS is calculated by dividing the net income (i.e., net earnings) of a company by its number of shares outstanding.

Earnings Release — A news release, typically distributed over a paid wire service, which reports the company's quarterly financial performance. The release may also include earnings guidance.

Earnout — A contractual agreement where the seller of a business will obtain additional future compensation if the acquired business achieves certain predetermined financial goals.

Economic Cycle — Economies go through natural periods of growth followed by decline and then growth again. This process of expansion and contraction is known as an economic cycle.

Economics — The study of the cause-and-effect relationships in an economy. While often now housed and taught in business schools around the world, economics is actually a social science.

Economists — Study the consequences of decisions that people make about the use of land, labor, capital, and other resources that go into producing the products that are bought and sold.

Economy — The total aggregate sum of all goods and services produced among market participants. An economy may be studied at a local, regional, national, or even international level.

EDGAR — All US public company disclosure documents are required to be made with the US Securities and Exchange Commission's EDGAR system. The full name is Electronic Data-Gathering, Analysis and Retrieval.

Employee Activism — The act of employees organizing and speaking out for or against their employer to bring about political or social change in the workplace and beyond.

Employment Report — Regular reports, often issued by government agencies, providing data on the state of employment and the employment rate for a particular region, such as a country.

Enterprise Value — This comprehensive valuation measure is the sum of the company's market capitalization (common stock) plus debt, any preferred stock, and minority interest, minus cash.

Environmental Scanning — The process of monitoring the environment in which organizations and clients operate for issues, trends, and factors which may impact future organizational decisions.

Environmental, Social, and Governance (ESG) — ESG refers to the various policies, disclosures, and behaviors that comprise an organization's environmental, societal, and governance performance.

Equity — A stock or other security that represents an underlying ownership interest in a company. More broadly, equity refers to ownership in an asset after all debts have been paid.

Equity Ownership Model — A form of compensation in which an agency or consultancy provides services to a client for a reduced fee in returning for earning an equity ownership stake in the client's business.

Ethics — A system or set of moral values or principles. As a discipline, ethics is a branch of philosophy concerned with what is morally good and bad and morally right and wrong.

Ethnography — Drawing from anthropology, a qualitative research technique in which the researcher observes, and potentially interacts with, participants in an area of their everyday lives.

Exchange Traded Fund (ETF) — An ETF is an investment fund that is bought and sold on an exchange like an individual stock, but which tracks the performance of a pool of securities or other assets.

Executive Committee — Also called the executive management committee or simply the management committee, this group comprises the most senior executives in an organization.

Exit, Voice, Loyalty — Framework developed by Albert Hirschman that explains how individuals will engage in either "exit" or "voice" when faced with declining quality in a relationship.

Expense — A cost that an organization incurs to generate revenue. This includes production, labor, leases, supplies, financing, and administration. Expenses are the opposite of revenue.

Expensed — Under accounting rules, an expenditure in which the total cost of the item is incurred all at once on the income statement. No amortization or depreciation is allowed.

Experimental Design — A quantitative research method that relies upon the manipulation and control of variables in a laboratory-like setting to establish causation between variables.

Federal Open Market Committee (FOMC) — The FOMC is an influential committee within the Federal Reserve System that makes decisions about monetary policy, including setting the fed funds rate.

Federal Reserve — Created in 1913 by the US Congress, the Federal Reserve is the central bank of the United States. The Fed sets monetary policy with a goal of full employment and stable prices.

Fee-based Work — Also known as fee-based income, this billing model charges clients fees based on the amount of time and number of employees working on the account, as well as the scope of the business that the agency handles. This labor and expertise fee-based model is prevalent across the professional services landscape.

Fiduciary — The highest legal and ethical duties of one party to another, a fiduciary is a person or organization that is bound to act in the other's best interest, rather than by self interests.

Fiduciary Duties — When referenced in the context of governance, this refers to the legal duties or obligations that directors have to act in the best interest of the organization's stakeholders.

Financial Accounting Standards Board (FASB) — FASB is an independent private organization which sets the generally accepted accounting principles for US financial reporting.

Financial Industry Regulatory Authority (FINRA) — The successor to the National Association of Securities Dealers, FINRA acts as a self-regulatory organization for financial securities firms that do business in the United States.

Financial Asset — Assets such as stocks, bonds, and cash that lack a physical embodiment, but are not considered intangibles since they basically represent claims on organizational assets.

Financial Communication — A specialty area of strategic communication concerned with communicating financial matters to the financial community and other stakeholders.

Financial Communication Society (FCS) — Founded in 1967, FCS is an association of financial services marketing and communication professionals. Chapters are in major financial center cities.

Financial Statements — Documents that state the financial health of an organization. The most well-known of these statements are the income statement, balance sheet, and cash flow statement.

Fiscal Year — The 12-month period that marks one full year of operations and financial reporting for an organization. Many organizations have a fiscal year that is the same as the calendar year.

Focus Group — A qualitative research approach in which a moderator leads a semi-structured discussion with a group of participants that is recorded and then later analyzed.

Fortune 500 — Compiled annually by Fortune magazine, this widely-followed list ranks America's largest companies by annual revenue. Together, these firms represent roughly two-thirds of the US economy.

Full-service Agency — This term refers to an agency that provides a full range of services and solutions to clients, rather than a specialty agency focused on a particular specialization area.

Charles Fombrun — Leading scholar on corporate reputation, founded Reputation Institute and led the development of the Reputation Quotient® and RepTrak® corporate reputation measures.

Form 4 — This document is required to be filed with the US Securities and Exchange Commission's EDGAR system whenever there are changes in an insider's ownership (i.e., a purchase or sale) of company securities.

Form 8-K — This document is required to be filed with the US Securities and Exchange Commission's EDGAR system whenever a material current event occurs in between a periodic report (i.e., 10-Qs and 10-K).

Form 990 — Most tax-exempt organizations must file this form annually with the Internal Revenue Service (IRS). This form's content is available to the public and discloses the organization's financial information.

Form 10-K — This document is required to be filed with the US Securities and Exchange Commission's EDGAR system. The 10-K reports a company's annual results and forms the foundation for a firm's annual report.

Form 10-Q — This document is required to be filed with the US Securities and Exchange Commission's EDGAR system. The 10-Q reports a company's quarterly results. Unlike the 10-K, these financials are *unaudited*.

Form S-1 — Also known as a prospectus, this registration document is required to be filed with the US Securities and Exchange Commission's EDGAR system and is used by companies that are planning to go public.

FORTUNE Most Admired Companies — Launched by FORTUNE in 1982, this annual list was the first attempt at measuring and ranking the reputations of America's largest companies.

Forward-looking Statement — A statement made by a company about future expectations and performance (i.e., earnings guidance). Safe-harbor language should accompany such a statement.

R. Edward Freeman — Business philosopher that is most closely associated with stakeholder theory, the concept of stakeholders, and the moral responsibility the firm has to stakeholders.

Milton Friedman — A winner of the Nobel Prize in Economic Sciences, this free market economist is most closely associated with shareholder theory and shareholder primacy.

Furlough — A temporary unpaid leave of absence in which an employee retains their position and sometimes retains their benefits. A furlough can become permanent and turn into a layoff.

Futures Contract — A standardized agreement where both parties agree to buy and sell an asset, such as a physical commodity, of a specified quantity at a specified future date and price.

General and Administrative Expenses — Also known as "G&A," these are expenses related to the day-to-day operations of a firm rather than expenses related to the direct production of goods.

General Counsel — Also known as the chief legal officer, this member of the C-suite is the senior most legal professional in an organization and heads up all legal affairs related matters.

Generally Accepted Accounting Principles (GAAP) — Set by the Financial Accounting Standards Board, GAAP are principles that help guide and provide consistency in US financial reporting.

General Data Protection Regulation (GDPR) — GDPR concerns the personal data of European Union (EU) citizens, wherever that data are held. If an organization is not based in the EU but has customers (or suppliers or other parties) within the EU whose data you hold, the GDPR applies.

Glass, Lewis & Co. — Founded in 2003 and owned by the Ontario Teachers' Pension Plan Board (OTPP) and Alberta Investment Management Corp., this organization is a provider of proxy advisory services and shareholder voting recommendations to institutional investors.

Global Reporting Initiative (GRI) — GRI is a non-profit organization that develops and promotes one of the most widely used sustainability reporting standards and frameworks for corporate social responsibility reporting.

GMI Ratings — A research firm that provides advisory services to institutional investors on environmental, social, and governance-related issues to help them manage risk.

Goal — A general statement rooted in the organization's mission and vision, stating what the organization intends to achieve; a goal tells stakeholders "*where* it is trying to go."

Golden Handcuffs — Special incentives provided to top executives that encourage them to remain with a company and not to go to work for a competitor.

Golden Parachute — An agreement, typically with a top executive, that the individual will receive certain significant benefits upon termination, often following a change in control.

Al Golin — The late founder of the global public relations agency GOLIN, owned by holding company IPG, Golin was the originator of the "trust bank" concept in which firms build up deposits of goodwill through giving back.

Goodwill — In a corporate accounting context, an asset that is based on the amount paid for a company over its stated book value. This figure places a value on the acquired firm's intangibles.

The Great Depression — Severe worldwide economic depression that started in 1930 for at least a decade. In the United States, the Great Depression sparked the first wave of federal securities laws.

Greenhouse Gases (GHGs) — GHGs are gases that trap heat in the atmosphere, such as carbon dioxide (CO_2), methane (CH_4), nitrous oxide (N_2O), and fluorinated gases. GHGs have far-ranging environmental and health effects, and contribute to climate change.

Greenwashing — Derogatory term for when a company is perceived as spending more resources promoting and touting sustainable business practices than actually engaging in such behaviors.

Gross Domestic Product (GDP) — GDP is a widely followed economic indicator of a country or region's economic health. GDP represents the market value of all goods produced over a certain period.

Gross Profit — Also called gross income, gross profit is a company's revenue minus its cost of goods sold. In other words, it is how much money is left over after deducting the direct expenses.

Guidance — The widespread practice of public companies attempting to improve transparency and manage investor expectations by releasing forecasts about future company performance.

Hedge Fund — A type of private investment fund that manages capital for high worth individuals and institutions. Hedge funds have traditionally faced less regulation than mutual funds.

Historical Analysis — A qualitative research method that seeks to learn from and about the past through the collection and analysis of historical artifacts related to the topic of study.

Hostile Takeover — The purchase of one company by another company that is accomplished by going directly to the target company's shareholders, rather than by coming to agreement with the target company's management.

Human Capital — Term that recognizes that an organization's employees are a key source of future benefits. Human capital is typically viewed as a specific type of intangible asset.

Imperfect Information — In an economics context, situations in which one party to a transaction has superior information than the other party, resulting in negative pricing and other actions.

Income Per Diluted Share — The value of earnings per share of a public company, assuming investors exercise all of the firm's convertible securities by turning them into common stock.

Income Statement — Also known as a profit and loss statement, this statement tracks how much money an organization made or lost, and spent, on an accounting basis for the stated time period.

Incubator — In a startup company context, an incubator is an entity that provides infrastructure, resources, and expertise that help to "incubate" and grow startup companies and innovations.

Independent Director — Also known as an outside director, this is an individual who is not an employee of the company and does not have a material relationship with the company.

Index Fund — A type of low cost investment product that tracks the performance of an index, such as the Standard & Poor's 500, the Dow Jones Industrial Average, or the NASDAQ Composite.

Individual Investor — A small private, non-professional investor that typically buys small blocks of stock when making investments. Individual investors are sometimes known as retail investors.

Inflation — The opposite of deflation. Inflation is when the prices for goods and services increase. Inflation decreases the value of money and reduces its purchasing power.

Information Asymmetry — A gap that occurs when one party to a potential transaction (i.e., the insider) is in possession of more and better information than the other party (i.e., the outsider).

Information Intermediary — Any entity that reports, interprets, and analyzes information for broader consumption. In corporate finance, this includes financial journalists and analysts.

Information Subsidy — Organizational communication vehicles and pre-packaged materials that lower the cost of information thereby increasing consumption by influencers and stakeholders.

In-house Agency — The concept of the in-house strategic communication department of an organization functioning and serving its internal clients like an internal agency of record.

In-house Side — In a communication context, this term refers to professionals that work internally for an organization's communication function rather than external or the agency side.

Initial Public Offering (IPO) — An IPO marks the first time that a company sells stock to the public and its shares are listed on a stock exchange and widely available for purchase by investors.

Innovation — A product, service, process, or practice that offers *significant* new value in solving problems for adopters, whether they be customers, employees, or other stakeholders.

Invention — Usually something which has not previously been in existence often originating from study or experiment into a problem. An innovation does not need to be an invention.

Insider Trading — The illegal practice of a company insider (i.e., executive or director), consultant, or related party trading on and profiting from non-public, material information.

Institute for Public Relations (IPR) — Founded in 1956, IPR is based at the University of Florida and is an independent non-profit foundation dedicated to the science beneath the art of public relations.

Institutional Investor — A professional investor, such as a mutual fund, hedge fund, pension fund, or endowment, that typically buys large blocks of stock when making investments.

Institutional Shareholder Services (ISS) — ISS, a portfolio company of Genstar Capital, is a provider of proxy advisory services and shareholder voting recommendations to institutional investors.

Intangible Asset — An asset that provides a source of future benefits, but lacks a direct physical embodiment. Examples include a firm's intellectual property, reputations, and relationships.

Integrated Reporting — A "one report" approach to company reporting in which financial and non-financial performance metrics are presented in a format conducive to all stakeholders.

Intellectual Property — A class of intangible assets that is generally the result of research and development activities. This includes patents, trademarks, copyrights, and trade secrets.

Interest Rate — The rate at which interest is paid by people or organizations to borrow money from lenders, such as banks. The Federal Reserve and other central banks impact interest rates.

International Accounting Standards Board (IASB) — The IASB is an independent body that is responsible for developing the International Financial Reporting Standards used around the world.

International Association for the Measurement and Evaluation of Communication (AMEC) — Founded in London in 1996, AMEC is a global trade group that played a lead role in the establishment of The Barcelona Declaration of Measurement Principles and other standards.

International Association of Business Communicators (IABC) — An association of approximately 15,000 business communication professionals located in over 80 countries.

International Communication Association (ICA) — Founded in 1950, ICA is an academic association for communication scholars with more than 4,500 members in 80 countries.

International Financial Reporting Standards (IFRS) — The IFRS accounting standards are overseen by the International Accounting Standards Board and are used in more than 100 countries.

Investment Bank — Financial organization that helps a company go public, sell stock or bonds, and advise it on financial transactions, such as mergers, acquisitions, or divestitures.

Investment Conference — Typically organized by an investment bank, public companies are invited to make a presentation to professional investors and analysts. Often is webcast.

Investor Relations (IR) — IR is a function in most public companies that serves as the primary interface for relationship building between the financial community, such as shareholders, and the company.

Islamic Finance — Also called Islamic banking or Shariah-compliant finance, refers to finance or banking activities that adhere to Shariah (Islamic law). Financial institutions need to follow Shariah when operating in Islamic countries and/or serving Islamic customers.

Jawboning — The planned, purposeful use of statements by government actors, such as the Federal Reserve, to try to influence economic behavior and conditions in the financial markets.

Jumpstart Our Business Startups Act — Passed in 2012 and known as the JOBS Act, this legislation loosened securities regulations on smaller companies and helped promote growth.

Kanban — A method used for knowledge work that was originally inspired by the original lean manufacturing system. Kanban also shares values and principles with the agile mindset.

Key Performance Indicator (KPI) — A KPI is a measure designed to gauge the performance of an organization or business unit at advancing or achieving a stated strategy, goal, or objective.

Lead Director — Also called a "presiding director," the lead director presides over meetings of the independent directors of the board; this position's level of power varies by company.

Lean — A set of manufacturing principles and practices that emphasize minimizing waste and constant improvement. Lean was adapted to software development and helped to inspire agile.

Leveraged Buyout (LBO) — LBO is typically associated with "going private" transactions and private equity firms. An LBO involves the use of a mix of debt and equity to acquire a company.

Liability — The opposite of an asset, a liability is an obligation that an organization takes on during the course of business, such as debt, accounts payable, or future incomes taxes payable.

Liquidity — A concept in corporate finance, liquidity is concerned with the ability to buy and sell a security, such as a stock, quickly and at a low cost with a limited effect on the market price.

Macroeconomics — Concerned with the study of the economy as a whole. Assesses the economy at a *macro-level* and studies the interactions of its various market participants.

Majority Voting — In the context of board of director elections, majority voting stipulates a director must receive majority shareholder support or otherwise tender their resignation.

Management, Discussion, and Analysis (MD&A) — MD&A is section of a company's proxy statement in which management discusses the company's prior year performance and discusses future plans.

Market Capitalization — Also known as "market cap," this valuation measure is calculated by multiplying the company stock price times the total number of shares of stock outstanding.

Market-to-Book Ratio — A valuation ratio calculated by taking a public company's total market capitalization and dividing it by the company's accounting book value (i.e., net asset value).

Market Maker — Specialists that stand ready to buy and sell a particular stock on a regular basis at the publicly quoted price. Market makers are essential to the functioning of stock exchanges.

MBA — The Master's in Business Administration is the most widely recognized graduate degree produced by business schools. Reportedly the first school to offer an MBA was Harvard University.

Material Information — In a public company context, information is considered *material* if a typical investor would likely view such information as important in affecting their investment decision-making. May also be referred to as *materiality*.

Media Clipping — Also known as a media placement or hit. The term goes back to when strategic communicators would "clip" articles and maintain records of media coverage in clip books.

Media Impressions — The maximum size of an audience that might have been exposed to a communication message as the result of a placement. Based on the publication's circulation size.

Media Placement — Also known as a hit or a clip. A placement is a news item or story that is attributed to strategic communication efforts, such as interactions with a journalist or influencer.

Metric — An informal term for a campaign or program measure or indicator. More specifically, a numeric value that should help determine whether a stated objective is being met.

Mezzanine Loan — A type of loan that generally includes both debt and equity financing. This type of financing sits between senior debt and equity in the capital structure of an organization.

Microeconomics — Concerned with the study of individual firms and households. Approaches economics from a *micro-level*, assessing the economic decisions of specific organizations.

Mission — A brief description that clarifies an organization's purpose: why it exists and what its goals are. The organizational mission may be codified in a written mission statement.

Mixed methods — A research approach in which multiple research techniques, specifically both quantitative methods and qualitative methods, are used to study and evaluate a topic of interest.

Moore's Law — The principle of exponential growth. In essence, Intel co-founder Gordon Moore posited that the speed and capability of computers can be expected to double every two years.

Multiple-step Flow Theory — Also known as the two-step flow theory, identifies the role of opinion leaders in the spread of information from the mass media to the general public.

Multipliers — The disputed notion that earned media coverage is worth more than or a "multiple of" paid advertising space in the same publication. Often used with ad value equivalencies.

Mutual Fund — A professionally managed investment fund that pools money from many people and invests it in a portfolio of stocks, bonds, and/or other assets. Investors buy shares in mutual funds. Each share represents an investors part ownership in the fund and its portfolio.

NASDAQ — Founded in 1971, the NASDAQ is the second largest stock exchange in the United States and the world, behind only the New York Stock Exchange. The NASDAQ is owned by the NASDAQ OMX Group.

National Investor Relations Institute — Founded in 1969 and based in the United States, it is the world's largest professional association of corporate investor relations officers and consultants.

Negative Equity — Also known as negative shareholders' equity, this occurs when total liabilities exceed total assets at a company. This indicates the firm may have trouble funding its operations.

Net Income — Also known as net profit, net earnings, or the "bottom line," this figure shows how much money a firm made after taking into account both operating and *non*-operating expenses.

Net Margin — A ratio of profitability calculated as net income or net profit divided by *all* expenses (both operating- and non-operating expenses, such as interest and taxes).

Net Revenue — Also known as net sales, this is the amount of revenue generated after the deduction of returns, allowances for damaged or missing goods, or any discounts allowed.

New York Stock Exchange (NYSE) — Also known as "the Big Board," the NYSE is the oldest and largest stock exchange in the world. The NYSE is operated by NYSE Euronext.

Non-deal Road Show — A series of meetings held in various financial center cities and/or virtually in which company management meets with current and prospective large shareholders.

Non-financial Information — Information that companies are generally not required to disclose, but which provides insights into the management and performance of intangible assets.

Non-governmental Organization (NGO) — An NGO is an organization that operates independently of government and has a mission committed to advancing environmental or social issues.

Non-organic Growth — In a business context, "non-organic" refers to business growth that is generated through acquisitions rather than through ownership of existing business operations.

Non-random Sample — A sample in which every member of a target population *does not* have an equal chance of being selected. Also known as a non-probability sample.

Objectives — Specific statements emerging from a goal presented in clear, measurable, realistic, and time-bounded terms; tells us "how we will know *if* and *when* we have gotten there."

Open Outcry — Also called pit trading, this form of trading relies on verbal bids, offers, and hand signals, unlike electronic trading which is fully computerized. The New York Stock Exchange still has open outcry.

Operating Income — Also called operating profit or income from operations, this figure shows how much money a firm made or lost after taking into account all of its operating expenses.

Operating Margin — A ratio of profitability calculated as operating income or operating profit divided by net revenue. This measure does not take into account non-operating expenses.

Options Contract — A contract that offers the buyer the right – but not the obligation – to buy ("call") or sell ("put") a security at a specified future date and price during a certain time period.

Organic Growth — In a business context, "organic" refers to growth that is generated *internally* via a company's existing operations rather than growth through *external* acquisitions.

Outcome — The most sophisticated level of evaluation; measures the establishment, change, or reinforcement in stakeholders' opinions, attitudes, or behaviors based on campaign messages.

Output — The most basic level of evaluation; measures the distribution of and possible exposure to campaign messages by stakeholders. Media analysis of third-party content falls under outputs.

Outtake — An intermediate level of evaluation; measures whether targeted stakeholders actually received, paid attention to, understood, and/or retained the campaign messages.

Over the Counter — A security, such as a stock, that is available for purchase, but is not listed on a formal stock exchange. Stocks traded "over the counter" are usually of higher risk.

P&L — This is an informal name for a profit and loss statement. The P&L is simply another name for the income statement, which tracks an organization's revenue and expenses on an accounting basis.

Page Principles — A set of seven principles adopted and embraced by the Page Society and its members. These principles are drawn from the writings and speeches of Arthur W. Page.

Page Up — Affiliated with the Arthur W. Page Society, this membership organization is for future potential chief communications officers and public relations agency chief executive officers.

Pay Ratio Rule — Part of the Dodd–Frank Act, the Securities and Exchange Commission implemented this rule starting in 2018 which requires US public companies to disclose the ratio of chief executive officer to median employee pay.

People Operations — Also referred to as people teams in some organizations, this term is growing in usage (vs human resources) and places a focus on maximizing employee value.

Performance-based Model — A fee-based model in which the agency or consultancy may earn incentive payments based upon agreed upon performance metrics being achieved for the client.

Pink Sheets — Originally a list of securities printed on sheets of pink paper, the securities quoted on the pink sheet system are not listed on a formal exchange and generally are speculative.

Plank Center for Leadership in Public Relations — Named after Betsy Plank, this center housed at The University of Alabama supports leadership in public relations education and practice.

Poison Pill — A type of anti-takeover provision, a poison pill limits the amount of stock that any one shareholder can own beyond a certain threshold, thereby giving more power to the board.

Preferred Stock — A special class of stock that has priority over common stockholders in the event of liquidation. Preferred shares generally have a fixed dividend, but no voting rights.

Price-to-Earnings Ratio — Also known as the earnings multiple, the *P/E* ratio is a widely used measure for valuing a company based on its share price relative to its earnings per share.

Primary Agency — Denotes the role of lead agency or consultancy for the client. The client may still work with other agencies for certain parts of the business. Not the same as agency of record.

Private Company — A private company is a company whose shares are *not* listed on a stock exchange and has a small number of shareholders. May also be called a closely held company.

Private Equity (PE) — PE is a type of alternative investment manager that may use leverage and invest capital in private companies and/or may engage in the buyout of public companies.

Private Equity Firm — A type of professional investor that invests in large, more established companies using a mix of debt and equity. May invest in public companies or buy them out.

Privileged Information — In a legal context, refers to information not subject to disclosure or discovery and that cannot be asked about in testimony due to the information being protected by a confidential relationship recognized by law (e.g., attorney-client).

Procurement and Sourcing — A function within larger organizations focused on supply chain partner selection, spending, and management. Depending on the organization, this function may play a role in the hiring of professional services firms, such as agencies and consultancies.

Profit Margin — A measure of operational efficiency which shows how much a company makes (i.e., earnings) on a percentage basis for each dollar of sales it generates after various expenses.

Project-based Work — The hiring of an agency or consultancy to work on a specific piece of business for a fixed period of time and defined scope, rather than a retainer-based relationship.

Project Management — The application of knowledge, skills, tools, and techniques to project activities to meet project requirements. Emerged as a distinct profession in the mid-twentieth century.

Project Management Office (PMO) — The PMO is a management structure that standardizes the project-related governance processes and the sharing of resources, methodologies, tools, and techniques.

Property, Plant, and Equipment (PP&E) — The "PP&E" line on the balance sheet records the estimated value of this broad category of physical assets, ranging from company real estate to equipment.

Prospectus — A legal document that offers for sale securities, such as stock in a company. The prospectus outlines the business, its financial performance, risks factors, and the use of funds.

Proxy Adviser — A specialized investment research firm hired by institutional investors to advise them on how to vote on corporate ballot issues, such as elections for board of director seats.

Proxy Contest — Also known as a proxy fight, such situation typically occurs when there is a contested election between a dissident investor and the company for one or more board seats.

Proxy Solicitor — A specialized communication and research firm hired by public companies or large shareholders to predict and influence the voting outcomes on corporate ballot issues.

Proxy Statement — Formally known as a DEF 14A filing with the Securities and Exchange Commission, this governance-oriented document is distributed annually in advance of a public company's annual meeting.

Public Relations Return on Investment (PR ROI) — PR ROI is the impact of a public relations (PR) program on business results. The outcome variable which demonstrates the impact of a PR investment on business.

Public Company — A public company is a company whose shares are listed on a stock exchange and is widely available for purchase by the public. May also be called a listed company.

Private Investment in Public Equity — Known as a PIPE deal or transaction, this is a private placement of securities of an already public company made to selected accredited investors.

Public Relations Society of America — With 21,000 members across the United States, it is the world's largest professional association for public relations and communication professionals.

Publicity Club of Chicago — Founded in 1941, it is the nation's largest independent public relations membership organization with a focus on Chicagoland and the Midwest.

Qualitative Research — A general research approach that collects non-numeric textual or image-based data (i.e., soft data) from relatively small samples to uncover deep, rich insights.

Quantitative Research — A general research approach that collects numeric data from random samples often with a goal of using statistics to generalize findings to a larger population.

Quarterly Earnings Call — A meeting held by a public company (and led by the chief executive officer and chief financial officer) that reviews quarterly earnings performance of the firm with the investor community. The earnings call normally includes prepared remarks by the company followed by a Q&A period.

Quarter-over-Quarter — QoQ or Q/Q is a growth rate measure that compares one quarter of data to the previous quarter of data to make a *sequential* comparison of performance.

Quiet Period — As mandated by US federal securities law, a company that has registered to sell stock (e.g., initial public offering) is limited in the public statements it can make. Many public companies also choose to voluntarily adopt "quiet periods" around the release of quarterly earnings reports.

Random Sample — A sample in which every member of a target population has an equal chance of being selected. Also known as a probability sample. Statistics assume random samples.

Recession — A period of economic decline and contraction during an economic cycle. A recession is officially defined as two consecutive quarters (six months) of negative gross domestic product growth.

Redundancy — In a business context, this term is used to refer to a reduction in workforce (i.e., layoffs) because a position is deemed to be no longer required and necessary by the organization.

Regulation Fair Disclosure — Also known as Reg FD, this federal regulation adopted by the Securities and Exchange Commission in August 2000 promotes the full and fair disclosure of material information by companies.

Reputation Management — The strategic communication and actions taken by a company to manage its reputation: an intangible asset that is co-owned by the company and its stakeholders.

Reputation Quotient (RQ)® — Launched in 1999, the RQ® is an annual measure of corporate reputation designed by scholar Charles Fombrun and market research firm Harris Poll.

Request for Information (RFI) — An RFI may be issued prior to the request for proposal. The RFI collect information about the capabilities of various vendors, such as agencies.

Request for Proposal (RFP) — An RFP is a document the client sends to a small group of vendors, such as agencies, outlining the work and inviting them to submit proposals if they wish to be considered for the work.

Research and Development (R&D) — R&D is an expense line on the income statement that tracks spending on the development of new products, processes, procedures, or related innovations.

Restricted Stock — Whether restricted stock awards or restricted stock units, this is a form of compensation that requires employees to meet specific vesting criteria, including length of employment. Restricted stock typically vests in increments over a period of several years.

Retained Earnings — Also known as retained profits or retained income. The profits left in an organization's bank accounts to invest back in the business after paying out any dividends.

Retainer — A fixed monthly base charge paid in advance by the client for a pre-determined minimum amount of agency or consultancy support and services.

Return on Expectations (ROE) — ROE is a metric that assesses the combined impact of financial and non-financial variables on stakeholder expectations, which leads to public relations return on investment.

Return on Investment (ROI) — ROI is an indicator of net financial performance based on a ratio of how much profit or cost savings is realized from an activity against its actual cost.

Reuters — Established in London in 1851, Reuters is an international news organization owned by Thomson Reuters that serves professionals in the corporate, finance, and media markets.

Revenue — The amount of money received for the sale of a good. Also known as sales, revenue is referred to as the "top line" since this figure appears near the top of the income statement.

Road Show — A series of meetings held online or in-person in which a company's management team, investment bankers, and other advisors meet with prospective large shareholders.

Rule 14(a)8 — A rule passed by the Securities and Exchange Commission in 1943, which allowed shareholders for the first time to submit some shareholder proposals for inclusion in public company's proxy materials.

Russell 2000 — A widely followed stock market index, the Russell 2000 is comprised of 2,000 small capitalization US companies. This index is a key measure of "small cap" performance.

Safe-harbor Language — As part of the Securities Litigation Reform Act of 1995, firms may list current risk factors when making forward statements to protect against frivolous lawsuits.

The Sarbanes–Oxley Act — Nicknamed "SOX" or "SarbOx," this US federal accounting reform and investor protection legislation was passed in 2002 in response to a wave of corporate accounting scandals (e.g., Adelphia, Enron, Tyco, and WorldCom).

Say-on-Frequency — A provision in the Dodd–Frank Act of 2010 gives shareholders the right to cast an advisory vote on how frequently shareholders should vote on executive compensation.

Say-on-Pay — A provision in the Dodd–Frank Act of 2010 gives shareholders the right to cast an advisory vote on executive compensation. This *nonbinding* vote is known as say-on-pay.

Same Store Sales (SSS) — SSS, also known as comparable store sales or simply "comps," is a metric that tracks revenue generated by retail stores and/or online operations that have been open a year or more.

Schedule 13D — A filing that is required to be made with the US Securities and Exchange Commission's EDGAR system within 10 days of whenever an investor acquires a more than 5% voting stake in a public company.

Schedule 13F — A filing that is required to be made with the US Securities and Exchange Commission's EDGAR system on a quarterly basis that discloses the equity investment holdings of large investment managers.

Schedule 13G — An alternative to the Schedule 13D, the 13G filing connotates that the investor tends to have only a *passive* (rather than active) ownership position in the public company.

S Corporation — An S Corp, so named under subchapter S of the Internal Revenue Service (IRS) code, is a legal structure with the benefits of a corporation, but is taxed as a partnership (i.e., avoids "double taxation"). Some small businesses are structured as S Corps.

Scrum — In an information technology and project management context, Scrum is one of the most widely used Agile frameworks and methods for product development and knowledge work.

Secondary Offering — Occurs when an already public company decides to sell additional shares of stock in order to raise money for the company and/or allow company insiders to sell shares.

Securities — Financial instruments that represent some type of financial value such as an ownership interest in a company (stock) or money that is borrowed and must be repaid (bond).

The Securities Act of 1933 — Also known as the Truth in Securities Act, this US federal legislation regulates the offer and sale of securities. The act promoted better disclosures.

Securities and Exchange Commission (SEC) — US federal government agency tasked with enforcing federal securities laws and regulating the securities industries and stock market.

The Securities Exchange Act of 1934 — This landmark US legislation governs the secondary trading of securities. The Securities and Exchange Commission was formed through this act.

Securities Laws — The laws that govern the offer and sale of securities. This includes the mandatory and voluntary disclosure of material, non-public information to the market.

Selective Disclosure — An illegal practice in which select market participants are made aware of material, non-public information about a public company ahead of the broader market.

Selling, General, and Administrative (SG&A) — "SG&A" is a broad expense category line that appears on an organization's income statement. Spending on strategic communication falls under SG&A.

Shareholder Activism — Attempt by one or more company shareholders to affect change at an organization through a variety of strategies, ranging from private meetings to proxy contests.

Shareholder Primacy — A perspective embedded in shareholder theory in which the board of directors and management make decisions based on how such actions affect shareholder value.

Shareholder Proposal — A proposal submitted by a shareholder for inclusion in a public company's proxy statement. Votes on shareholder proposals are typically advisory/non-binding.

Shareholder Theory — Most closely associated with economist Milton Friedman, this theory posits that a company should maximize profits for shareholders, while following rules and laws.

Shareholders' Equity — Also known as net worth or book value, this line on the balance sheet is equal to total assets minus total liabilities. This is share capital invested plus retained earnings.

Shares Outstanding — Shown on a company's balance sheet, this figure represents the total number of shares currently outstanding and owned by shareholders, including insiders.

Signaling Theory — A theory into the process of how and why market participants engage in costly and observable behaviors, known as "signals," which reduce information asymmetry.

Six Sigma — A set of techniques and tools for process improvement. Popularized by General Electric and other large companies, Six Sigma is associated with lean manufacturing.

Adam Smith — A father of modern economics and the author of *The Wealth of Nations*, which argued that, by operating out of self-interest, individuals and firms inadvertently benefit others.

Socialism — An economic and political system characterized by full or partial social ownership of the means of production by the community.

Socially Responsible Companies (SRC) — The idea of SRC moves beyond corporate social responsibility (CSR) initiatives toward embedding CSR into the core of a firm's business model.

Sovereign Wealth Fund (SWF) — A SWF is a government-owned investment fund or entity that is funded by a country's foreign currency reserves. These funds invest in securities and other assets.

Special Meeting — When a major corporate event occurs, such as a pending merger or acquisition, a special meeting of shareholders may be called before the next annual meeting.

Special Purpose Acquisition Company (SPAC) — A SPAC, also known as a "blank check company," is a publicly traded acquisition vehicle that provides an alternate way for private firms to go public.

Specialty Agency — Also called a specialist agency, an alternative to a full-service agency, the specialty agency has deep expertise and knowledge in a specific industry, sector, or area.

Spin-off — In a corporate context, refers to when a company separates off one or more of its operating units into a newly established standalone business. This is also known as a "spin-out."

Sprints — Under the Scrum methodology, these are development iterations which can last 2–4 weeks. During each iteration, the team completes the selected requirements set for that period.

Staggered Board — A board of directors is said to be "staggered" when board seats come up for vote over a multi-year period rather than all seats coming up for vote on an annual basis.

Stakeholder — Individuals or groups that have a shared interest or "stake" in the performance of an organization. This includes customers, employees, suppliers, investors, and the community.

Stakeholder Theory — Most closely associated with business ethicist R. Edward Freeman, this theory posits that firms have a responsibility to *all* stakeholder groups, *not* just shareholders.

Standard — In a communication measurement context, an agreed upon approach, process, or idea used as a norm or model that facilitates comparative evaluations against and across campaigns.

Standard & Poor's 500 (S&P 500) — The S&P 500 is a widely followed broad measure of the US market. This stock market index is comprised of 500 large capitalization or "large cap" companies.

Statistics — A field of mathematics concerned with the collection and analysis of numeric data, often for purposes of making inferences from a sample data set onto the population of study.

Stock — A security that represents an ownership interest in a company and its future earnings. The two main classes of stock are common stock and preferred stock.

Stock Chart — Also called a price chart, this chart plots and visually displays the performance of a company's share price over a period of time, such as weekly, monthly, annually, or even longer.

Stock Exchange — A market where securities, such as shares of stock in a company, are bought and sold. A company must meet listing requirements to have its stock listed on an exchange.

Stock Index — A collection of stocks that represent the change in value of a particular industry, sector or the overall stock market. The Dow Jones Industrial Average and Standard & Poor's 500 are widely tracked stock indexes.

Stock Market — Also known as the equity market or the share market, the collection of stock exchanges where shares of publicly listed companies are traded (i.e., shares are bought and sold).

Stock Option — An instrument that gives someone, whether a company employee or an investor, the right to buy a specific number of shares of stock at a pre-set price on a future date. Stock options often have a one-year "cliff" from the grant date and a four-year vesting period.

Stock Split — An action in which a company divides its existing shares outstanding into additional shares. A stock split in itself does not change the total dollar value of the company.

Stock Ticker Symbol — In the US market, a series of unique letters (or single letter) used to identify the publicly traded stock of a company. Goes back to the days of ticker tape machines.

Strategic Communication — The purposeful use of communication to help advance an organization's mission and create value for the organization and its stakeholders.

Strategy — An overall plan or method employed to achieve an organizational goal; not to be confused with *tactics*, which are specific elements implemented in support of a strategy.

Supermajority Voting — In the context of corporate governance, a provision that states that proposed bylaw amendments must receive a high percentage (67% or greater) of total votes.

Supply-and-Demand — A core tenet of economic theory and the pricing of goods and services. In a free market environment, shifts in supply and demand play a key role in affecting prices.

Survey — A quantitative research method that uses a standard series of questions to collect data from respondents to gauge the sample and/or population's beliefs, attitudes, and/or behaviors.

Sustainability — In a corporate context, refers to business practices and performance that meet current needs, while not compromising the environment and society for future generations.

Sustainability Reporting Frameworks — Standards developed by non-profit organizations to guide company sustainability reporting practices so that they are comparable across firms.

Sustainable, Responsible, and Impact (SRI) Investing — SRI is an investment discipline that considers environmental, social, and governance criteria to generate long-term competitive financial returns and positive societal impact. SRI may also stand for socially responsible investing.

Talent Development — The organizational human resources processes designed to recruit, develop, motivate, and retain employees through skill, competency, and career development.

Tangible Asset — An asset that has a direct physical embodiment such as real estate, factories and fixtures, equipment, vehicles, or product inventory. Also known as "hard" assets.

Third-party Endorsement — Recommendation, verification, or similar action provided by a seemingly independent, objective third party, whether the news media or another influencer.

Top Line — Refers to an organization's revenue or sales. The name "top line" comes from the fact that revenue is generally the first line at the top of an organization's income statement.

Transformation — The process of strategic change with a goal of driving significant and sustained – rather than simply incremental – organizational growth, efficiency, and performance.

Transparency — In a communication context, the proactive efforts taken by an organization to be open, visible, and accessible to stakeholders about organizational policies and actions.

Triple Bottom Line — A core concept of corporate social responsibility. Companies have a responsibility to profits, people, and the planet, rather than solely the traditional bottom line.

Trust Barometer — An annual global survey conducted by public relations firm Edelman into the concept of trust by country on institutions, industry sectors, and informational sources.

Turnover — In an accounting context (particularly the United Kingdom), this term refers to the amount of net revenue or sales an organization generates over a time period. In a different context, turnover can refer to how quickly the inventory of a business is sold and moved.

Underwriter — An investment bank that is responsible for the distribution, pricing, and sale of securities by a company, such as during an initial public offering of a company's stock.

Unemployment Rate — A percentage calculated from employment report data, which represents the ratio of unemployed people looking for work versus those that are currently employed.

USC Center for Public Relations — Housed at the University of Southern California (USC), this academic center seeks to bridge the gap between the public relations profession and academia.

Utilization Rate — The total *actual* billable hours divided by the baseline hours (i.e., total *available* billable hours) expressed as a percentage for a certain time period (e.g., month, quarter, and year).

Valuation — An estimation of the economic worth of a business asset, unit, or the entire enterprise. There are many different valuation metrics that are used by investors.

Value Proposition — In the context of business models and entrepreneurship, this refers to the value offered by an organization's product or service to solving a customer's want or need.

Values — In an organizational context, these are the guiding ethical ideals and principles that an organization holds as important. Such values should guide the organization's mission and vision.

Venture Capital — Capital that generally invests in private, fast-growing ventures with a goal of generating an eventual return through a liquidity event, such as a sale of the business or an initial public offering.

Venture Capital Firm — A type of professional investment manager that typically invests in private, fast-growing companies. Venture capital firms are often investors in pre-initial public offering companies.

Vesting Period — In the context of corporate finance, refers to the time that an employee must wait until they are able to exercise stock incentives. Vesting encourages loyalty by employees.

Vicious Cycle — The opposite of a *virtuous* cycle. In economics, a vicious cycle is the result of a chain of events which *negatively* intensify a situation, leading to worsening conditions.

Virtue Signaling — A pejorative term that refers to efforts to garner praise for expressions that signal one's high moral standing and convictions, but that often are not backed by actual *actions*.

Virtuous Cycle — The opposite of a *vicious* cycle. In economics, a virtuous cycle is the result of a chain of events which *positively* intensify a situation, leading to improving conditions.

Vision — The core tenets and values driving what an organization hopes to become and achieve.

VUCA — An acronym used in business management and leadership circles that stands for: volatility, uncertainty, complexity, and ambiguity. The concept has its roots in military education.

Wall Street — A street in Lower Manhattan that is the heart of New York's financial district. Wall Street or simply "the street" is also used to refer to the US financial industry as a whole.

Warrant — Similar to an option, only that a warrant is a longer-dated instrument that gives the holder the right to purchase a security, usually a stock, at a specific price within a certain time.

Written Consent — In the context of corporate governance, written consent allows shareholders to take various corporate actions without having to wait for voting at the next annual meeting.

Year-over-Year — YoY or Y/Y is a standard growth rate measure that compares one period of data (e.g., quarter or full year) to the prior year's same period of data to make an *annual* comparison of performance.

Zero-based Budgeting (ZBB) — ZBB is a budgeting method in which all expenses must be justified for each new period. ZBB starts from a "zero base" rather than budget history as a starting point.

REFERENCES

Abelson, M., & Gillette, F. (2018, September 28). Insider trading's odd couple: The Goldman banker and the NFL linebacker. *Bloomberg.com*. Retrieved from https://bloom.bg/3an2aTi

Ad Age Studio 360. (2019, December 23). Amazon challenges Google and Facebook's hold on digital ad share. *AdAge*. Retrieved from https://bit.ly/2VGHhfT

Adesina, F., & Mizell, J. (2020, July 9). The American public wants companies to take action on advancing racial equity – Especially Black Americans. *JUSTCapital. com*. Retrieved from https://bit.ly/391Ewfr

AFL-CIO. (2019, June 25). *AFL-CIO releases 2019 executive paywatch report* [Press release]. Retrieved from http://bit.ly/34D3LBi

Aflac Incorporated, Inc. (2020, June 10). *Aflac named a top 50 civic-minded company in America* [Press release]. Retrieved from https://bit.ly/3jJWiYK

Aghina, W., De Smet, A., Lackey, G., Lurie, M., & Murarka, M. (2018). *The five trademarks of agile organizations*. New York, NY: McKinsey & Company.

Aghina, W., Handscomb, C., Ludolph, J., West, D., & Yip, A. (2019). *How to select and develop individuals for successful agile teams: A practical guide*. New York, NY: McKinsey & Company.

Agilemanifesto.org. (2001). Manifesto for agile software development. Retrieved from https://agilemanifesto.org/

Albanese, J. (2019, July 28). Defining the chief growth officer: Does a CGO have a place in your organization? *Inc*. Retrieved from https://bit.ly/3d4tW8c

Alpha IR Group. (2020). *COVID-19 brings new realities & priorities for your 2020 IR program*. Chicago, IL: Alpha IR Group.

Altman, D., & Berman, J. (2011). *The single bottom line*. New York, NY: Department of Economics, Stern School of Business, New York University.

Anthony, S. D., Viguerie, S. P., Schwartz, E. I., & Van Landeghem, J. (2018). *2018 corporate longevity forecast: Creative destruction is accelerating*. Boston, MA: Innosight.

APCO Worldwide. (2016, November). *Chief corporate communicator survey*. Chicago, IL: APCO Worldwide.

APCO Worldwide. (2018). *Corporate advocacy in five acts: When corporate brands are called to take a stand, how do you inspire loyalty and ensure success?* Washington, DC: APCO Worldwide.

Appleby, J. (2011). *The relentless revolution: A history of capitalism.* New York, NY: W. W. Norton & Company.

Aguinis, H., & Glavas, A. (2012). What we know and don't know about corporate social responsibility: A review and research agenda. *Journal of Management, 38*(4), 932–968.

Argenti, P. A. (2017). Strategic communication in the C-suite. *Journal of Business Communication, 54*(2), 146–160. doi:10.1177/2329488416687053

Arthur W. Page Society. (2012). *Building belief: A new model for activating corporate character & authentic advocacy.* New York, NY: Arthur W. Page Society.

Arthur W. Page Society. (2013). *Corporate character: How leading companies are defining, activating & aligning values.* New York, NY: Arthur W. Page Society.

Arthur W. Page Society. (2016a). *The CCO as builder of digital engagement systems.* New York, NY: Arthur W. Page Society.

Arthur W. Page Society. (2016b). *The new CCO: Transforming enterprises in a changing world.* New York, NY: Arthur W. Page Society.

Arthur W. Page Society. (2017). *The CEO view: Communications at the center of the enterprise.* New York, NY: Arthur W. Page Society.

Arthur W. Page Society. (2019a). *The CCO as pacesetter: What it means, why it matters, how to get there.* New York, NY: Arthur W. Page Society.

Arthur W. Page Society. (2019b). The Page principles. *Page.org.* Retrieved from https://page.org/site/the-page-principles

Arthur W. Page Society. (2020). About Page. *Page.org.* Retrieved from https://page.org/site/about

The Aspen Institute. (2014). *Unpacking corporate purpose: A report on the beliefs of executives, investors and scholars.* Washington, DC: The Aspen Institute Business & Society Program.

Asper, S., McCoy, C., & Taylor, G. K. (2019, July). The expanding use of non-GAAP financial measures: Understanding their utility and regulatory limitations. *The CPA Journal.* Retrieved from https://bit.ly/2xyT3AH

Avella, J. R. (2016). Delphi panels: Research design, procedures, advantages, and challenges. *International Journal of Doctoral Studies, 11*, 305–321.

Babcock, A. F., & Williamson, S. (2018). *Quarterly earnings guidance – A corporate relic? Director notes.* New York, NY: The Conference Board, Inc.

Baer, J. (2019, December 25). State Street CEO takes the long view on shareholder activism. *The Wall Street Journal.* Retrieved from https://on.wsj.com/2rOxfOK

Bain, M. (2018). Understanding the corporate legal department. In M. W. Ragas & R. Culp (Eds.), *Mastering business for strategic communicators: Insights and advice from the C- suite of leading brands* (pp. 115–121). Bingley: Emerald Publishing.

Barrett, S. (2020, April 21). A new normal for the agency world. *PRWeek*. Retrieved from https://www.prweek.com/article/1679488/new-normal-agency-world

Battan, C. (2018, April 11). The cult brand whisperer behind Casper, Allbirds, and Birchbox. *FastCompany*. Retrieved from https://bit.ly/2zhenLH

Beattie, A. (2019, June 25). The birth of stock exchanges. *Investopedia.com*. Retrieved from https://www.investopedia.com/articles/07/stock-exchange-history.asp

Beer, J. (2019, November 20). The agencies behind Warby Parker launch a new project to find the next great brand. *FastCompany*. Retrieved from https://bit.ly/2YKVmvW

Beiser, K. (2018). Taking the numb out of numbers: Working with the office of the CFO. In M. W. Ragas, & R. Culp (Eds.), *Mastering business for strategic communicators: Insights and advice from the C-suite of leading brands* (pp. 49–55). Bingley: Emerald Publishing.

Benham, F., & Obregon, R. (2019, July 12). Commentary: The decreasing number of public companies – An elephant in the markets? *Pensions&Investments*. Retrieved from http://bit.ly/2RWB5Qi

Benioff, M., & Langley, M. (2019). *Trailblazer: The power of business as the greatest platform for change*. New York, NY: Currency.

Bennett, N., & Lemoine, G. J. (2014). What VUCA really means for you. *Harvard Business Review*, 92(1–2), 27.

Berger, B. K. (2019). Leadership. In C. M. Kim (Ed.), *Public relations: Competencies and practice* (pp. 12–29). New York, NY: Routledge.

Berger, B. K., & Meng, J. (Eds.). (2014). *Public relations leaders as sensemakers: A global study of leadership in public relations and communication management*. New York, NY: Routledge.

Berry, L. L., & Seltman, K. D. (2014). The enduring culture of Mayo. *Mayo Clinic Proceedings*, 89(2), 144–147. doi:10.1016/j.mayocp.2013.10.025

Blakey, J. (2016, January 7). What's the purpose of your business? *Management-issues.com*. Retrieved from http://bit.ly/2JE7CXc. Accessed on July 17, 2019.

Block, E. M. (2019). Historical perspective: The legacy of public relations excellence behind the name. *Page.org*. Retrieved from https://page.org/site/historical-perspective. Accessed on June 10, 2019.

Bloomenthal, A. (2020, April 15). Gross profit margin definition. *Investopedia.com*. Retrieved from https://www.investopedia.com/terms/g/gross_profit_margin.asp

BNY Mellon. (2020, February). *Global trends in investor relations* (12th ed.). New York, NY: BNY Mellon.

BoardSource. (2017). *Leading with intent: 2017 national index of nonprofit board practices*. Washington, DC: BoardSource.

Bolton, R., Stacks, D. W., & Mizrachi, E. (Eds.). (2018). *The new era of the CCO: The essential role of communication in a volatile world*. New York, NY: Business Expert Press.

Bomkamp, S. (2018, March 7). Processed-food stalwart Kraft Heinz creates unit to go after health-conscious consumers. *Chicago Tribune*. Retrieved from http://bit.ly/2IQewb9

Borneman, J. (2019). First principles of executive pay: Setting effective performance goals. *Directors & Boards, 43*(2), 18–20.

Boston Consulting Group. (2010, January 14). Indra K. Nooyi on performance with purpose. *BCG.com*. Retrieved from https://on.bcg.com/32TQbZI

Boston Consulting Group. (2020). *The most innovative companies 2020: The serial innovation imperative*. Boston, MA: Boston Consulting Group.

Bowen, S. A. (2005). Mission and vision statements. In R. L. Heath (Ed.), *Encyclopedia of public relations* (pp. 535–537). Thousand Oaks, CA: SAGE.

Bowen, S. A. (2008). A state of neglect: Public relations as corporate conscience or ethics counsel. *Journal of Public Relations Research, 20*(3), 271–296. doi:10.1080/10627260801962749

Bowen, S. A., Hardage, G., & Strong, W. (2018). Managing the corporate character of the enterprise: Identity, purpose, culture, and values. In R. Bolton, D. W Stacks, & E. Mizrachi (Eds.), *The new era of the CCO: The essential role of communication in a volatile world* (pp. 53–70). New York, NY: Business Expert Press.

Bowen, S. A., Rawlins, B., & Martin, T. R. (2019). *An overview of the public relations function* (2nd ed.). New York, NY: Business Expert Press.

Bradley, D. (2019, March 8). Lenovo picks BCW for China corporate PR, brand reputation support. *PRWeek*. Retrieved from http://bit.ly/2Y8FKSR

Brancato, C. K., & Plath, C. A. (2005). *Corporate governance handbook 2005: Developments in best practices, compliance, and legal standards*. New York, NY: The Conference Board, Inc.

Breuninger, K., Mangan, D., & Higgins, T. (2020). Ex-New York congressman Chris Collins sentenced to 26 months for insider-trading tip to son. *CNBC.com*. Retrieved from https://cnb.cx/3arX48g

Bronn, P. S., Romenti, S., & Zerfass, A. (Eds.). (2016). *The management game of communication*. Bingley: Emerald Publishing.

Brown, K. A., Waymer, D., & Zhou, Z. (2019). Racial and gender-based differences in the collegiate development of public relations majors: Implications for underrepresented recruitment and retention. *Journal of Public Relations Education, 5*(1), 1–30.

Bucy, M., Hall, S., & Yakola, D. (2016). Transformation with a capital T. *McKinsey Quarterly*. Retrieved from https://mck.co/2xjfLck

Budd, C. S., & Cooper, M. (2004). A project management approach to increasing agency margins. *Journal of Promotion Management, 11*(1), 21–49. doi:10.1300/J057v11n01_03

Buerkle, A., Change, K., & Storto, M. (2018). *Just good business: An investor's guide to B Corps.* New Haven, CT: Yale Center for Business and the Environment, Patagonia, Inc. and The Caprock Group.

Burson, H. (2017). *The business of persuasion: Harold Burson on public relations.* New York, NY: RosettaBooks.

Burton, K. (2019). The road to convergence. *Strategies & Tactics, 2*(1), 11–13.

Business Roundtable. (2018, June 7). *Business Roundtable supports move away from short-term guidance* [Press release]. Retrieved from https://bit.ly/3aJZ4sA

Business Roundtable. (2019a). *Statement on the purpose of a corporation.* Washington, DC: Business Roundtable.

Business Roundtable. (2019b, August 25). Redefined purpose of a corporation: Welcoming the debate. *Medium.com.* Retrieved from http://bit.ly/2qIi1dk

Butters, J. (2020, February 21). *S&P 500 forward P/E ratio hits 19.0 for the first time since 2002.* Norwalk, CT: FactSet. Retrieved from https://bit.ly/2VRtrHE

Cahill, J. (2019, August 20). What's really behind CEOs' common-good-over-profits pledge. *Crain's Chicago Business.* Retrieved from http://bit.ly/2NjI2XZ

Cappelli, P., & Tavis, A. (2018). HR goes agile. *Harvard Business Review, 96*(2), 46–52.

Carnegie, A. (1889). Wealth. *North American Review, 148*(391), 653–665.

Castillo, E. A. (2018, November 20). Why are we still struggling with diversity, equity, and inclusion in nonprofit governance? *Nonprofit Quarterly.* Retrieved from http://bit.ly/39JfIsk

Castillo, M. (2017, May 23). Reed Hastings' story about the founding of Netflix has changed several times. *CNBC.com.* Retrieved from https://cnb.cx/37ypqLQ

Catalyst. (2018, August). Why diversity and inclusion matter: Quick take. *Catalyst.org.* Retrieved from https://www.catalyst.org/research/why-diversity-and-inclusion-matter/

CBINSIGHTS. (2018, March 13). Hungry for investment: Big food races toward startups. *CBinsights.com.* Retrieved from http://bit.ly/2XH81Qx

Charan, R. (2017). *What the CEO wants you to know: How your company really works.* New York, NY: Currency.

Chatterji, A. K., & Toffel, M. W. (2018). The new CEO activists. *Harvard Business Review, 96*(1), 78–89.

Chatterji, A. K., & Toffel, M. W. (2019). Assessing the impact of CEO activism. *Organization & Environment, 32*(2), 159–185. doi:10.1177/1086026619848144

Chen, J. (2018, May 1). Street expectations. *Investopedia.com*. Retrieved by https://www.investopedia.com/terms/s/streetexpectation.asp

Chen, J. (2020a, March 23). Stockholders' equity. *Investopedia.com*. Retrieved from https://www.investopedia.com/terms/s/stockholdersequity.asp

Chen, J. (2020b, March 29). Private securities litigation reform act (PSLRA). *Ivestopedia.com*. Retrieved from https://www.investopedia.com/terms/p/pslra.asp

Chitkara, A. (2018, April 12). PR agencies need to be more diverse and inclusive. Here's how to start. *Harvard Business Review*. Retrieved from https://bit.ly/3hg5weN

Christ, M., & Sandor, R. (2015, July 23). Advice from two millennials on how businesses can do good. *PRWeek*. Retrieved http://bit.ly/2G8GNba

Christ, M., Sandor, R., & Tonne, A. (2015). *Cigarettes out. Health in: An analysis of the rebrand of CVS Health*. New York, NY: Arthur W. Page Society.

Christian, R. C. (1997). Foreword. In C. L. Caywood (Ed.), *The handbook of strategic public relations and integrated communications* (pp. iii–v). New York, NY: McGraw-Hill.

Christensen, C. M. (1997). *The innovator's dilemma: When new technologies cause great firms to fail*. Boston, MA: Harvard Business School Press.

Christensen, C. M., & Raynor, M. E. (2003). *The innovator's solution: Creating and sustaining successful growth*. Boston, MA: Harvard Business School Press.

Clark, K. (2020, March 26). What does negative shareholders' equity mean? *Investopedia.com*. Retrieved from https://bit.ly/2RZjxCJ

Clarke, T., & Branson, D. (Eds.). (2012). *The SAGE handbook of corporate governance*. London: SAGE Publications Ltd.

Claussen, D. (2008). On the business and economics education of public relations students. *Journalism & Mass Communication Educator, 63*(3), 191–194. doi:10.1177/107769580806300301

Clifford, C. (2018, September 20). Whole Foods turns 38: How a college dropout turned his grocery store into a business Amazon bought for $13.7 billion. *CNBC.com*. Retrieved from http://cnb.cx/3reUPy6

Cohen, W. (2011, March 7). *The purpose of business is not to make a profit*. Tampa, FL: HR Exchange Network. Retrieved from http://bit.ly/2SaHAgD

Colgate-Palmolive Company. (2020). About Colgate-Palmolive. *Colgatepalmolive.com*. Retrieved from https://www.colgatepalmolive.com/en-us/about

Collier, P. (2018). *The future of capitalism: Facing the new anxieties*. New York, NY: Harper Collins.

Commission on Public Relations Education. (2018). *Fast forward: Foundations + future state. Educators + practitioners*. New York, NY: Commission on Public Relations Education.

Cone, C. (2019, August 23). It's time for companies to treat purpose like a verb. *PRWeek*. Retrieved from http://bit.ly/2NltpTT

Cone Communications. (2016). *2016 Cone Communications millennial employee engagement study*. Boston, MA: Cone Communications.

The Conference Board. (2019, January 17). *In 2019, CEOs are most concerned about talent and a recession* [Press release]. Retrieved from https://prn.to/2YzTYZg

Conger, K. (2019, February 28). Uber and Lyft said to offer drivers a chance to participate in I.P.O.s. *The New York Times*. Retrieved from https://nyti.ms/3aaxe8j

Cooley LLP. (2019). Fiduciary duties. *Cooleygo.com*. Retrieved from h ttps://www.cooleygo.com/glossary/fiduciary-duties/

Coombs, W. T., & Holladay, S. J. (2012). *Managing corporate social responsibility: A Communication approach*. Malden, MA: Wiley-Blackwell.

Coombs, W. T., & Holladay, S. J. (2018). Social issues qua wicked problems: The role of strategic communication in social issues management. *Journal of Communication Management, 22*(1), 79–95. doi:10.1108/JCOM-11-2016-0093

Cooperrider, D. (2008, July 1). Sustainable innovation. *BizEd*. Retrieved from https://bized.aacsb.edu/articles/2008/07/sustainable-innovation

Cope, K. (2012). *Seeing the big picture: Business acumen to build your credibility, career and company*. Austin, TX: Greenleaf Book Group.

Coren, M. J. (2019, June 19). After Slack, the IPO market might never be the same. *QUARTZ*. Retrieved from http://bit.ly/381wxN3

Costco Wholesale Corporation. (2020). What is Costco's mission statement and code of ethics? *Costco.com*. Retrieved from http://bit.ly/2Lf0IcM

Council of Institutional Investors. (2019, August 19). *Council of Institutional Investors responds to Business Roundtable statement on corporate purpose* [Press release]. Retrieved from http://bit.ly/2qSbLjf

Covey, S. R. (2004). *The 7 habits of highly effective people: Powerful lessons in personal change*. New York, NY: Simon & Schuster.

Creswell, J., Draper, K., & Maheshwari, S. (2018, September 26). Before running with Kaepernick, Nike considered cutting him loose. *The New York Times*, p. B9.

CristKolder Associates. (2019). *CristKolder volatility report of America's leading companies*. Downers Grove, IL: Crist Kolder Associates.

Cummins Inc. (2020). About us. *Cummins.com*. Retrieved from https://www.cummins.com/kr/about-us

Cutlip, S. M. (1994). *The unseen power: Public relations: A history*. Hillsdale, NJ: Erlbaum.

Cutlip, S. M. (1995). *Public relations history: From the 17th to the 20th century*. Hillsdale, NJ: Erlbaum.

CVS Health. (2015, January 15). We quit tobacco, here's what happened next. *CVSHealth.com*. Retrieved from https://cvshealth.com/about/purpose-statement

CVS Health. (2019). Working towards a tobacco-free future. *CVSHealth.com*. Retrieved from https://cvshealth.com/about/purpose-statement

CVS Health. (2020a). 2019 corporate social responsibility report. *CVSHealth.com*. Retrieved from https://cvshealth.com/sites/default/files/2019-csr-report.pdf

CVS Health. (2020b). Purpose statement. *CVSHealth.com*. Retrieved from https://cvshealth.com/about/purpose-statement

Daly, F., Teague, P., & Kitchen, P. (2003). Exploring the role of internal communication during organisational change. *Corporate Communications: An International Journal*, 8(3), 153–162. doi:10.1108/13563280310487612

Damodaran, A. (2020, January). Margins by sector (US). *Pages.Stern.NYU.edu*. Retrieved from http://pages.stern.nyu.edu/~adamodar/New_Home_Page/datafile/margin.html

Daneshkhu, S., & Barber, L. (2017, December 3). Paul Polman: How I fended off a hostile takeover bid. *Financial Times*. Retrieved from https://on.ft.com/2PdGoK8

Daniel J. Edelman Holdings, Inc. (2020). About Edelman. *Edelman.com*. Retrieved from https://www.edelman.com/about-us

Daniels, C. (2017, March). 2017 salary survey: Opportunities to advance in position and salary abound. PR pros who have the right skill sets number among the winners. *PRWeek*, pp. 28–34.

Daniels, C. (2018, March). Smarter investments: 2018 salary survey. *PRWeek*, pp. 30–36.

Daniels, C. (2019a, October 3). Bellwether survey: C-suite dinosaurs hold back communications. *PRWeek*. Retrieved from https://bit.ly/2WfiEbt

Daniels, C. (2019b, March–April). Evidence of progress: 2019 salary survey. *PRWeek*, pp. 40–46.

Daniels, C. (2020, March 9). An industry ready to move: 2020 salary survey. *PRWeek*. Retrieved from https://bit.ly/3gaL6U2

Davis & Gilbert LLP. (2019). *Public relations industry 2019 survey trends and highlights*. New York, NY: Davis & Gilbert LLP.

Deloitte. (2016). *Framing the future of corporate governance: Deloitte governance framework*. New York, NY: Deloitte Center for Board Effectiveness.

Deloitte. (2019a). *Data-driven change: Women in the board room, a global perspective* (6th ed.). New York, NY: Deloitte Global Center for Corporate Governance.

Deloitte. (2019b). *The Deloitte global millennial survey 2019*. New York, NY: Deloitte.

Deloitte & Alliance for Board Diversity. (2019). *Missing pieces report: The 2018 board diversity census of women and minorities on Fortune 500 boards*. New York, NY: Deloitte & Alliance for Board Diversity.

Deloitte Development LLC. (2015). *Zero-based budgeting: Zero or hero?* New York, NY: Deloitte Consulting LLP.

Deloitte Development LLC. (2020). *Advancing environmental, social, and governance investing: A holistic approach for investment management firms.* New York, NY: Deloitte Center for Financial Services.

Denning, S. (2017, October 15). What is Agile? The four essential elements. *Forbes.com.* Retrieved from http://bit.ly/2K8supN

Denning, S. (2019, February 20). The irresistible rise of agile: A paradigm shift in management. *Forbes.com.* Retrieved from http://bit.ly/32RL7nG

Detrixhe, J. (2017, September 26). Why robot traders haven't replaced all the humans at the New York Stock Exchange—Yet. *QUARTZ.* Retrieved from http://bit.ly/31QdFPI

Detrixhe, J. (2020, March 22). For the first time in 228 years, the New York Stock Exchange will open with its trading floor. *QUARTZ.* Retrieved from https://bit.ly/2y4iRVf

Dimon, J. (2018). Chairman and CEO letter to shareholders. *JPMorganChase.com.* Retrieved from http://bit.ly/318lor0

Dimon, J., & Buffett, W. E. (2018). Short-termism is harming the economy. *The Wall Street Journal.* Retrieved from https://on.wsj.com/39ngidQ

DiStaso, M. W. (2012). The annual earnings press release's dual role: An examination of relationships with local and national media coverage and reputation. *Journal of Public Relations Research, 24*(2), 123–143.

DiStaso, M. W., & Bortree, D. S. (2012). Multi-method analysis of transparency in social media practices: Survey, interviews and content analysis. *Public Relations Review, 38*(3), 511–514.

Dodd, M. (2018). Globalization, pluralization, and erosion: The impact of shifting societal expectations for advocacy and public good. *Journal of Public Interest Communications, 2*(2), 221–238.

Dodd, M. D., & Supa, D. W. (2014). Conceptualizing and measuring the influence of "corporate social advocacy" communication on consumer purchase intention, corporate financial performance. *Public Relations Journal, 8*(3), 1–23.

Dodd, M. D., & Supa, D. W. (2015). Testing the viability of corporate social advocacy as a predictor of purchase intention. *Communication Research Reports, 32*(4), 287–293. doi:10.1080/08824096.2015.1089853

D'Onfro, J. (2016, August 17). The incredible rise of Ruth Porat, CFO at one of the most valuable companies in the world. *Business Insider.* Retrieved from http://bit.ly/3mI8euQ

Dozier, D. M. (1992). The organizational roles of communications and public relations practitioners. In J. E. Grunig (Ed.), *Excellence in public relations and communication management* (pp. 395–417). Hillsdale, NJ: Erlbaum.

Dozier, D. M., & Broom, G. M. (2006). The centrality of practitioner roles to public relations theory. In C. H. Botan & V. Hazelton (Eds.), *Public relations theory II* (pp. 137–170). New York, NY: Erlbaum.

Dozier, D. M., & Grunig, L. A. (1992). The organization of the public relations function. In J. E. Grunig (Ed.), *Excellence in public relations and communication management* (pp. 395–417). Hillsdale, NJ: Erlbaum.

Drucker, P. F. (2002). The discipline of innovation. *Harvard Business Review, 80*(8), 95–103.

Drucker, P. F. (2014). *Innovation and entrepreneurship: Practice and principles.* London: Routledge.

Duhé, S. (2013, December 12). *Teaching business as a second language.* Gainesville, FL: Institute for Public Relations. Retrieved from http://bit.ly/1cGKcsw

Eaglesham, J., & Brown, E. (2019, October 7). WeWork investors turned off by 'sloppy' IPO filings. *The Wall Street Journal.* Reviewed from https://on.wsj.com/34JsODK

Ebrahimji, A. (2020, May 30). Nike is saying 'don't do it' in a message about racism in America. *CNN.com.* Retrieved from https://cnn.it/3esJfsu

Edelman. (2018a, October). *2018 Edelman earned brand: Brands take a stand.* New York, NY: Edelman.

Edelman, R. (2018b, December 21). Zeno at 20. *Edelman.com.* Retrieved from https://www.edelman.com/insights/zeno-20-year-anniversary

Edelman. (2019, January). *2019 Edelman trust barometer: Global report.* New York, NY: Edelman.

Edelman. (2020, June). *Special report: Brands and racial justice in America. Edelman trust barometer 2020.* New York, NY: Edelman.

Edgecliffe-Johnson, A. (2018, February 27). Unilever chief admits Kraft Heinz bid forced compromises. *Financial Times.* Retrieved from https://on.ft.com/362nI5M

Edgecliffe-Johnson, A. (2019, November 9). Stephen Badger: Balancing profit with creating value for society. *Financial Times.* Retrieved from https://on.ft.com/2yyBCR9

Elkington, J. (2018, June 25). 25 years ago I coined the phrase "triple bottom line." Here's why it's time to rethink it. *Harvard Business Review.* Retrieved from http://bit.ly/2N6OQrQ

Ericsson, K. A., Krampe, R. T., & Tesch-Römer, C. (1993). The role of deliberate practice in the acquisition of expert performance. *Psychological Review, 100*(3), 363–406. doi:10.1037/0033-295X.100.3.363

ESPN. (2020). 'The last dance': The untold story of Michael Jordan's Chicago Bulls. *ESPN.com.* Retrieved from https://es.pn/2WIGwE7

EY Beacon Institute. (2015). *The business case for purpose*. Brighton, MA: Harvard Business School Publishing.

Fama, E. F. (1980). Agency problems and the theory of the firm. *Journal of Political Economy*. 88(2), 288–307. doi:10.1086/260866

Fama, E. F., & Jensen, M. C. (1983). Agency problems and residual claims. *Journal of Law and Economics*, 26(2), 327–349. doi:10.1086/467038

Farr, C., & Elias, J. (2019, October 21). Alphabet CFO Ruth Porat opens up about her bouts with cancer and Google's work in early disease detection. *CNBC.com*. Retrieved from https://cnb.cx/3cRy8rF

Farrell, M. (2019, February 28). Some Uber, Lyft drivers to get stock in IPOs. *The Wall Street Journal*. Retrieved from https://on.wsj.com/2HZyEGz

Federal Register. (2020). Agencies. *FederalRegister.gov*. Retrieved from https://www.federalregister.gov/agencies

Feldman, B. (2016, November 28). Dear comms exec: Basic business skills are still required. *PRWeek*. Retrieved from http://bit.ly/2ovUmWt

Feldman, B. (2019, January 25). CCOs can get the comms funds they need, if they know where to look. *PRWeek*. Retrieved from http://bit.ly/2SQMmAp

Fidlin, D. (2011, December 17). 10 notable retail stores that went out of business. *Listosaur.com*. Retrieved from http://bit.ly/2J3pnO5

Fildes, N. (2019, March 14). Martin Sorrell to earn £2m bonus from WPP even after departure. *Financial Times*. Retrieved from https://on.ft.com/2ZD7QnK

Financial Accounting Standards Board. (n.d.). Comparability in international accounting standards – A brief history. *FASB.org*. Retrieved from https://www.fasb.org/jsp/FASB/Page/SectionPage&cid=1176156304264

Fink, L. (2018). Larry Fink's annual letter to CEOs: A sense of purpose. *BlackRock.com*. Retrieved from http://bit.ly/2XBRzll

Fink, L. (2019). Larry Fink's 2019 letter to CEOs: Purpose and profit. *BlackRock.com*. Retrieved from http://bit.ly/2XBRzll

Fink, L. (2020). Larry Fink's 2020 letter to CEOs: A fundamental reshaping of finance. *BlackRock.com*. Retrieved from http://bit.ly/2XBRzll

Finkbeiner, E., Lecher, N., Sowa, N., & Ohm, A. (2018). *Unilever and Kraft Heinz: A global clash of corporate purpose and profits*. New York, NY: Arthur W. Page Society.

Forbes. (2019). America's largest private companies. *Forbes.com*. Retrieved from https://www.forbes.com/largest-private-companies/list/#tab:rank

Forbes, M., & McGrath, M. (2019, December 12). The world's 100 most powerful women. *Forbes.com*. Retrieved from https://www.forbes.com/power-women/#18ccf78c5e25

Ford, P. (2019, May 6). Lessons from leaders: More progress, fewer platitudes. *PRWeek*. Retrieved from https://bit.ly/2WIUXZC

Fortune. (2019). Most powerful women. *Fortune.com*. Retrieved from https://fortune.com/most-powerful-women/

Fortune. (2020a). Fortune 500: Alphabet. *Fortune.com*. Retrieved from https://fortune.com/company/alphabet/fortune500/

Fortune. (2020b). Fortune 500: Walmart. *Fortune.com*. Retrieved from https://fortune.com/company/walmart/fortune500/

Francis, T. (2020, June 3). Coronavirus crisis dents salaries, not stock awards for many CEOs. *The Wall Street Journal*. Retrieved from https://on.wsj.com/30NaVUJ

Francis, T., & Gryta, T. (2020, March 25). Coronavirus shows cash is king, even for biggest U.S. companies. *The Wall Street Journal*. Retrieved from https://on.wsj.com/2ywS7gC

Freberg, K. (2019). *Social media for strategic communication: Creative strategies and research-based applications*. Thousand Oaks, CA: SAGE Publications, Inc.

Freeman, R. E. (2010). *Strategic management: A stakeholder approach*. New York, NY: Cambridge University Press.

Freeman, R. E., Harrison, J. S., & Wicks, A. C. (2007). *Managing for stakeholders: Survival, reputation, and success*. New Haven, CT: Yale University Press.

Freeman, R. E., Harrison J. S., Wicks, A. C., Parmar, B. L., & de Colle, S. (2010). *Stakeholder theory: The state of the art*. New York, NY: Cambridge University Press.

Freeman, R. E., Harrison, J. S., & Zyglidopoulos, S. (2018). *Stakeholder theory: Concepts and strategies*. New York, NY: Cambridge University Press.

Friedman, M. (1965, August 24). Social responsibility: A subversive doctrine. *National Review*, pp. 721–723.

Friedman, M. (1970, September 13). The social responsibility of business is to increase its profits. *The New York Times Magazine*, pp. 32–33, 122, 124, 126.

Friedman, M., Mackey, J., & Rodgers, T. J. (2005, October). Rethinking the social responsibility of business. *Reason*. Retrieved from http://bit.ly/2XJhBOF

Friess, E. (2018). "Filling to capacity": An exploratory study of project management language in agile scrum teams. *Technical Communication, 65*(2), 169–180.

Fry, R. (2018, April 11). *Millennials are the largest generation in the U.S. labor force*. Washington, DC: Pew Research Center. Retrieved from https://pewrsr.ch/2YL7EBJ

Gaines-Ross, L. (2019, September 20). 4 in 10 American workers consider themselves social activists. *QUARTZ*. Retrieved from https://qz.com/work/1712492/

Gallant, C. (2019, May 8). Will I lose my shares if a company is delisted? *Investopedia.com*. Retrieved from https://bit.ly/2KcjT4g

Gallo, C. (2019, October 22). Netflix co-founder says entrepreneurs should constantly remind themselves that 'nobody knows anything.' *Inc*. Retrieved from http://bit.ly/2Hqes0p

Gandel, S. (2017, June 21). Whole Foods' CEO pay discount expires. *Bloomberg News*. Retrieved from https://bloom.bg/2NKHKtv

Garrahan, M. (2018, April 14). Martin Sorrell resigns after 33 years as WPP chief. *Financial Times*. Retrieved from https://on.ft.com/2QBEjXu

Gartner, Inc. (2019). *2019 CEO survey: The year of challenged growth*. Stamford, CT: Gartner, Inc.

Garton, E., & Noble, A. (2017, July 19). How to make agile work for the C-suite. *Harvard Business Review*. Retrieved from http://bit.ly/3129Vcg

Gelles, D. (2014, May 8). At odds, Omnicom and Publicis end merger. *The New York Times*, p. B1.

Gelles, D. (2017, August 20). The moral voice of corporate America. *The New York Times*, p. B1.

Gelles, D. (2019, September 1). To drive change, look past the bottom line. *The New York Times*, p. B4.

Geller, M., & Naidu, R. (2019). Kraft Heinz' problems shine light on controversial budget tool. *Reuters*. Retrieved from https://reut.rs/2Yv9M1i

Gelles, D., Stewart, J. B., Silver-Greenberg, J., & Kelly, K. (2018, August 17). Musk details 'excruciating' year of sleepless nights and turmoil. *The New York Times*, p. A1.

George, B. (2017, March 24). The battle for the soul of capitalism explained in one hostile takeover bid. *CNBC.com*. Retrieved from https://cnb.cx/2BAJxvq

George, B. (2019, February 26). Responsible capitalism will be the U.S.'s saving grace. *Fortune.com*. Retrieved from http://bit.ly/2JgR0nI

Gilbert, J. C., Kassoy, A., & Houlahan, B. (2019, August 22). Don't believe the Business Roundtable has changed until its CEOs' actions match their words. *Fast Company*. Retrieved from http://bit.ly/2ph0rwL

Gladwell, M. (2011). *Outliers: The story of success*. New York, NY: Little, Brown and Company.

Glazer, E., Stevens, L., & Andriotis, A. (2019, January 5). Jeff Bezos and Jamie Dimon: Best of frenemies. *The Wall Street Journal*. Retrieved from https://on.wsj.com/316h7Es

Goldman, L. (2011, July 20). The incredible story of Walmart's expansion from five & dime to global megacorp. *Business Insider*. Retrieved from http://bit.ly/2KCskrR

Goldstein, M. (2018, September 29). Elon Musk steps down as chairman in deal with S.E.C. over tweet about Tesla. *The New York Times*. Retrieved from http://nyti.ms/2KrfnD7

Goldstein, M. (2019, June 6). Elon Musk and S.E.C. reach new accord, lifting cloud over Tesla. *The New York Times*. Retrieved from http://nyti.ms/2WIHlMZ

Golin, A. (2006). *Trust or consequences: Build trust today or lose your market tomorrow*. New York, NY: AMACOM.

GOLIN. (2017, April 9). Al Golin built a PR firm based on Midwestern values. *Golin.com.* Retrieved from https://bit.ly/2YKPaE5

Goodman, M. (2019). Corporate and agency public relations. In C. M. Kim (Ed.), *Public relations: Competencies and practice* (pp. 272–294). New York, NY: Routledge.

Gotlieb, M. R., McLaughlin, B., & Cummins, R. G. (2017). 2015 survey of journalism and mass communication enrollments: Challenges and opportunities for a changing and diversifying field. *Journalism & Mass Communication Educator*, 72(2), 139–153.

Gould+Partners. (2019a). *PR agency industry 2019 best practices benchmarking report: By agency size and selected regions.* New York, NY: Gould+Partners.

Gould+Partners. (2019b). *PR agency industry 2019 billing rates and utilization report: By agency size and selected regions.* New York, NY: Gould+Partners.

Gould+Partners. (2020). *PR industry turnover report: Impact and implications of staff and client turnover.* New York, NY: Gould+Partners.

Governance & Accountability Institute, Inc. (2019, September 4). Flash report: 60% of Russell 1000® are publishing sustainability reports, G&A Institute's inaugural benchmark survey shows. *GA-Institute.com.* Retrieved from http://bit.ly/32ZCE2H

Governance & Accountability Institute, Inc. (2020, July 16). Flash report: 90% of S&P 500® index companies publish sustainability/responsibility reports in 2019. *GA-Institute.com.* Retrieved from https://bit.ly/2ClrNYX

Green, D. (2019, July 5). Jeff Bezos has said that Amazon has had failures worth billions of dollars – Here are some of the biggest ones. *Business Insider.* Retrieved from http://bit.ly/2GCP6fD

Grothaus, M. (2019, August 26). Patagonia, Ben & Jerry's, and 30 other companies tell the Business Roundtable CEOs to put up or shut up. *Fast Company.* Retrieved from http://bit.ly/30h1omO

Grove, A. S. (1999). *Only the paranoid survive: How to exploit the crisis points that challenge every company.* New York, NY: Currency.

Grunig, J. E. (Ed.). (1992). *Excellence in public relations and communication management.* Mahwah, NJ: Routledge.

Grunig, L. A., Grunig, J. E., & Dozier, D. M. (2002). *Excellent public relations and effective organizations: A study of communication management in three countries.* Mahwah, NJ: Erlbaum.

Gupta, A. H. (2019, December 17). California companies are rushing to find female board members. *New York Times.* Retrieved from https://nyti.ms/2ZLVqKs

Hamilton, I. A. (2019, July 5). Amazon turned 25 today, which according to Jeff Bezos means it will die in as little as 5 years' time. *Business Insider.* Retrieved http://bit.ly/2yT3XOU

Handley, L. (2019, March 4). Firms are taking more marketing functions in-house. Here's why. *CNBC.com*. Retrieved from https://cnb.cx/2NklfhM

Haqqi, T. (2020, August 9). 20 largest stock exchanges in the world. *Insider Monkey*. Retrieved from https://www.yahoo.com/news/20-largest-stock-exchanges-world-175549152.html

Haran, L., & Sheffer, G. (2015, March 24). Is the chief communications officer position going the way of the dodo? *PRWeek*. Retrieved from http://bit.ly/1OLpY3z

Harrison, E. B., & Mühlberg, J. (2015). *Leadership communication: How leaders communicate and how communicators lead in today's global enterprise*. New York, NY: Business Expert Press.

Haski-Leventhal, D., Pournader, M., & McKinnon, A. (2017). The role of gender and age in business students' values, CSR attitudes, and responsible management education: Learnings from the PRME international survey. *Journal of Business Ethics, 146*(1), 219–239. doi:10.1007/s10551-015-2936-2

Hastings, R., & Meyer, E. (2020). *No rules rules: Netflix and the culture of reinvention*. New York, NY: Penguin Press.

Hayes, A. (2019, April 22). Business valuation. *Investopedia.com*. Retrieved from https://www.investopedia.com/terms/b/business-valuation.asp

Henderson, R. (2019, July 9). Slack and Spotify debuts tempt companies to cut out the middlemen. *Financial Times*. Retrieved from https://on.ft.com/2vdroEA

Hengeveld, M. (2019, January 4). Big business has a new scam: The 'purpose paradigm.' *The Nation*. Retrieved from http://bit.ly/2S8o7xc

Hinds, J., Hayes, A., Sanderson, R., Sachar, H., & Samson, M. (2016). *The emergence of the chief growth officer in consumer packaged goods*. London: Russell Reynolds Associates.

Hine, C. (2018). Telling the story of value creation. In M. W. Ragas & R. Culp (Eds.), *Mastering business for strategic communicators: Insights and advice from the C-suite of leading brands* (pp. 99–105). Bingley: Emerald Publishing.

Hodgson, L. (2020, June 10). Virtual IPO roadshows could become the new post-crisis standard. *Pitchbook.com*. Retrieved from https://bit.ly/2BrU1k6

Hodgson, P. (2017, January 12). The pros and cons of issuing quarterly guidance. *IR magazine*. Retrieved from https://bit.ly/2JqmNSK

Human, T. (2020, May 29). IR teams embrace Zoom for virtual meetings, finds poll. *IR magazine*. Retrieved from https://bit.ly/2Nn9C7g

Hynes, A. (2017, June 8). Actions make your words matter more. *LinkedIn*. Retrieved from http://bit.ly/30CeUjP

Hynes, A. (2018, April 13). Becoming our clients' conscience. *LinkedIn*. Retrieved from http://bit.ly/2xWxk2r

Institute for Public Relations (n.d.). About IPR. *InstituteforPR.org*. Retrieved from https://instituteforpr.org/about/

Intel Corporation. (n.d.). Over 50 years of Moore's law. Retrieved from https://intel. ly/2NkpMki

Investopedia. (2019, August 15). The difference between a capital market and the stock market. Retrieved from http://bit.ly/2RXqhS1

Investopedia. (2020, February 4). If you invested right after Netflix's IPO (NFLX). Retrieved from http://bit.ly/37wMTNF

Ives, N. (2019, June 6). Average tenure of CMO slips to 43 months. *The Wall Street Journal*. Retrieved from http://on.wsj.com/38tqao0

Jain, R., & Bain, M. (2017). Delivering higher value through higher performance: Insights on performance evaluation and talent management in corporate communication. *Public Relations Journal*, *11*(1), 1–18.

Jensen, M. C., & Chew, D. (2000). *A theory of the firm: Governance, residual claims and organizational forms*. Cambridge, MA: Harvard University Press.

Jensen, M. C., & Meckling, W. F. (1976). Theory of the firm: Managerial behavior, agency costs, and ownership structure. *Journal of Financial Economics*, *3*(4), 305–360. doi:10.1016/0304-405X(76)90026-X

John, S. (2019, April 8). How Walmart keeps its prices so low. *Business Insider*. Retrieved from https://www.businessinsider.com/walmart-low-price-strategy-tips-2019-4. Accessed on June 24, 2019.

Johnson, B. (2020a, May 8). Ad business cuts 36,400 jobs in April. *AdAge*. Retrieved from https://adage.com/article/datacenter/ad-business-cut-36400-jobs-april/2255426

Johnson, B. (2020b, May 11). 2019 was the weakest year for agency growth since the Great Recession. But the bad news is 2020. *AdAge*. Retrieved from https://bit. ly/2Lr6NAP

Johnson, D. (2020, May 4). Michael Jordan's teammate Bill Wennington: 'He would be on top at the end'. *WTOPnews*. Retrieved from https://bit.ly/3jtThwc

Johnson & Johnson Services, Inc. (2020). Our credo. *Jnj.com*. Retrieved from https://www.jnj.com/credo/

Jones, R. W., & Kostyak, C. (Eds.). (2011). *Words from a page in history: The Arthur W. Page speech collection*. University Park, PA: The Arthur W. Page Center for Integrity in Public Communications, Bellisario College of Communications, Pennsylvania State University.

JUST Capital. (2017, November). *Roadmap for corporate America: JUST Capital's 2017 survey results*. New York, NY: JUST Capital.

JUST Capital. (2019, October). *A roadmap for stakeholder capitalism: JUST Capital's 2019 survey results*. New York, NY: JUST Capital.

JUST Capital, & The Harris Poll. (2020). SURVEY: What Americans want from corporate America during the response, reopening, and rest phases of the Coronavirus crisis. *JUSTCapital.com*. Retrieved from https://bit.ly/393RkBP

Kandell, J. (2018, May 21). Jamie Dimon is not messing around. *Institutional Investor*. Retrieved from http://bit.ly/2GAWRTy

Kaplan, D. A. (2013). Mars Incorporated: A pretty sweet place to work. *Fortune.com*. Retrieved from https://on.ft.com/2yyBCR9

Karaian, J. (2014, March 23). Another chapter in the long, slow decline of the chief operating officer. *QUARTZ*. Retrieved from https://bit.ly/2xUJYCL

Keating, G. (2013). *Netflixed: The epic battle for America's eyeballs*. New York, NY: Portfolio/Penguin.

Kelleher, T. (2020). *Public relations: Engagement, conversation, influence, transparency, trust*. (2nd ed.). New York, NY: Oxford University Press.

Kenton, W. (2019a, April 2). Schedule 13D. *Investopedia.com*. Retrieved from https://www.investopedia.com/terms/s/schedule13d.asp

Kenton, W. (2019b, July 13). Operating margin definition. *Investopedia.com*. Retrieved from https://www.investopedia.com/terms/o/operatingmargin.asp

Kenton, W. (2020a, February 27). Book value. *Investopedia.com*. Retrieved from https://www.investopedia.com/terms/b/bookvalue.asp

Kenton, W. (2020b, March 21). Fiscal year-end. *Investopedia.com*. Retrieved from https://www.investopedia.com/terms/f/fiscalyearend.asp

Kerrigan, K. (2020). *Our future in public relations: A cautionary tale in three parts*. Bingley : Emerald Publishing.

Kim, E. (2018, November 15). Jeff Bezos to employees: 'One day, Amazon will fail' but our job is to delay it as long as possible. *CNBC.com*. Retrieved from https://cnb.cx/2KGB4Lf

Kim, E. (2019, May 29). Jeff Bezos's elite Amazon 'S-team' just got a new addition – Here's a full rundown of everybody on it. *CNBC.com*. Retrieved from https://cnb.cx/35wmDC9

Kishan, S. (2020, August 31). California lawmakers approve racial quotas for corporate boards. *BloombergQuint.com*. Retrieved from https://bit.ly/3hazkbr

Kolberg, B. (2014, March). Getting down to business at public relations agencies. *PR Update, 49*(2), 6–7.

Kolbert, E. (2018, August 20). Gospels of giving for the gilded age. *The New Yorker*. Retrieved from http://bit.ly/2Prv3Ge

Kolchin, K. (2019, October). *Q: Who owns stock in America? A: Individual investors*. New York, NY: SIFMA.

Kolchin, K., & Podziemska, J. (2019). *Capital markets fact book 2019*. New York, NY: SIFMA.

Korn Ferry. (2019, April 17). *Korn Ferry analysis of largest U.S. companies shows percentage of women in C-suite roles inches up from previous year* [Press release]. Retrieved from http://bit.ly/36J1FS3

Korn Ferry. (2020a). *2020 pulse survey: CCAO.* New York, NY: Korn Ferry.

Korn Ferry. (2020b, January 21). *Age and tenure in the C-suite: Korn Ferry study reveals trends by title and industry* [Press release]. Retrieved from https://bit.ly/2N0m1h4

Korn Ferry. (2020c). *Chief communications officers: The pandemic's new business leaders.* New York, NY: Korn Ferry.

Kostov, N., & Vranica, S. (2019, January 25). WPP asked ex-CEO Martin Sorrell to repay expenses. *The Wall Street Journal.* Retrieved from https://on.wsj.com/2QgZxuV

KPMG International. (2016). *Global transformation study 2016: Succeeding in disruptive times.* New York, NY: KPMG International.

KPMG International. (2018). *Growing pains: 2018 global CEO outlook.* New York, NY: KPMG International.

KPMG International. (2019). *Agile or irrelevant: Redefining resilience.* New York, NY: KPMG International.

Kramer, M. R. (2020, January 20). Larry Fink isn't going to read your sustainability report. *Harvard Business Review.* Retrieved from https://bit.ly/2wMYUCk

Krishna, A., Wright, D. K., & Kotcher, R. L. (2020). Curriculum rebuilding in public relations: Understanding what early career, mid-career, and senior PR/communications professionals expect from PR graduates. *Journal of Public Relations Education*, 6(1), 33–57.

Kroc, R. A. (1992). *Grinding it out: The making of McDonald's.* New York, NY: Contemporary Books.

Kulp, P. (2019, June 17). Why Aflac's animatronic duck, which comforts young cancer patients, is a speaker at Cannes. *ADWEEK.* Retrieved from http://bit.ly/36gETAK

Kurzweil, R. (2006). *The singularity is near: when humans transcend biology.* New York, NY: Viking.

Kwoh, L. (2012, May 23). You call that innovation? *The Wall Street Journal.* Retrieved from https://on.wsj.com/2IMV3br

LaBranche, G. A. (2019, September 17). A legacy of advocacy. *IR Update Weekly.* Retrieved from http://news.content.smithbucklin.com/NIRI/091719.html

The LAGRANT Foundation. (2020). About The LAGRANT Foundation. *LAGRANT-Foundation.org.* Retrieved from https://www.lagrantfoundation.org/About

Lambiase, J. (2018). Advice from chief communication officers to master business and change for success. *Communication Booknotes Quarterly*, 49(4), 132–133. doi:10.1080/10948007.2018.1548201

Landis, K. (2019, March 19). The public relations industry is too white and the solution starts with higher education. *INSIGHT Into Diversity*. Retrieved from https://bit.ly/37gofCq

Laskin, A. V. (2014). Investor relations as a public relations function: A state of the profession in the United States. *Journal of Public Relations Research*, 26(3), 200–214. doi:10.1080/1062726X.2013.864244

Laskin, A. V. (2018). Investor relations and financial communication: The evolution of the profession. In A. V. Laskin (Ed.), *The handbook of financial communication and investor relations* (pp. 3–22). New York, NY: Wiley-Blackwell.

Leder, M. (2003). *Financial fine print: Uncovering a company's true value*. Hoboken, NJ: John Wiley & Sons, Inc.

Lenovo. (2020). Diversity & inclusion. *Lenovo.com*. Retrieved from https://www.lenovo.com/us/en/about/diversity

Lev, B. (2012). *Winning investors over: Surprising truths about honesty, earnings guidance, and other ways to boost your stock price*. Boston, MA: Harvard Business Review Press.

Lev, B., & Gu, F. (2016). *The end of accounting and the path forward for investors and managers*. Hoboken, NJ: Wiley.

Lewis, M. (2015). *Flash boys: A Wall Street revolt*. New York, NY: W. W. Norton.

Liker, J. K. (2004). *The Toyota way: 14 management principles from the world's greatest manufacturer*. New York, NY: McGraw-Hill.

Lim, D. (2020, January 15). BlackRock's assets blow past $7 trillion in milestone for investment giant. *The Wall Street Journal*. Retrieved from https://on.wsj.com/31RBFUl

Lincoln, M. (n.d.). *Your duties as a director: The basics*. Palo Alto, CA: Cooley LLP. Retrieved from https://www.cooleygo.com/director-fiduciary-duties/

Luttrell, R. M. (2019). *Social media: How to engage, share, and connect* (3rd ed.). Lanham, MD: Rowman & Littlefield.

Luttrell, R. M., & Capizzo, L. W. (2019a). *Public relations campaigns: An integrated approach*. Thousand Oaks, CA: SAGE.

Luttrell, R. M., & Capizzo, L. W. (2019b). *The PR agency handbook*. Thousand Oaks, CA: SAGE.

M Booth. (2019). Culture is everything. Retrieved from https://www.mbooth.com/culture/

Machan, T. R. (2011, February 12). Profit: The right standard for business. *Barron's*. Retrieved from http://on.barrons.com/hAGqpL

Mackey, J., McIntosh, S., & Phipps, C. (2020). *Conscious leadership: Elevating humanity through business*. New York, NY: Portfolio.

Mackey, J., & Sisodia, R. (2014). *Conscious capitalism: Liberating the heroic spirit of business*. Boston, MA: Harvard Business School Press.

Macnamara, B. N., & Maitra, M. (2019). The role of deliberate practice in expert performance: Revisiting Ericsson, Krampe & Tesch-Römer (1993). *Royal Society Open Science, 6*(8), 1–19. doi:10.1098/rsos.190327

Macnamara, B. N., Moreau, D., Hambrick, D. Z. (2016). The relationship between deliberate practice and performance in sports: A meta-analysis. *Perspectives on Psychological Science, 11*(3), 333–350. doi:10.1177/1745691616635591

Maheshwari, S. (2019, April 3). Accenture is buying Droga5, an ad agency, making a bet on creativity. *The New York Times*, p. B1.

Mahler, D. (2016, June 30). Zero-based budgeting is not a wonder diet for companies. *Harvard Business Review*. Retrieved from https://bit.ly/3fmfoSB

Marcec, D. (2018, February 12). CEO tenure rates. *Harvard Law School Forum on Corporate Governance*. Retrieved from https://corpgov.law.harvard.edu/2018/02/12/ceo-tenure-rates/

Marriage, M., & Garrahan, M. (2018, June 11). Martin Sorrell's downfall: Why the ad king left WPP. *Financial Times*. Retrieved from https://on.ft.com/2F6uk74

Mars, Incorporated. (2020). All about Mars. *Mars.com*. Retrieved from https://www.mars.com/about

Marszalek, D. (2020, June 2). Edelman laying off 390 employees across global workforce. *PRovoke*. Retrieved from http://bit.ly/3mMDVmP

Martin, D. (2020). *Marilyn: A woman in charge*. New York, NY: PRMuseum Press, LLC.

Martin, J. (2017). Agile organizational change: Leveraging learnings from software development. *OD Practitioner, 49*(3), 39–41.

Matthews, T. (2018, April 18). Jelinek on shareholders, Costco.com, and hot dogs. *425Business*. Retrieved from https://425business.com/costco-ceo-craig-jelinek/

May, S. K. (2016). Corporate social responsibility. In C. E. Carroll (Ed.), *The SAGE encyclopedia of corporate reputation* (pp. 217–220). Thousand Oaks, CA: SAGE Publications.

Mayo Clinic. (2019a). Mayo Clinic facts. *Mayoclinic.org*. Retrieved from https://www.mayoclinic.org/about-mayo-clinic/facts-statistics

Mayo Clinic. (2019b). Mayo Clinic mission and values. *Mayoclinic.org*. Retrieved from http://history.mayoclinic.org/impact/mayo-clinic-values.php

McCann, D. (2018, June 12). Want to be a nonprofit CFO? Much will be familiar. *CFO.com*. Retrieved from https://bit.ly/2zyK9nv

McCorkindale, T., & Cody, S. (2020, May 5). CCOs shine during an otherwise dark period in human history. *Page.org*. Retrieved from https://bit.ly/3diHrRg

McCorkindale, T., Hynes, A., & Kotcher, R. (2018). The changing business landscape. In R. Bolton, D. W Stacks, & E. Mizrachi (Eds.), *The new era of the*

CCO: *The essential role of communication in a volatile world* (pp. 1–18). New York, NY: Business Expert Press.

McGinnis, K. (2018). Building communications' influence during corporate transformation. In M. W. Ragas, & R. Culp (Eds.), *Mastering business for strategic communicators: Insights and advice from the C-suite of leading brands* (pp. 177–183). Bingley: Emerald Publishing.

McLaughlin, D., & Massa, A. (2020, January 13). The great index fund takeover. *Bloomberg Businessweek*, pp. 20–25.

McTavish, E. (2018, December 21). The rise of belief-driven buying. *14EAST*. Retrieved from http://bit.ly/2JB9wqb

Men, R. L. (2019). *It's the best time for internal communicators!* Gainesville, FL: Institute for Public Relations. Retrieved from http://bit.ly/2Ncc42T

Men, R. L., & Bowen, S. A. (2017). *Excellence in internal communication management*. New York, NY: Business Expert Press.

Men, R. L., Robinson, K., & Thelen, P. (2019). Measurement and evaluation in public relations. In C. M. Kim (Ed.), *Public relations: Competencies and practice* (pp. 115–128). New York, NY: Routledge.

Meng, J. (2014). Unpacking the relationship between organizational culture and excellent leadership in public relations: An empirical investigation. *Journal of Communication Management*, 18(4), 363–385. doi:10.1108/JCOM-06-2012-0050

Merle, R. (2020, March 24). SEC warns of risk of insider trading during coronavirus market turbulence. *The Washington Post*. Retrieved from https://wapo.st/33Q3xYb

Miller, J. A. (2017, October 19). What is a project management office (PMO) and do you need one? *CIO*. Retrieved from http://bit.ly/2ylsZpI

Mishel, L., & Wolfe, J. (2019, August 14). *CEO compensation has grown 940% since 1978*. Washington, DC: Economic Policy Institute

Monllos, K. (2019, August 6). 'The fee model has not changed': Why agencies' biggest problem is their business model. *Digiday*. Retrieved from https://digiday.com/?p=342655

Moorhead, P. (2019, June 18). Salesforce.com's Tableau acquisition: Admitting organic innovation failure? *Forbes.com*. Retrieved from http://bit.ly/2X6LP2r

Monks, R. A. G., & Minow, N. (2011). *Corporate governance* (5th ed.). Hoboken, NJ: John Wiley & Sons.

Morgan, G. (1986). *Images of organization*. Beverly Hills, CA: SAGE Publications.

Morrill, D. C. (1995). Origins of NIRI. *NIRI.org*. Retrieved from https://www.niri.org/about-niri/history-of-niri-(origins)

Mundy, D. E. (2016). Bridging the divide: A multidisciplinary analysis of diversity research and the implications for public relations. *Research Journal of the Institute for Public Relations*, 3(1), 1–28.

Mundy, D. E. (2019). Diversity and inclusion: A core public relations mandate. In C. M. Kim (Ed.), *Public relations: Competencies and practice* (pp. 29–42). New York, NY: Routledge.

Murphy, C. B. (2020, April 22). Enterprise value – EV. *Investopedia.com*. Retrieved from https://www.investopedia.com/terms/e/enterprisevalue.asp

Murray, A. (2019, August). A new purpose for the corporation. *Fortune, 180*(3), 88–94.

Musk, E. [elonmusk]. (2018, August 7). *Am considering taking Tesla private at $420. Funding secured* [Tweet]. Retrieved from https://twitter.com/elonmusk/status/1026872652290379776?lang=en

Nasdaq, Inc. (2020). MarketSite at Times Square. *Nasdaq.com*. Retrieved from https://www.nasdaq.com/marketsite

National Investor Relations Institute. (2013). *Standards of practice: Earnings release content*. Alexandria, VA: National Investor Relations Institute.

National Investor Relations Institute. (2014). *NIRI earnings process practices research report*. Alexandria, VA: National Investor Relations Institute.

National Investor Relations Institute. (2016). *Standards of practice: Disclosure*. Alexandria, VA: National Investor Relations Institute.

National Investor Relations Institute. (2017). *NIRI IR counselor profession and compensation research report*. Alexandria, VA: National Investor Relations Institute.

National Investor Relations Institute. (2018, June 7). *NIRI 2018 policy statement – Guidance practices* [Press release]. Retrieved from https://bit.ly/2UPiNR7

National Investor Relations Institute. (2019). *Investor relations: The disruption opportunity*. Alexandria, VA: National Investor Relations Institute.

Neatby, J. (2016, July 21). The ballooning executive team. *Harvard Business Review*. Retrieved from https://hbr.org/2016/07/the-ballooning-executive-team

Neill, M. S. (2015). Beyond the C-suite: Corporate communications' power and influence. *Journal of Communication Management, 19*(2), 118–132. doi:10.1108/JCOM-06-2013-0046

Neill, M. S. (2018). Change management communication: Barriers, strategies & messaging. *Public Relations Journal, 12*(1), 1–26.

Neill, M. S. (2019). Public relations ethics: responsibility and necessary skills. In C. M. Kim (Ed.), *Public relations competencies and practice* (pp. 58–69). New York, NY: Routledge.

Neill, M. S., & Barnes, A. O. (2018). *Public relations ethics: Senior PR pros tell us how to speak up and keep your job*. New York, NY: Business Expert Press.

Neill, M. S., & Schauster, E. (2015). Gaps in advertising and public relations education: Perspectives of agency leaders. *Journal of Advertising Education, 19*(2), 5–17. doi:10.1177/109804821501900203

Neptune, T. (2020, September 10). Racial inequality in PR is deplorable. *PRWeek*. Retrieved from https://bit.ly/33CypMn

Netflix, Inc. (2020). Company profile. *Netflixinvestors.com*. Retrieved from https://www.netflixinvestor.com/ir-overview/profile/default.aspx

The New York Times. (2002, May 23). Offering of Netflix brings in $82.5 million, 6C.

Nguyen, J. (2019, June 25). How do I value the shares that I own in a private company? *Investopedia.com*. Retrieved from https://bit.ly/34Yxy8K

Nickelsburg, M. (2019, December 5). Amazon expands Bezos' elite 'S-team,' adding 6 execs from emerging branches of the company. *GeekWire*. Retrieved from http://bit.ly/2FpfmsW

Nivedita, C., Franklin, J., & Hussain, N. Z. (2020, September 9). Palantir goes on Wall Street charm offensive ahead of public listing. *Reuters*. Retrieved from https://reut.rs/3m5PJ4u

Nooyi, I. (2019). Profit and purpose. *Directors & Boards*, 43(2), 18–20.

Nothhaft, H., Werder, K. P., Vercic, D., & Zerfass, A. (Eds.). (2020). *Future directions of strategic communication*. London: Routledge.

O'Bryan, M. (2013). Innovation: The most important and overused word in America. *Wired*. Retrieved from http://bit.ly/2RBQh3a

Omnicom Group, Inc. (2020a). Overview. *Omnicomgroup.com*. Retrieved from https://www.omnicomgroup.com/about/

Omnicom Group, Inc. (2020b). OPEN 2.0 – For global distribution. Retrieved from https://bit.ly/35NKzEO

Osipovich, A. (2020, December 1). Nasdaq CEO pushes corporate boards to diversify. *The Wall Street Journal*. Retrieved from http://on.wsj.com/2WwUWaa

Osterwalder, A., & Pigneur, Y. (2010). *Business model generation: A handbook for visionaries, game changers, and challengers*. Hoboken, NJ: John Wiley & Sons, Inc.

Osterwalder, A., & Pigneur, Y., Bernarda, G., & Smith, A. (2014). *Value proposition design: How to create products and services customers want*. Hoboken, NJ: John Wiley & Sons, Inc.

Osterwalder, A., & Pigneur, Y., Smith, A., & Etiemble, F. (2020). *The invincible company: How to constantly reinvent your organization with inspiration from the world's best business models*. Hoboken, NJ: John Wiley & Sons, Inc.

OTC Markets Group, Inc. (2020). Our company. *OTCMarkets.com*. Retrieved from https://www.otcmarkets.com/about/our-company

Owens, J. C. (2017, May 24). 15 years after IPO, Netflix has changed drastically—And is worth nearly 22,000% more. *MarketWatch*. Retrieved from https://on.mktw.net/2StcOl0

Page, J. T., & Parnell, L. J. (2019). *Introduction to strategic public relations: Digital, global, and socially responsible communication*. Thousand Oaks, CA: SAGE.

Parker, K., & Fry, R. (2020, March 25). *More than half of U.S. households have some investment in the stock market*. Washington, DC: Pew Research Center. Retrieved from https://pewrsr.ch/3aipqSz

Pasquarelli, A. (2019, August 19). Allstate beefs up its internal agency as more work goes in- house. *AdAge*. Retrieved from https://bit.ly/2VLybQ5

Pathak, S. (2019, March 29). DTC brands force agencies to think of new ways to get paid. *Digiday*. Retrieved from https://digiday.com/?p=327898

Penning, T., & Bain, M. (2018). High-performing corporate communications teams: Views of top CCOs. *Public Relations Journal, 11*(3), 1–22.

Peppercomm, & Institute for Public Relations. (2020a). *COVID-19: How businesses are handling the crisis*. New York, NY: Peppercomm.

Peppercomm, & Institute for Public Relations. (2020b). *Special report: How companies are engaging during COVID-19*. New York, NY: Peppercomm.

Pettigrew, J. E., & Reber, B. (2013). Corporate reputation and the practice of corporate governance. In C. E. Carroll (Ed.), *The handbook of communication and corporate reputation* (pp. 334–346). Malden, MA: Wiley-Blackwell.

Phillips, J. (2019). *PMI-ACP agile certified practitioner exam guide*. New York: McGraw-Hill.

Piper, M. (2013). *Accounting made simple: Accounting explained in 100 pages or less*. Lexington, KY: Simple Subjects, LLC.

Place, K. R. (2019). Listening as the driver of public relations practice and communication strategy within a global public relations agency. *Public Relations Journal, 12*(3), 1–18.

Pollack, J. (2019, April 3). Behind Accenture's groundbreaking Droga5 deal. *AdAge*. Retrieved from https://adage.com/article/agency-news/accenture-interactive-set-buy-droga5/317215

Pompper, D. (2015). *Corporate social responsibility, sustainability and public relations: Negotiating multiple complex challenges*. London: Routledge.

Porter, M. E., & Kramer, M. R. (2006). Strategy and society: The link between competitive advantage and corporate social responsibility. *Harvard Business Review, 84*(12), 78–92.

Porter Novelli. (2018). *2018 Porter Novelli/Cone purpose premium index*. New York, NY: Porter Novelli.

Porter Novelli. (2019). *Feeling purpose: 2019 Porter Novelli/Cone purpose biometrics study*. New York, NY: Porter Novelli.

Posner, C. (2019, September 3). It's been eons since the SEC last did this—Brought a Reg FD enforcement action, that is. *Cooley PubCo*. Retrieved from https://cooley-pubco.com/2019/09/03/sec-brings-reg-fd-enforcement-action-that-is/

Posner, C. (2020, June 4). What's the latest on virtual shareholder meetings? *Cooley PubCo*. Retrieved from https://bit.ly/2zRYpIu

PM Solutions. (2018). *The adaptive organization 2018: A benchmark of changing approaches to project management*. Glen Mills, PA: PM Solutions.

PQ Media. (2020). *Global advertising & marketing revenue forecast 2019–23*. Stamford, CT: PQ Media.

PR Council. (2019). *How to build a request for proposal (RFP)*. New York, NY: PR Council.

PRovoke. (2019). The 2019 influence 100. *Provokemedia.com*. Retrieved from https://www.provokemedia.com/ranking-and-data/influence-100/the-influence-100-2019

PRovoke. (2020). The 2020 influence 100. *Provokemedia.com*. Retrieved from https://www.provokemedia.com/ranking-and-data/influence-100/the-influence-100-2020

PRWeek. (2015). Betsy Plank: Hall of Fame 2015. *PRWeek.com*. Retrieved from https://www.prweek.com/article/1362637/betsy-plank-hall-fame-2015

PRWeek. (2016). Hall of fame 2016. *PRWeek.com*. Retrieved from https://www.prweek.com/us/halloffame2016

PRWeek. (2020, July 7). PRWeek US power list 2020. *PRWeek.com*. Retrieved from https://www.prweek.com/article/1688049/prweek-us-power-list-2020

Prang, A. (2020, March 6). California law pressures small-company boards to include women. *The Wall Street Journal*. Retrieved from https://on.wsj.com/33SUK84

Project Management Institute, Inc. (2017a). *Agile practice guide*. Newtown Square, PA: Project Management Institute, Inc.

Project Management Institute, Inc. (2017b). *A guide to the project management body of knowledge (PMBOK GUIDE®)* (6th ed.). Newtown Square, PA: Project Management Institute.

Public Company Accounting Oversight Board. (2020). About the PCAOB. *PCAOBUS.org*. Retrieved from https://pcaobus.org/About/Pages/default.aspx

Public Relations Society of America, Inc. (2019). Betsy Plank. *PRSSA.PRSA.org*. Retrieved from https://prssa.prsa.org/about-prssa/history/betsy-plank/

Public Relations Society of America, Inc. (2020). MBA/business school. *PRSA.org*. Retrieved from https://www.prsa.org/about/mba-business-school

PwC. (2016). *Putting purpose to work: A study of purpose in the workplace*. New York, NY: PwC.

PwC. (2019a). *CEOs' curbed confidence spells caution: 22nd annual global CEO survey*. New York, NY: PwC.

PwC. (2019b). *Global top 100 companies by market capitalisation*. London: PwC.

Ragas, M. W. (2013, February 8). Require business 101 for every student. *The Chronicle of Higher Education, 59*(22), p. A25.

Ragas, M. W. (2016a). Financial intermediaries. In C. E. Carroll (Ed.), *The SAGE encyclopedia of corporate reputation* (pp. 315–318). Thousand Oaks, CA: SAGE.

Ragas, M. W. (2016b). Public relations means business: Addressing the need for greater business acumen. *Journal of Integrated Marketing Communications, 17*, 34.

Ragas, M. W. (2018). Corporate proxy contests: Overview, application and outlook. In A. Laskin (Ed.), *The handbook of financial communication and investor relations* (pp. 187–196). New York, NY: Wiley-Blackwell.

Ragas, M. W. (2019a). Defining 'business acumen': A Delphi study of corporate communications leaders. *Public Relations Journal, 13*(1), 1–19.

Ragas, M. W. (2019b). Financial communications and investor relations: Speaking and translating the language (and issues) of business and finance. In C. M. Kim (Ed.), *Public relations: Competencies and practice* (pp. 232–248). New York, NY: Routledge.

Ragas, M. W., & Culp, R. (2014a). *Business essentials for strategic communicators: Creating shared value for the organization and its stakeholders.* New York, NY: Palgrave Macmillan.

Ragas, M. W., & Culp, R. (2014b, December 22). *Public relations and business acumen: Closing the gap.* Gainesville, FL: Institute for Public Relations. Retrieved from http://www.instituteforpr.org

Ragas, M. W., & Culp, R. (2015, May 1). Business weak: Five ways to build greater business acumen. *Public Relations Tactics*, 17.

Ragas, M. W., & Culp, R. (2018a, March 28). C-suite issues PR a license to lead. *PRWeek*. Retrieved from http://www.prweek.com

Ragas, M. W., & Culp, R. (Eds.). (2018b). *Mastering business for strategic communicators: Insights and advice from the C-suite of leading brands.* Bingley: Emerald Publishing.

Ragas, M. W., Laskin, A. V., & Brusch, M. D. (2014). Investor relations measurement and evaluation: A survey of professionals. *Journal of Communication Management, 18*(2), 176–192. doi:10.1108/JCOM-03-2013-0020

Ragas, M. W., & Ragas, T. H. (forthcoming). Understanding Agile for strategic communicators: Foundations, implementations, and implications. *International Journal of Strategic Communication.*

Ragas, M. W., & Tran, H. L. (2015). The financial news ecosystem: Journalists' perceptions of group hierarchy. *Journalism: Theory, Practice, and Criticism, 16*(6), 711–729. doi:10.1177/1464884914540441

Ragas, M. W., Uysal, N., & Culp, R. (2015). "Business 101" in public relations education: An exploratory survey of senior communication executives. *Public Relations Review, 41*(3), 378–380. doi:10.1016/j.pubrev.2015.02.007

Ramanujam, K. (2019, February 7). The CFO's crucial role in digital transformation. *CFO.com*. Retrieved from http://bit.ly/2FZbcbS

Randolph, M. (2019). *That will never work: The birth of Netflix and the amazing life of an idea*. New York, NY: Little, Brown and Company.

Rappeport, A., & Chokshi, N. (2020, April 29). Crippled airline industry to get $25 billion bailout, part of it as loans. *The New York Times*. Retrieved from https://nyti.ms/2zL2nCs

Rawlins, B. L. (2005). Corporate social responsibility. In B. Heath (Ed.), *Encyclopedia of Public Relations* (Vol. 1, pp. 210–214). Thousand Oaks, CA: SAGE Reference.

Rawlins, B. L. (2006). *Prioritizing stakeholders for public relations*. Gainesville, FL: Institute for Public Relations.

Rawlins, B. L. (2008). Measuring the relationship between organizational transparency and employee trust. *Public Relations Journal*, 2(2), 1–21.

Rawlins, B. L. (2009). Give the emperor a mirror: Toward developing a stakeholder measurement of organizational transparency. *Journal of Public Relations Research*, 21(1), 71–99.

Remund, D. L., & Kuttis, K. (2018). Securities law for financial communication and investor relations in the United States, 1929–2016. In A. Laskin (Ed.), *The handbook of financial communication and investor relations* (pp. 127–136). New York, NY: Wiley-Blackwell.

Rennie, K. D., Byrum, K., Tidwell, M., & Chitkara, A. (2018). Strategic communication in MBA curriculum: A qualitative study of student outcomes. *Journal of Management Education*, 42(5), 594–617. doi:10.1177/1052562918774593

RFP Associates, LLC. (2019). *The impact of the agency selection process on public relations programs & outcomes*. Washington, DC: RFP Associates, LLC, CommunicationsMatch, & Researchscape.

Ries, E. (2011). *The lean startup: How today's entrepreneurs use continuous innovation to create radically successful businesses*. New York, NY: Crown Business.

Rickard, A. (2019, Spring). NIRI celebrates 50 years of success. *IR Update*, pp. 10–19.

Rigby, D. K., Elk, S., & Berez, S. (2020). The agile C-suite. *Harvard Business Review*, 98(3), 64–73.

Rigby, D. K., Sutherland, J., & Noble, A. (2018). Agile at scale: How to go from a few teams to hundreds. *Harvard Business Review*, 96(3), 88–96.

Rigby, D. K., Sutherland, J., & Takeuchi, H. (2016). Embracing agile: How to master the process that's transforming management. *Harvard Business Review*, 94(5), 40–50.

Ritholtz, B. (2017, July 6). The world is about to change even faster. *Bloomberg View*. Retrieved from https://bloom.bg/2Ft2JO8

Rittenhouse, L. (2020a, May 4). Pitching in a remote world. *AdAge*. Retrieved from https://bit.ly/3fRzDZe

Rittenhouse, L. (2020b, July 28). Omnicom Group's John Wren finally releases workforce diversity data in staff memo. *AdAge*. Retrieved from https://bit.ly/30U1Mbv

Rittenhouse, L., & Pasquarelli, A. (2020, April 25). Allstate severs six-decade relationship with Leo Burnett. *Crain's Chicago Business*. Retrieved from https://bit.ly/2xgKlXI

Roberts, S. (2017, April 14). Al Golin, PR man whose vision helped make McDonald's a success, dies at 87. *The New York Times*. Retrieved from https://nyti.ms/2oJ67g9

Rodrigues, K. (2018, August 3). Building an agile business. *JPMorgan.com*. Retrieved from http://bit.ly/2YzcIrD

Rogers, E. M. (1962). *Diffusion of innovations*. New York, NY: Free Press of Glencoe.

Rose, D. (2015). *Leading agile teams*. Newtown Square, PA: Project Management Institute, Inc.

Rossman, J. (2019). *Think like Amazon: 50 ½ ideas to become a digital leader*. New York, NY: McGraw-Hill Education.

Roush, C. (2006). The need for more business education in mass communication schools. *Journalism & Mass Communication Educator, 61*(2), 195–204.

Roush, C. (2016). *Show me the money: Writing business and economic stories for mass communication* (3rd ed.). New York, NY: Routledge.

Russell, J. J. (1989, April). A boy and his airline. *TexasMonthly*. Retrieved from https://www.texasmonthly.com/articles/a-boy-and-his-airline/

Rutherford, L. (2018). Collaborating with strategy and innovation: Taking on the challenge to "communicate the amoeba." In M. W. Ragas & R. Culp (Eds.), *Mastering business for strategic communicators: Insights and advice from the C-suite of leading brands* (pp. 91–97). Bingley: Emerald Publishing.

Safire, W. (1968). *The New language of politics: An anecdotal dictionary of catchwords, slogans, and political usage*. New York, NY: Random House.

Salmon, F. (2019, January 28). Gen Z prefers "socialism" to "capitalism." *AXIOS*. Retrieved from http://bit.ly/2NVtotI

Salter, M. S. (2019). *Rehabilitating corporate purpose*. Working Paper 19-104, Harvard Business School. Retrieved from https://hbs.me/2JqE7I2

Sandler, R. J. (2012, October 15). *Securities offerings during blackout periods and following a quarter-end*. Harvard Law School Forum on Corporate Governance. Retrieved from https://bit.ly/3aoRd3L

Santilli, P. (2020, December 21). Tesla stock joins the S&P 500: A game changer. *The Wall Street Journal*. Retrieved from http://on.wsj.com/38rRSBu

Satell, G. (2014). A look back at why Blockbuster really failed and why it didn't have to. *Forbes.com*. Retrieved from http://bit.ly/2ucrVpA

Sax, D. (2018, December 7). End the innovation obsession. *The New York Times*, p. SR9.

Schad, T. (2018, August 29). Browns LB Mychal Kendricks admits to insider trading after federal charges. *USA Today*. Retrieved from https://bit.ly/3bwx7Vj

Scott, S. (2019). Nine business transformation stats you can't afford to ignore in 2019. *Institute for Public Relations*. Retrieved from http://bit.ly/2FvmCUz

Schultz, E. J. (2017, May 1). The race is on! How IBM, Accenture, PwC and Deloitte are shaking up the marketing industry. *AdAge*. Retrieved from https://adage.com/article/news/consultancies-rising/308845

Schwartz, E. I. (2019, January). Corporate longevity update: Creative destruction rides high. *Innosight.com*. Retrieved from http://bit.ly/2YLqbl7

SD Learning Consortium. (2016). *The entrepreneurial organization at scale: Report of the SD Learning Consortium*. New York, NY: SD Learning Consortium.

SD Learning Consortium. (2017). *2017 report of the SD Learning Consortium*. New York, NY: SD Learning Consortium.

Segal, T. (2020, April 5). Profit margin. *Investopedia.com*. Retrieved from https://www.investopedia.com/terms/p/profitmargin.asp

Skonieczny, M. (2012). *The basics of understanding financial statements*. Schaumburg, IL: Investment Publishing.

Smith, R. D. (2017). *Strategic planning for public relations* (5th ed.). New York, NY: Routledge.

Society for Human Resource Management. (2019, July 26). All S&P \500 companies now have women on boards. *SHRM.org*. Retrieved from http://bit.ly/2FrUAJv

Soriano, M. (2019, June 17). *Communicating with purpose: Best practices for executive leaders*. Gainesville, FL: Institute for Public Relations. Retrieved from http://bit.ly/2xF5sjf

Sorkin, A. R. (2018, January 15). A demand for change backed up by $6 trillion. *The New York Times*, p. B1.

Sorkin, A. R. (2019a, January 16). Top investor says C.E.O.s can bridge global rifts. *The New York Times*, p. B1.

Sorkin, A. R. (2019b, April 19). War of words in capitalism vs. socialism. *The New York Times*, p. B1.

Sorkin, A. R. (2019c, September 18). Profits or public interest? *The New York Times*, p. F2.

Sorkin, A. R. (2020, September 11). A free market manifesto that changed the world, reconsidered. *DealBook*. Retrieved from https://nyti.ms/3kbGqyd

Southwest Airlines. (2020a). Southwest corporate fact sheet. *SWAmedia.com*. Retrieved from https://www.swamedia.com/pages/corporate-fact-sheet

Southwest Airlines Co. (2020b). Purpose, vision, values and mission. *Investors.southwest.com*. Retrieved from https://swa.is/2XRgQY1

Sowell, T. (2011). *Basic economics: A common sense guide to the economy* (4th ed.). New York, NY: Basic Books.

Spangler, J. (2014, June 2). *Valued communicators understand the business.* Gainesville, FL: Institute for Public Relations. Retrieved from http://bit.ly/1xiYB8n. Accessed on June 6, 2014.

Spector, S., & Spector, B. (2018). *Diverse voices: Profiles in leadership.* New York, NY: PRMuseum Press, LLC.

Spencer Stuart. (2018a). *2018 United States Spencer Stuart board index.* Chicago, IL: Spencer Stuart.

Spencer Stuart. (2018b). *Chief communications officers in the boardroom—A rarity today, but could that change?* Chicago, IL: Spencer Stuart.

Spencer Stuart. (2020, May 27). *Women & minorities make significant gains within the CMO ranks in 2019.* [Press release]. Retrieved from https://bit.ly/2TRDtbn

Spencer Stuart, & Weber Shandwick. (2016). *The rising CCO VI: Chief communications officers: Roles & perspectives.* Chicago, IL: Spencer Stuart.

Staley, O. (2017, August 14). To fill 70,000 jobs, chocolate giant Mars will have to overcome its deeply secretive past. *QUARTZ.* Retrieved from https://qz.com/1047136/mars-recruiting/

State Street Global Advisors. (2020, March 5). *State Street Global Advisors marks third anniversary and progress of Fearless Girl campaign, reports 681 companies added female board members* [Press release]. Retrieved from https://bit.ly/3h82zvz

Stein, L. (2017, November 13). How much are agencies' ideas worth? *AdAge.* Retrieved from https://adage.com/article/agency-news/ideas-worth/311267

Stern, J. M., & Chew, D. H. (Eds.). (2003). *The revolution in corporate finance* (4th ed.). Malden, MA: Blackwell Publishing.

Sternberg, J. (2019, June 28). The rise of the chief growth officer. *ADWEEK.* Retrieved from https://www.adweek.com/brand-marketing/the-rise-of-the-chief-growth-officer/

Stoll, J. D. (2019, September 6). A reminder for CEOs considering a shift in focus: Shareholders are still king. *The Wall Street Journal.* Retrieved from https://on.wsj.com/39X9fud

Stone, B. (2013a, June 7). Costco CEO Craig Jelinek leads the cheapest, happiest company in the world. *Bloomberg Businessweek.* Retrieved from https://bloom.bg/2Y7z4EO

Stone, B. (2013b). *The everything store: Jeff Bezos and the age of Amazon.* New York, NY: Little, Brown and Company.

Stone, B. (2017). *The upstarts: Uber, Airbnb, and the battle for the new Silicon Valley.* New York, NY: Back Bay Books.

Stout, L. (2012). *The shareholder value myth: How putting shareholders first harms investors, corporations, and the public.* San Francisco, CA: Berrett-Koehler Publishers.

Strine, L. E. (2016). *The dangers of denial: The need for a clear-eyed understanding of the power and accountability structure established by the Delaware general corporation law* (Research Paper No. 15-08). Philadelphia, PA: Institute for Law and Economics.

Strine, L. E. (2017). Corporate power is corporate purpose I: Evidence from my hometown. *Oxford Review of Economic Policy, 33*(2), 176–187. doi:10.1093/oxrep/grx027

Strine, L. E. (2019). *Toward fair and sustainable capitalism: A comprehensive proposal to help American workers, restore fair gainsharing between employees and shareholders, and increase American competitiveness by reorienting our corporate governance system toward sustainable long-term growth and encouraging investments in America's future* (Research Paper No. 19-39). Philadelphia, PA: Institute for Law and Economics.

Sudhaman, A. (2017, August 18). Lenovo rethinks PR approach with big budget global agency review. *The Holmes Report*. Retrieved from http://bit.ly/30BspAe

Sudhaman, A. (2018, May 18). Barby Siegel profile: Fearless leader. *The Holmes Report*. Retrieved from http://bit.ly/2TPp1j0

Sudhaman, A. (2019, June 18). Cannes: Aflac opens up about risks from successful purpose shift. *The Holmes Report*. Retrieved from http://bit.ly/2NiV7Rm

Sundaram, A. (2019, June 26). A stock exchange for sneakers is now worth $1 billion and it just hired a former eBay exec as CEO. *CNBC.com*. Retrieved from https://cnb.cx/2SmNdKp

Sustainability Accounting Standards Board. (2020, July 12). Promoting clarity and compatibility in the sustainability landscape. *SASB.org*. Retrieved from https://bit.ly/3fvvCZg

Swann, P. (2014). *Cases in public relations management: The rise of social media and activism* (2nd ed.). New York, NY: Routledge.

Swartz, J. (2020, April 17). Google braved one recession, and Alphabet is more diversified as coronavirus roils rivals. *MarketWatch*. Retrieved from https://on.mktw.net/3aq4msi

Swerling, J., Thorson, K., Tenderich, B., Yang, A., Li, Z., Gee, E., & Savastano, E. (2014). *GAP VIII: Eighth communication and public relations generally accepted practices study*. Los Angeles, CA: USC Annenberg School for Communication and Journalism, Strategic Communication and Public Relations Center.

Tabuena, J. A. (2006, December). The chief compliance officer vs the general counsel: Friend or foe? *Compliance & Ethics*, pp. 4–7, 10–15.

Tahmincioglu, E. (2019). Profit and purpose. *Directors & Boards, 43*(2), 16–17.

Taparia, J. (2004). *Understanding financial statements: A journalist's guide*. Portland, OR: Marion Street Press, Inc.

Tai, Y. (2018, February 23). 1871 ranks 1st in the world in global study of business incubators. *blog.1871.com*. Retrieved from http://bit.ly/2Ng6WLa

Tett, G. (2019, September 5). Does capitalism need saving from itself? *Financial Times*. Retrieved from https://on.ft.com/2MKMyhL

Thomas, J. M. (2017, November 16). Where have all the public companies gone? *The Wall Street Journal*. Retrieved from https://on.wsj.com/2SrPxyP

Thomas, L. (2018, December 7). Here's the one photo Walmart's CEO keeps on his phone to stoke 'healthy paranoia' in race against Amazon. *CNBC*. Retrieved from https://cnb.cx/31SU4xS

Thomas, L. (2020, June 5). Read Nike CEO John Donahoe's note to employees on racism: We must 'get our own house in order.' *CNBC.com*. Retrieved from https://cnb.cx/3fNQo6R

Tindall, N. T. J. (2018). Beyond the classroom. In C. Roush (Ed.), *Master class: Teaching advice for journalism and mass communication instructors* (pp. 143–153). Lanham, MD: Rowman & Littlefield.

Tindall, N. T. J., & McWilliams, M. S. (2011). The myth and mismatch of balance: Black female professors' construction of balance, integration, and negotiation of work and life. In E. Gilchrist (Ed.), *Experiences of single African-American female professors: With this Ph.D., I thee Wed* (pp. 59–82). Lanham, MD: Lexington.

Tonello, M., & Brancato, C. K. (2007). *Corporate governance handbook 2007: Legal standards and board practices*. New York, NY: The Conference Board, Inc.

Tortoriello, R. (2018, March). *In the money: What really motivates executive performance?* New York, NY: S&P Global Market Intelligence.

Toth, E. (Ed.). (2006). *The future of excellence in public relations and communication management: Challenges for the next generation*. Mahwah, NJ: Erlbaum.

Tran, H., & Ragas, M. W. (2018). Peer perceptions of media elites and hierarchical differentiation among financial journalists. *Journalism & Mass Communication Quarterly, 95*(1), 258–277. doi:10.1177/1077699017691249

Trentmann, N., & Broughton, K. (2020, April 21). Companies that don't cut executive pay now could pay for it later. *The Wall Street Journal*. Retrieved from https://on.wsj.com/3fciXLV

Twitter, Inc. (2020). Form 10-K. Retrieved from https://bit.ly/3aH0CE5

U.S. Bureau of Labor Statistics. (2020). *Occupational outlook handbook*. Washington, DC: U.S. Department of Labor.

U.S. Securities and Exchange Commission. (n.d.-a). Form 8-K. *Investor.gov*. Retrieved from https://www.investor.gov/introduction-investing/investing-basics/glossary/form-8-k

U.S. Securities and Exchange Commission. (n.d.-b). Shareholder voting. *Investor.gov*. Retrieved from https://www.investor.gov/research-before-you-invest/research/shareholder-voting

U.S. Securities and Exchange Commission. (2004). Selective disclosure (Reg. FD). *SEC.gov*. Retrieved from https://www.sec.gov/hot/regfd.htm

U.S. Securities and Exchange Commission. (2012a). *Investor bulletin: How to read an 8-K*. Washington, DC: SEC Office of Investor Education and Advocacy.

U.S. Securities and Exchange Commission. (2012b). Spotlight on proxy matters – Corporate elections generally. *SEC.gov*. Retrieved from https://www.sec.gov/spotlight/proxymatters/corporate_elections.shtml

U.S. Securities and Exchange Commission. (2013, April 2). *SEC says social media OK for company announcements if investors are alerted* [Press release]. Retrieved from https://www.sec.gov/news/press-release/2013-2013-51htm

U.S. Securities and Exchange Commission. (2017). Quiet period. *SEC.gov*. Retrieved from https://www.sec.gov/fast-answers/answersquiethtm.html

U.S. Securities and Exchange Commission. (2018). Non-GAAP financial measures. *SEC.gov*. Retrieved from https://www.sec.gov/divisions/corpfin/guidance/nongaapinterp.htm

U.S. Securities and Exchange Commission. (2019). Going public. *SEC.gov*. Retrieved from https://www.sec.gov/smallbusiness/goingpublic

U.S. Securities and Exchange Commission. (2020). About EDGAR. *SEC.gov*. Retrieved from https://www.sec.gov/edgar/about

United States Census Bureau. (2020). Quick facts: United States. *Census.gov*. Retrieved from https://www.census.gov/quickfacts/fact/table/US/PST045219

US SIF Foundation. (2020). *Report on US sustainable, responsible and impact investing trends*. Washington, DC: US SIF Foundation.

USC Annenberg Center for Public Relations. (2019). *2019 global communications report*. Los Angeles, CA: USC Annenberg School for Communication and Journalism.

USC Annenberg Center for Public Relations. (2020a). *2020 global communications report*. Los Angeles, CA: USC Annenberg School for Communication and Journalism.

USC Annenberg Center for Public Relations. (2020b). *Relevance report 2020*. Los Angeles, CA: USC Annenberg School for Communication and Journalism.

Uysal, N. (2016). Social collaboration in intranets: The impact of social exchange and group norms on internal communication. *International Journal of Business Communication, 53*(2), 181–199. doi:10.1177/2329488415627270

Uysal, N., & Tsetsura, K. (2015). Corporate governance on stakeholder issues: Shareholder activism as a guiding force. *Journal of Public Affairs, 15*(2), 210–219. doi:10.1002/pa.1529

van Ruler, B. (2014). *Reflective communication scrum: Recipe for accountability*. The Hague: Eleven International Publishing.

van Ruler, B. (2015). Agile public relations planning: The Reflective communication scrum. *Public Relations Review, 41*(2), 187–194. doi:10.1016/j.pubrev.2014.11.008

van Ruler, B. (2018). Communication theory: An underrated pillar on which strategic communication rests. *International Journal of Strategic Communication*, 12(4), 367–381. doi:10.1080/1553118X.2018.1452240

Vigna, P. (2013, April 2). SEC clears Netflix's Reed Hastings; Says social media's OK for sharing. *Blogs.WSJ.com*. Retrieved from https://on.wsj.com/33UF9F1

Vista Equity Partners Management, LLC. (2020). *The evolving role of the chief growth officer*. Austin, TX: Vista Equity Partners Management, LLC.

Wallington, C. F. (2020). Barriers, borders, and boundaries: Exploring why there are so few African-American males in the public relations profession. *Public Relations Journal*, 12(3), 1–16.

Washkuch, F. (2020, December 21). MDC Partners, Stagwell reach agreement to combine. *Campaign*. Retrieved from http://bit.ly/3pfD1Rx

Weber Shandwick. (2017). *CEO activism in 2017: High noon in the C-suite*. New York, NY: Weber Shandwick & KRC Research.

Weber Shandwick. (2018). *CEO activism in 2018: The purposeful CEO*. New York, NY: Weber Shandwick & KRC Research.

Weber Shandwick. (2019a). *CEO activism: Inside comms & marketing*. New York, NY: Weber Shandwick & KRC Research.

Weber Shandwick. (2019b). *Employee activism in the age of purpose: Employees (up)rising*. New York, NY: Weber Shandwick, United Minds, & KRC Research.

Weindruch, B. (2016). *Start with the future and work back: A heritage management manifesto*. Lanham, MD: Hamilton Books.

Wessel, M., & Christensen, C. M. (2012). Surviving disruption. *Harvard Business Review*, 90(12), 56–64.

Whitaker, M. (2019, October 24). The American public agrees that capitalism is broken—And on how to fix it. *FastCompany*. Retrieved from http://bit.ly/2Wr38rp

Wigglesworth, R. (2020, January 28). State Street vows to turn up the heat on ESG standards. *Financial Times*. Retrieved from https://on.ft.com/2XPXOAX

Wilcox, D. L., Cameron, G. T., & Reber, B. H. (2015). *Public relations: Strategies and tactics* (11th ed.). Upper Saddle River, NJ: Pearson.

Winkler, R. (2020a, March 16). Startups race to shore up balance sheets as panic spreads. *The Wall Street Journal*. Retrieved from https://on.wsj.com/34UxTcI

Winkler, R. (2020b, April 18). Coronavirus forces tech startups founders to grow up fast. *The Wall Street Journal*. Retrieved from https://on.wsj.com/2VuXbLy

Wisner, F. (2012). *Edelman and the rise of public relations*. New York, NY: Daniel J. Edelman, Inc.

Wladawsky-Berger, I. (2018, November 2). It's all about business model innovation, not new technology. *WSJ.com CIO Journal*. Retrieved from https://on.wsj.com/2IQoVnt

WPP plc. (2020). About. *WPP.com*. Retrieved from https://www.wpp.com/about

Wohl, J. (2017, July 17). Everything, including the kitchen sink: Inside Kohler's in-house agency. *AdAge*. Retrieved from https://bit.ly/3bQSX6t

Workday, Inc. (2016). *6 top CEO priorities and how to address them*. Pleasanton, CA: Workday, Inc.

The World Federation of Exchanges. (2019). *World-exchanges.org*. The World Federation of Exchanges publishes 2018 full year market highlights. Retrieved from http://bit.ly/2uHhgDu

Youn, S. (2019, December 21). Nike sales booming after Colin Kaepernick ad, invalidating critics. *ABC News*. Retrieved from https://abcn.ws/2SgcbZF

Zacharek, S., Dockterman, E., & Sweetland Edwards, H. (2017, December 18). *TIME* person of the year: The silence breakers. *TIME*. Retrieved from http://bit.ly/36pBPBW

Zerfass, A., & Volk, S. C. (2018). How communication departments contribute to corporate success: The communications contributions framework. *Journal of Communication Management*, 22(4), 397–415. doi:10.1108/JCOM-12-2017-0146

Zillman, C. (2019, May 16). The Fortune 500 has more female CEOs than ever before. *Fortune.com*. Retrieved from http://bit.ly/30mKzXH

ABOUT THE SIDEBAR CONTRIBUTORS

Valerie Barker Waller is a seasoned leader with experience in strategy, branding and integrated marketing and communications and has worked in Fortune 100 companies, non-profit and civic organizations and advertising agencies. She is currently the Chief Marketing and Communications Officer at YMCA of the USA (Y-USA) where she is responsible for identifying and creating opportunities to build the Y's brand through strategic partnerships and public engagement. Over the last 10 years, she has held brand, marketing and communications leadership roles at United Way of Metropolitan Chicago, United Airlines and Chicago 2016 – the organization formed to deliver Chicago's bid for the 2016 Olympic and Paralympic Games. She holds a bachelor's degree in finance and business economics from the University of Notre Dame and earned an MBA from the University of Michigan Ross School of Business.

Katie Boylan is the Chief Communications Officer for Target Corporation. In her role, she leads the company's internal and external communications, overseeing employee engagement, executive positioning and corporate, financial and brand communications. She joined Target in January 2011. Prior to Target, she was a Senior Vice President at Edelman, a global communications marketing firm. Earlier in her career, she held roles at Weber Shandwick and Burson Marsteller where she developed communications programming for leading companies such as Coca-Cola, McDonald's, Burger King, Land-O-Lakes and Hormel. She also held a public relations role at Marshall Field's, a regional department store. She earned a BA from the College of St. Benedict and currently serves on its Board of Trustees. She and her husband, Steve, have two sons and live in Minneapolis, MN.

Joe Cohen is Chief Marketing and Communications Officer at AXIS, a global provider of specialty insurance and reinsurance with a presence that spans North America, Europe, Latin America, Middle East, Asia-Pacific and Bermuda. He leads the company's global in-house marketing and communications team. He is responsible for guiding brand reputation, marketing and advertising, digital, financial communications and internal/change management communications. He previously served as Senior Vice President (SVP) of Communications at KIND Healthy Snacks where he was responsible for guiding the company's communications strategy and leading its in-house team. Prior to that, he spent 15 years at the MWW public relations firm where he rose from an entry-level position to SVP and held leadership positions in the firm's consumer marketing and corporate communications practices. He served as 2014 National Chair of Public Relations Society of America and is a graduate of the S.I. Newhouse School of Public Communications at Syracuse University.

Carol Cone, Chief Executive Officer, Carol Cone ON PURPOSE, is internationally recognized for her work in purpose and corporate social responsibility. She is cited as one of the industry's pioneers of social purpose and the person who today, continues to lead the work and conversation on purpose. Called the "Mother of Social Purpose," for over 30 years, she's embraced a steadfast commitment to building lasting partnerships between companies, brands and social issues for deep business and societal impact. Initiatives she has created include: Aflac's My Special Aflac Duck, American Heart Association's Go Red for Women, Avon Breast Cancer Crusade; P&G's Live, Learn and Thrive; PNC Grow Up Great; Reebok's Human Rights Program; and Vaseline Healing Project. Her signature initiatives have raised more than $3 billion for various social causes, won hundreds of awards for excellence around the globe and are the subject of four Harvard Business School cases.

Bob Feldman is Vice Chair of ICF Next, a global transformation and engagement firm with deep competencies in marketing, communications and technology. In 2007, he founded PulsePoint Group, a communications management consulting firm, and then sold that company in 2014 to ICF. Before PulsePoint, he held senior positions with DreamWorks Animation SKG, GCI Group, Ketchum and Burson-Marsteller. His areas of expertise include reputation and issues management and organizational design of the communications and marketing functions. Companies he has advised over the years include Anthem, Bristol-Myers Squibb, Chevron, CVS Health,

Disney, DuPont, GE, HPE, Johnson & Johnson, Kaiser Permanente, Netflix, SeaWorld Parks & Entertainment, Toyota and Wells Fargo. He serves on the Board of Trustees of the Page Society and is the recipient of Page's 2019 Distinguished Service Award and the Plank Center's 2018 Milestones in Mentoring Legacy Award.

Catherine Hernandez-Blades is the former Senior Vice President, Chief ESG and Communications Officer at Aflac. She served in the chief marketing officer (CMO) and chief communications officer (CCO) roles simultaneously at two Fortune 500 companies. She is in the inaugural class of the Women in Communications Hall of Fame and the first recipient of the *PRWeek's* Most Purposeful CCO award. A PR News Hall of Famer, Forbes Top 50 Most Influential Global CMO, inducted into the PR Week Hall of Femme in 2017, she is the first American to win the Relations 4 the Future Medal at the Communications 4 the Future awards at Davos. The 2019 Latina Style Corporate Executive of the Year, and on The Holmes Report's Influence 100, she is the 2018 Innovation SABRE recipient for Most Innovative Marketing/Communications Professional – Brand, and *PRWeek's* 2018 Outstanding In-House Professional of the Year. She is a four-time Top Woman in PR, and four-time Bulldog Star of PR.

Shelly Lazarus is Chairman Emeritus of Ogilvy & Mather and served as Chairman of the company from 1997 to June 2012. She has appeared multiple times in *Fortune* magazine's annual ranking of America's 50 Most Powerful Women in Business since the list's inception in 1998. She was the first woman to receive Columbia Business School's Distinguished Leader in Business Award, as well as the Advertising Educational Foundation's Lifetime Achievement Award. She was inducted into the American Advertising Federation Hall of Fame in 2013 and is also a Hall of Fame member of the Direct Marketing Association, American Marketing Association and Crain's New York Business. She serves on many boards including, Merck, The Blackstone Group, New York Presbyterian Hospital, World Wildlife Fund, Partnership for New York City and Lincoln Center for the Performing Arts. She is a member of the Board of Overseers of Columbia Business School where she received her MBA.

Maril MacDonald, Founder & Chief Executive Officer of Gagen MacDonald, is a pioneer in communication, strategy execution and business transformation who is nationally recognized for successfully collaborating with leaders to energize and mobilize their workforce to deliver on company strategy. Her clients have included world leading companies such as Bristol-Myers Squibb, Coca-Cola, DuPont, GE, Johnson & Johnson and United Airlines. Previously, she was chief communication officer at Navistar where she played a critical role in its resurgence from the brink of bankruptcy to one of *Wall Street Journal's* "Top 10 Performers." She is the recipient of the Page Society's Hall of Fame and Distinguished Service Awards.

Kelly McGrail, Vice President of Leadership Communications, Mars, is known for her business perspective and crafting communications strategies that remove roadblocks, unlock opportunities and show impact. Accordingly, she has developed communications strategies and capabilities at multiple organizations – from Oil-Dri Corporation and the Wm. Wrigley Jr. Company to Mars. For the last 10 years, she has helped Mars build its Corporate Communications practice and stewarded organizational firsts for the private company including: shaping a corporate brand strategy; public sustainability reporting; change communication programming in support of a strategic change agenda and major acquisitions; and securing high-profile media engagements for C-suite and Mars family members. With 25+ years' experience as a problem-solver, writer, spokesperson and coach, she excels in helping leaders and teams across Mars achieve their business goals through strategic and authentic communication.

John Onoda consults with corporations, universities, non-governmental organizations and government agencies on a wide range of communications issues. He is the former Head of Communications for General Motors, Levi Strauss, Charles Schwab and Visa USA; and he was Global Head of Media Relations for McDonalds, Holiday Inn Hotels and Harrah's casinos. Most of his work relates to corporate brands and reputation, strategic planning, organizational change, purpose, corporate culture and the professional development of communications professionals. He received the Milestones in Mentoring Award from the Plank Center for Leadership in Public Relations for his decades of coaching corporate and agency professionals. He has also received the Arthur Page Society's Distinguished Service Award and the Integrity Award from the Page Center for Integrity in Public Communications.

A significant portion of his career has been dedicated to corporate social responsibility and sustainability issues.

Linda Rutherford, a 30+ year veteran of journalism and communication, currently serves as Senior Vice President & Chief Communications Officer for Dallas-based Southwest Airlines. During her career, she has spent time working with teams on evolving the airline's communications and social business functions as well as nurturing its iconic corporate culture through periods of great change. She is currently helping the airline map the employee experience, identify what gets in the way of doing great work and advocate for changes across the enterprise. A point of pride is the development of a "social topics" committee and a discussion framework to help the airline maneuver the expectations of various stakeholders to "take a stand" or articulate where it creates societal value. She serves on the National Advisory Board for Texas Tech University's College of Media & Communication, where she received her undergraduate degree, and serves on the Board of Trustees for the Page Society.

Rodrigo A. Sierra is Chief Communications Officer and Senior Vice President of the American Medical Association (AMA). There, he is leading the transformation of the 170-year-old organization to reclaim a leadership position in shaping the evolving healthcare system for the nation. The brand repositioning, media and public affairs expert is responsible at the AMA for public relations, internal communications, executive leadership positioning and social responsibility. He also serves as executive sponsor of the AMA's Latinx employee resource group, on the steering committee of the AMA Center for Health Equity, and as liaison to the AMA Foundation. Over a distinctive and award-winning career, he has been instrumental in achieving meaningful results in high-profile corporate, media, government and regulatory positions. He has led change for Johnson Publishing Company, Integrys Energy Group, Peoples Energy, Chicago Mayor Richard M. Daley, WGN Radio and ABC News. He earned an MBA from the Kellogg School of Management and a bachelor's degree in Philosophy from Northwestern University.

Grant Toups is Chief Client Officer at ICF Next where he leads client impact/service, growth and marketing for the firm. Prior to ICF Next, he led

PulsePoint Group, a communications management consulting firm, spending a decade there after joining the firm at its founding. He is regarded as an expert on business strategy, organizational design and the transformation of communications and marketing functions into agile organizations built for tomorrow. He has counseled C-suite leaders across a wide range of companies including Bristol-Myers Squibb, Chevron, Disney, GE, HPE, Johnson & Johnson, Kaiser Permanente, Novartis, Pfizer, Toyota and Wells Fargo, among others. Prior to joining PulsePoint Group, he worked in strategic communications and marketing roles in Cape Town, South Africa, Boston and New York. He is an alum of the Freeman School of Business at Tulane University and the Annenberg School for Communication at the University of Southern California.

Karen van Bergen is Executive Vice President of Omnicom Group and Dean of Omnicom University. In her role, she oversees the holding company's pre-eminent management development program. She joined Omnicom in 2007, holding leadership roles at FleishmanHillard and Porter Novelli. In 2016, she was named the Chief Executive Officer of Omnicom Public Relations Group, focusing on strategic growth areas including talent, innovation and cross-agency collaboration. Prior to Omnicom, she spent 13 non-consecutive years with McDonald's across Europe and Asia. She also worked with The Coca-Cola Company and Outboard Marine Corporation. Her leadership has been recognized with honors including *Ad Age* "Woman to Watch" and *New York Business Journal* "Woman of Influence." She was 2017 PR jury president at the Cannes International Festival of Creativity and was the first woman ranked #1 on the PRWeek Power List. She is a Founding Member of Omniwomen and serves on the board of the New York Pops.

INDEX

Printed in the United States
by Baker & Taylor Publisher Services